# Stock
# Market
# Arithmetic

# Stock Market Arithmetic

Revised and Enlarged Edition

## A Home Study Course for Investors

Regnery Gateway
Washington, DC

To my wife, Karen . . .
always there with encouragement
and support

Regnery Books is an imprint of Regnery Gateway, Inc. All
inquiries concerning this book should be directed to Regnery
Gateway, Inc., 1130 17th Street NW, Washington, DC 20036.

**Library of Congress Cataloging-in-Publication Data**

Caes, Charles J.
　Stock market arithmetic.

　Bibliography: p.
　Includes index.
　1. Investments—Mathematics.　2. Business
Mathematics.　I. Title.
　　HG4515.3.C33　1985　　332.63′22　　87-14457
　　ISBN 0-89526-780-2

# ACKNOWLEDGMENTS

In the course of compiling any document, a writer finds himself leaning on any number of individuals who can supply him with the source material, instruction, or additional information which he needs to launch and complete his work. A writer puts his name to a book because the way of presenting the material, the idea of it, and the responsibility for its content are his. But from its inception to its final printing, many people will have contributed to the project, not the least of whom are the editors and project coordinators who supervise the publishing.

I am particularly grateful to those professionals who took the time to answer my calls or correspondence, especially the public information and relations personnel at the U.S. and foreign exchanges who responded quickly and with quality and quantity to my queries.

Very special thanks belongs to Dennis McAlpine (Oppenheimer & Co.), whose review of the manuscript resulted in important corrections to formulas and computations. As this book is actually a synthesis of the original *Stock Market Arithmetic* and two other manuscripts originally prepared for separate publication, the margin for error during compilation and abridgement was somewhat wide, and Dennis' history of experience in business finance, as well as in writing about business subjects, has been extremely valuable.

But, in the final analysis, any errors in fact or arithmetic that may have made it past the final proofing belong to the man whose name appears on the title page, as he caused them in the first place.

Though the dedication page bears her name, I still cannot close without once again mentioning my wife, Karen, who continually goes about her responsibilities as wife and mother with such efficiency and with such concern for everyone's individual needs that I have never had to worry about finding the time or the place to complete my research or writing. She is one in a million.

# PREFACE

Although this revised and expanded edition goes deeper into the fundamentals of stock investing than ordinary investment primers and takes on topics not usually covered in such books—topics such as opportunity cost, types of margin, business ratios—its objective remains the same: *This book is designed to simplify the arithmetic used in the business of buying and selling securities.* It has been prepared especially with the new investor in mind but not in disregard of the more experienced stock trader.

In fact, much of the information contained in the twelve chapters and the dictionary at the end of the text will also be of special interest to the independent investor who has been dealing in the market for sometime, for even the experienced trader is not usually on top of many of the fundamentals related to margin purchases, short selling, the effects of dividends on stockholders' equity, warrants, and stock rights. There is something surprising in every chapter for almost everyone.

There is a lot to the game of buying and selling stocks. Knowing the fundamentals will never assure success, but not knowing them assures failure except where pure luck intervenes. *It is easy to lose money in the stock market.* Every investor needs to keep informed, needs to be thoroughly familiar with the basics. But many are not. In fact, while you peruse this book, deciding whether or not it is for you, turn to Chapter Eleven; read some of the common misconceptions many investors have about the market and see if any apply to you. Even the most experienced investor is guilty of one or more of them.

No book can make you a successful investor, just as no book can make you a successful tennis player. Skill and experience brewed with expert instruction are required for success. But a book can let you know the ground rules and how to keep score. And that's what this book does.

# CONTENTS

## CHAPTER 1

# Stock
# Markets

The stock market is probably the best example of what a free enterprise system is all about. Stock prices are governed strictly by the law of supply and demand. When demand exceeds supply, stock prices climb; when supply exceeds demand, stock prices tumble. Of course, there are a lot of variables which affect that supply and demand, which affect investor interest. The stock market is a complicated financial theater; there is a lot to learn about it before that first share of stock should be purchased.

The term "stock market" is in itself somewhat confusing to the would-be investor who would like to explore it. Actually, when people talk about the stock market, what they are actually referring to is that market for corporate stocks which is created by the various stock exchanges around the world. Stock exchanges are actually auction markets which provide a convenient means through which individuals can invest in business enterprises at almost anytime. The amount of trading that is accomplished every day in these exchanges is phenomenal, as Table 1.1 well indicates; the table shows stock sales on registered exchanges from 1960 through 1983. In 1986 and 1987, the New York Stock Exchange was trading frequently above 100 million shares a day, so annual sales from all exchanges now far exceed the 1983 figures.

Stock exchanges are nothing new to the financial world. They have been around for hundreds of years. In the United States, informal exchanges were formed as long ago as the early part of the eighteenth century, the first ones having evolved in New

York City. In those days, exchanges not only dealt in corporate stocks and certain commodities but also in human beings; slave traders made up the membership as well as the usual merchants and brokers. The first truly organized exchange in the United States was actually established in the city of Philadelphia in the year 1790. The members of this exchange were highly experienced businessmen who brought the trading in corporate securities to new levels of sophistication; they were far ahead of that loosely knit group of New York auctioneers who never really organized their operation formally until decades after the

### Table 1.1
### Sales of Stocks on Registered Exchanges
### 1960-83

| Year | Market Value ($ billion) | Shares (millions) |
|------|--------------------------|-------------------|
| 1960 | 45 | 1,389 |
| 1965 | 89 | 2,587 |
| 1970 | 131 | 4,539 |
| 1973 | 179 | 5,723 |
| 1974 | 118 | 4,846 |
| 1975 | 157 | 6,231 |
| 1976 | 195 | 7,036 |
| 1977 | 187 | 7,023 |
| 1978 | 249 | 9,483 |
| 1979 | 300 | 10,863 |
| 1980 | 476 | 15,486 |
| 1981 | 491 | 15,910 |
| 1982 | 602 | 22,423 |
| 1983 | 957 | 30,147 |

From tables in the 1980 & 1985 *Statistical Abstract of The United States*, p. 545 and p. 507 respectively. Original source: U.S. Securities & Exchange Commission. When the figures for 1986 and 1987 are in, they will be phenomenal.

Philadelphia group was formed. But despite their informalities, as early as 1792 the New York group of brokers began to charge fees for representing others in the purchase and sale of corporate stocks.

Back in those days, New York was hardly the metropolis that it is today; its population had not yet reached fifty thousand. Once this fact is realized, it is no surprise to learn that the first indoor headquarters for these merchants and traders was a coffee house—the Tontine Coffee House.

As this nation of ours began to grow, government obligations increased markedly and so, too, did the banking and insurance communities. And in the twenty-five years since that informal start in 1790, there was created such interest in stocks and bonds that the brokerage community also grew steadily as it grew wealthy. Before long it was clear to securities dealers that what was needed was a constitution to both guide their business activities and limit their membership. They drafted that constitution, put that limit on membership, and called themselves the "New York Stock Exchange Board." From that time on each new member would have to be sponsored by a present member and his application would have to be approved by the entire membership.

As conditions continued to become more and more crowded, the members of the New York Stock Exchange Board decided that it would be necessary to rent indoor quarters and they subsequently made 40 Wall Street their first real home. By this time they were charging new members a membership fee; that fee was based on exactly where the newcomer's seat would be located in the trading room. They also levied fines and expelled those who did not adhere to the rules.

Today, on any of the exchanges, there are no seats. In fact, the exchanges today bear hardly any resemblance to old 40 Wall Street. But the term "seat" is still used.

With the advent of the Civil War, new interest was created in the securities market. Creation or improvement of any market attracts greater numbers of entrepreneurs. Accordingly, applications for "seats" in the exchange skyrocketed. Not all applicants could be accepted, however. Memberships had to be limited.

Not to be lost to any money-making opportunity, those brokers on whom the door was shut organized their own exchange which they called the "Open Board of Brokers." There was competition for awhile, but the two exchanges were soon to merge into what today is known as the "New York Stock Exchange."

At the time this exchange was created, there was another group of brokers who had been conducting business in the open since 1849. They were the hard-dealing members of the New York Curb Exchange. "Curb" was a fitting part of the name, since that exchange's members were literally conducting business—actually buying and selling securities—right on the sidewalk curb. This little group of businessmen continued to do their business with the sky for a roof until they finally moved their exchange indoors in 1921. Now the New York Curb Exchange is the American Stock Exchange.

While the New York Stock Exchange and the American Stock Exchange are by far the best known in the United States, they are by no means the only exchanges in our country, though they do tend to get the most publicity. An investor eventually stumbles across the other exchanges in the course of his full-time or part-time quest for capital gains or dividend income. In fact, an investor is likely to go beyond the U.S. borders in his search for stock investment opportunities. There are, actually, more than a hundred stock exchanges around the world. Of course, many of them are so small and remote or else associated with countries whose political future is highly uncertain that most investors pay little or no attention to them. But there are a number of other U.S. and foreign exchanges which list securities of major interest to the investment public at the same time that they offer highly visible and competitive markets for their equity issues. It is beyond the plan of this chapter to introduce all of those other exchanges, but an introduction to some of them is in order, as such introduction will enhance the reader's awareness of these marketplaces.

## U.S. Exchanges

In the United States, the largest exchange outside the boundaries of New York City is the Pacific Stock Exchange. It was founded just a few decades ago, in 1957. It came about because some far-sighted administrators saw the advantage of combining two small California exchanges, the Los Angeles and the San Francisco, into one exchange offering a viable auction market for what now amounts to more than a thousand equity issues. The San Francisco Stock Exchange dated back to 1882; and the Los Angeles Exchange, actually the Los Angeles Oil Exchange, dated back to 1899. Though the operations were consolidated on paper, the physical locations remained separate, and the exchange still has two different "trading floors" hundreds of miles apart. But these floors are connected by telecommunications systems which allow buyers and sellers from each location to be in touch with each other in seconds. Income for the exchange comes from dues to members and fees received for the use of facilities and services.

The second largest regional exchange in the United States is the Midwest Exchange which was organized in December of 1949 when the Chicago, Cleveland, Minneapolis-St. Paul, and St. Louis stock exchanges merged. Many of the issues traded here are also listed on other exchanges. Annual trading volume of the Midwest Exchange is 18 hundreds of million of shares per year.

Another large regional exchange in the United States is the Boston Stock Exchange which was organized back in 1834 and which has operated since that time on a continuing basis except for a brief period at the outset of World War I when all exchange activities were suspended. It has, however, only been since 1965 that the Boston Exchange has had a full-time president and staff to oversee trading activities and the management of the exchange.

There are, in additon to the New York, American, Pacific, Midwest, and Boston exchanges, six other stock exchanges registered under the Securities Exchange Act as meeting the requirements of a national securities exchange. These

**Figure 1.** The New York Stock Exchange Building at 11 Wall Street, New York. (Photo by Edward C. Topple, N.Y. Stock Exchange photographer.)

exchanges are listed in Table 1.2. Some very small regional exchanges have been exempted from registration, it must be noted, because the Securities and Exchange Commission (SEC) judges the volume of trading activity to be so limited that it is not necessarily in the public interest to require registration. Registered exchanges listed in Table 1.2 are required by the SEC to supply copies of their rules and regulations, constitution, articles of incorporation; are required to agree to comply with all rules and regulations of the Securities Act of 1934 and its amendments; are required to supply all data related to operational and organizational procedure.

All trading at any of these exchanges can only be conducted by the exchange's members, and membership is always strictly limited. Membership still can only be obtained by purchasing another member's seat on an exchange.

An applicant has a choice of a number of types of memberships on an exchange. There are memberships for commission brokers, floor brokers, registered traders, specialists, odd-lot dealers, and block positioners.

Commission brokers handle buy-and-sell transactions for the general public. Their fee is a percentage of the amount of the transaction.

Floor brokers ($2 brokers) conduct transactions for other members of the same exchange in return for a commission. These floor brokers serve an important role as backups for the other brokers. They handle excess orders that otherwise could not be handled at all or efficiently and they fill in for other brokers when those brokers cannot be available.

Registered traders are members of an exchange who buy and sell securities for their own account. They neither handle orders for other brokers nor do they handle orders for the general public. They buy a seat and pay the related costs so they can personally buy and sell for their own profit. Strict parameters are established to guide these registered traders so that their activities will in no way conflict with the trading public.

Specialists handle "limit" orders for other brokers. This is to say that if a customer has given instructions to his broker to buy a stock currently selling at $11.50 for no more than $10.00, the broker will call on a specialist to "stay with" the stock and execute the order at the very first opportunity which is presented. Specialists have another and very important responsibility. This is to maintain what is called an "orderly market." To do this they must buy and sell for their own accounts whenever there is an unusual trading situation developing, usually buying against the flow, they keep a notebook of orders at specified prices, in strict order of receipt, which have been placed by brokers.

Odd-lot dealers are those exchange members who buy from or sell to customers of commission brokers dealing in fewer than 100 shares. These odd-lot dealers do not work on a usual-type commission. Rather, they earn their income on the difference between buy and sell prices on the shares they may be trading.

Block positioners handle trades of a thousand or more shares of stock, though the trading is not usually done on the "floor," and is usually done at risk.

### The Over-the-Counter Market

There is another "marketplace" for securities in the United States called the OTC Market, or Over-the-Counter Market. This is the market for those securities that are not listed on any of the major exchanges. OTC securities, though not all of them, are listed daily in the financial papers and in the financial sections of the larger daily newspapers like *The New York Times*. The listings, though not complete, are usually quite extensive, and many of the issues are worth researching. Through the creation of an organization titled the *National Association of Securities Dealers (NASD), the OTC market has developed into a well-organized electronic auction center representing millions of dollars in trade each day. This has come about through the creation of NASDAQ, or the National Association of Securities Dealers Automatic Quotation system.* OTC

---

**Table 1.2**
**Stock Exchanges Registered Under**
**the Securities & Exchange Act**

| American | Intermountain | Pacific |
|----------|---------------|--------------|
| Boston | Midwest | Philadelphia |
| Cincinnati | New York | Spokane |

---

stocks are now divided into two main categories, those that subscribe to the automatic quotation system and those that do not. Subscribers must meet certain financial and market requirements. NASD, through its quotation system, has brought order to a once unruly and confusing market arena for unlisted stocks. NASDAQ system continues to grow rapidly, affecting more than 10 billion stock traders each year.

**Foreign Exchanges**
Just as is the case for the smaller U.S. exchanges, major foreign exchange listings are published daily in all the financial papers and in the financial sections of major daily newspapers. Among these listings of foreign exchanges you will find the Montreal, London, and Paris exchanges.

The Montreal Exchange is not the only exchange in Canada; there are also exchanges in Calgary, Toronto, Vancouver, and Winnipeg. Similarly, the Paris and London exchanges are not the only ones in France and the United Kingdom; there are also exchanges in Bordeaux, Lille, Lyon, Marsailles, Nancy, Nnantes, and in Belfast. And there are many other exchanges in other countries. The table on the last page of this chapter lists all countries in which there are more than one stock exchange.

The Montreal Exchange, or la Bourse de Montreal, was established in 1874. But like some of its U.S. counterparts, it had actually begun on open streets and in coffee houses during the early part of the eighteenth century. While, as mentioned, it

# Foreign Markets
### *Closing Prices of Selected Issues*

Wednesday, March 25, 1987

| LONDON (in pence) | Close | Prev. Close |
|---|---|---|
| Allied Lyons | 403 | 400 |
| Babcock | 195 | 197 |
| Barclays Bk | 515 | 520 |
| Bass Ltd | 940 | 944 |
| BOC Group | 459 | 465 |
| British GE | 223 | 223.5 |
| Britoil | 229 | 235 |
| BTR PLC | 326 | 329 |
| Cable&Wi | 367 | 368 |
| Cadbury Sch | 245.5 | 250 |
| Charter Con | 335 | 331 |
| Coats Viyella | 612 | 618 |
| Consol Gold | 923 | 864 |
| Dalgety | 350 | 351 |
| Glaxo | 1,514 | 1,539 |
| Grand Metro | 487 | 488.5 |
| Guest Keen | 335 | 337 |
| Guinness | 334 | 339 |
| HansonTrust | 163.5 | 164.5 |
| Johnson Mat | 318 | 319 |
| Legal Gen | 300 | 309 |
| Lonrho | 275 | 267 |
| Lucas Indust | 592 | 593 |
| MIM Hold | 108 | 102 |
| Nat'l WestBk | 609 | 610 |
| Nrthrn Food | 308 | 315 |
| Racal Elect | 238 | 239 |
| Redland | 474 | 475 |
| Reed Int'l | 414 | 419 |
| Rio Tinto | 758 | 726 |
| Royal Ins | 935 | 943 |
| STC | 263 | 259 |
| Tate&Lyle | 788 | 791 |
| TaylrWoodrw | 393 | 384 |
| Thorn EMI | 613 | 618 |
| Trust House | 239 | 235 |
| T I Group | 692 | 693 |
| Ultramar | 235 | 249 |
| Utd Biscuit | 288 | 292 |
| Vickers | 490 | 490 |
| Wellcome | 452 | 487 |

| South African Mines (in U.S. currency) ADR | Close | Prev. Close |
|---|---|---|
| Bracken | 3.10 | 3.00 |
| Deelkraal | 4.45 | 4.38 |
| Doornfontein | 17.75 | 15.50 |
| DurbanDeep | 12.88 | 13.00 |
| East Rand Gold | 8.50 | 8.00 |
| East Rand | 8.00 | 7.63 |
| Elandsrand | 12.25 | 12.00 |
| Elsburg | 3.65 | 3.50 |
| Grootvlei | 5.13 | 4.75 |
| Harmony | 12.87 | 12.50 |
| Hartebeest | 8.40 | 7.80 |
| Impala | 14.05 | 13.37 |
| Kinross | 18.75 | 17.75 |
| Leslie | 9.50 | 9.50 |
| Libanon | 26.50 | 24.00 |
| Loraine | 8.13 | 7.50 |
| Randfontein | 13.90 | 13.10 |
| Rustnbg Plat | 14.65 | 14.00 |
| Southvaal | 63.00 | 59.00 |
| Stilfontein | 7.75 | 7.50 |
| Unisel | 10.50 | 10.00 |
| West Areas | 5.87 | 5.62 |
| Winkelhaak | 28.00 | 25.50 |
| *in British pounds* | | |
| General Mng | 11.63 | 10.88 |

| TOKYO (in yen) | Close | Prev. Close |
|---|---|---|
| Ajinomoto | 3,480 | 3,180 |
| Asahi Chem | 878 | 859 |
| Bk of Tokyo | 1,420 | 1,430 |
| BridgestnTire | 750 | 765 |
| C. Itoh | 821 | 828 |
| Daiwa House | 1,940 | 1,890 |
| Daiwa Secur | 2,930 | 2,910 |
| Eisai | 2,100 | 2,100 |
| Fuji Bank | 2,990 | 2,940 |
| Fujitsu | 850 | 875 |
| Isuzu Mot Ltd | 325 | 339 |
| Kajima Corp | 1,590 | 1,560 |
| Kansai Elec | 4,140 | 4,200 |
| Komatsu Ltd | 595 | 619 |
| MaruiDeptStr | 2,520 | 2,580 |
| Marubeni | 463 | 470 |
| Mazda | 371 | 382 |
| MitsubishiEst | 2,710 | 2,700 |
| MitsubishiInd | 606 | 620 |
| Mitsui & Co | 625 | 635 |
| MitsuiRealE | 2,290 | 2,310 |
| Nikko Secur | 2,490 | 2,420 |
| NipponKogaku | 683 | 715 |
| NipponGakki | 1,580 | 1,620 |
| NipponSteel | 378 | 380 |
| NomuraSecur | 4,850 | 4,830 |
| Ricoh | 845 | 865 |
| Sekisui House | 1,730 | 1,700 |
| Sharp El | 1,000 | 1,020 |
| SumitomoBk | 3,590 | 3,580 |
| SumitomoCh | 890 | 830 |
| Taisei Const | 1,060 | 1,030 |
| Takeda Chem | 2,990 | 3,010 |
| Teijin | 792 | 804 |
| Tokyo Elec | 8,000 | 8,030 |
| Toshiba | 698 | 711 |
| YamaichiSec | 2,210 | 2,240 |
| Yasuda F&M | 1,110 | 1,110 |

| PARIS (in French francs) | Close | Prev. Close |
|---|---|---|
| AirLiq | 773 | 765 |
| Aquitaine | 355 | 351 |
| BSNGrD | 5,250 | 5,170 |
| Club Med | 725 | 727 |
| Imetal | 121 | 121 |
| L'Oreal | 4,445 | 4,455 |
| Hachette | 3,272 | 3,279 |
| LafargeCoppee | 1,660 | 1,600 |
| Machines Bull | 55 | 54.70 |
| Michelin | 3,405 | 3,408 |
| MoetHen | 2,537 | 2,540 |
| PeugtCtn | 1,490 | 1,500 |
| Source Perrier | 819 | 819 |
| Total CFP | 486 | 483 |

| SWITZERLAND (in Swiss francs) Zurich | Close | Prev. Close |
|---|---|---|
| Brown Bov | 1,750 | 1,730 |
| Ciba-Geigy | 3,350 | 3,300 |
| Credit Suisse | 3,120 | 3,080 |
| Nestle | 9,300 | 9,250 |
| Sandoz | 11,350 | 11,300 |
| Sulzer | 519 | 520 |
| Swissair | 1,185 | 1,160 |
| Swiss Alum | 462 | 456 |
| Swiss Bancp | 461 | 457 |
| Union Bank | 5,225 | 5,125 |
| **Basel** | | |
| vHoffmn-LaR | 13,950 | 13,850 |
| Pirelli Intl | 441 | 435 |
| *v-1/10 share.* | | |

| FRANKFURT (in marks) | Close | Prev. Close |
|---|---|---|
| AEG | 310.50 | 302 |
| Allianz Vers | 1,605 | 1,590 |
| BASF | 256 | 257 |
| Bayer | 295.50 | 295.60 |
| BMW | 482 | 480.50 |
| Cont'l Gummi | 315.50 | 311 |
| Commerzbnk | 266 | 264.50 |
| Daimler-Benz | 937 | 923 |
| Degussa | 450 | 450 |
| Deutsche Bk | 643 | 640.50 |
| Dresdner Bk | 330 | 329.50 |
| Hoechst | 260.50 | 259.20 |
| Lufthansa | 184 | 187.50 |
| Nixdorf | 716.20 | 717.80 |
| Porsche | 843 | 840 |
| RWE | 211.50 | 214 |
| Schering | 578 | 559.50 |
| Siemens | 651.50 | 647.50 |
| Thyssen-Hut | 123.50 | 125 |
| Veba | 259 | 261 |
| Volkswagen | 334.50 | 339 |

| BRUSSELS (in Belgian francs) | Close | Prev. Close |
|---|---|---|
| ARBED | 1,496 | 1,498 |
| Gevaert | 6,690 | 6,600 |
| GB-Inno-Bm | 1,158 | 1,158 |
| GrpBrLambrt | 3,780 | 3,890 |
| Metal Hobokn | 7,190 | 7,150 |
| Petrofina | 10,450 | 10,425 |
| SocGenerale | 3,560 | 3,590 |
| Solvay | 10,250 | 10,050 |

| MILAN (in Lire) | Close | Prev. Close |
|---|---|---|
| Buitoni | 7,200 | 7,250 |
| Ciga | 4,631 | 4,598 |
| Fiat | 12,970 | 12,890 |
| Generali | 136,300 | 136,000 |
| La Rinas | 1,268 | 1,210 |
| Mont Ed | 2,850 | 2,877 |
| Olivetti | 13,295 | 13,160 |
| Pirelli | 5,388 | 5,325 |
| Snia Visc | 4,888 | 4,899 |

| STOCKHOLM (in Swedish krona) | Close | Prev. Close |
|---|---|---|
| AGA b | 195 | 186 |
| Alfa Laval b | 296 | 298 |
| Electrolux b | 309 | 307 |
| Kone oy | 285 | 285 |
| Svenska Cel b | 327 | 320 |

| AMSTERDAM (in guilders) | Close | Prev. Close |
|---|---|---|
| AKZO | 141 | 143.40 |
| Ahold | 107.60 | 110.60 |
| Algemene Bk | 511 | 518.50 |
| Amst-Rot Bk | 80 | 81.10 |
| Elsevier | 251.50 | 253 |
| Fokker | 45.50 | 45.30 |
| Heineken's | 172.50 | 174 |
| Holec | 32.80 | 32.80 |
| Hoogovens | 34.10 | 35 |
| Nation Neder | 72.40 | 72.50 |
| Nedlloyd | 173 | 173.50 |
| Robeco | 101.70 | 101.90 |
| Rolinco | 90.90 | 90.60 |
| Rorento | 51.20 | 51.20 |
| Wessanen | 80 | 79.80 |
| *a-Ex-dividend.* | | |

| HONG KONG (in Hong Kong dollars) | Close | Prev. Close |
|---|---|---|
| Bk of East Asia | 19.80 | 19.80 |
| Cheung Kong | 45.50 | 44.75 |
| Hang Seng Bk | 53 | 53 |
| Hong Kong El | 14.10 | 14.20 |
| Hong Kong Lnd | 8.05 | 8.05 |
| HongkongShBk | 10.10 | 10 |
| Hutchsn Whmp | 55 | 54 |
| Jardine Mathsn | 25.10 | 25 |
| SunHungKaiP | 26.20 | 25.80 |
| Swire Pacific | 23.50 | 23.80 |
| World Intl | 3.825 | 3.825 |
| *z-Not quoted.* | | |

| SYDNEY (in Australian dollars) | Close | Prev. Close |
|---|---|---|
| ANZ Bk Grp | 5.30 | 5.36 |
| Central Norse | 16.80 | 16.10 |
| Coles GJ | 6.40 | 6.40 |
| CRA | 6.84 | 6.76 |
| CSR | 3.93 | 3.86 |
| LeightonHld | 0.96 | 0.96 |
| Natl Aust Bk | 5.26 | 5.34 |
| News Corp | 22.80 | 22.80 |
| Pacific Dunlop | 4.75 | 4.70 |
| RensnGoldFlds | 13.40 | 13.50 |
| Santos | 4.80 | 4.58 |
| SouthrnPacPet | 0.25 | 0.25 |
| Westrn Mining | 7.44 | 7.20 |
| Westpac | 4.70 | 4.74 |
| Woodside Pete | 2.45 | 2.60 |
| Woolworth Ltd | 3.42 | 3.25 |

*Figure 2.* Listings of Foreign Exchange issues from the Wall Street Journal

**Figure 3.** *The trading floor of the Montreal Stock Exchange. (Courtesy Montreal Stock Exchange.)*

is not the only exchange in Canada, it was the first to create honorary governorships committed to the purpose of looking out for the public's interest as well as monitoring exchange operations. In 1974, the Montreal and Canadian stock exchanges merged under the Montreal name, thus bringing about a powerful, more sophisticated, and more competitive marketplace for trading in Canada.

The London Stock Exchange began, too, with informal groups gathered at coffee houses. While informal U.S. stock markets can be traced back to the eighteenth century, informal marketplaces can be traced even furhter back in England, and there are records of daily price lists going as far back as 1698. But the first formal site of the London Exchange was near Threadmill Street in London and it was as far back as 1773 that the exchange set up operations. Currently there are more than four thousand members of the London Stock Exchange; and the exchange lists more than seven thousand securities. Its operations are free of all government involvement. Because of the way in which the exchange is organized to provide a free and continuing market even in relatively small corporate issues, it leaves little room for the equivalent of a U.S. OTC market. The London Exchange recently ended its program of fixed commissions that dates back to the latter part of the 19th century, and now its brokers can act as traders, market makers and underwriters instead of performing only as middlemen who bring buyers and sellers together. This has all been part of a deregulation program begun on October 27, 1986. Expecting that deregulation will not only stir competition but possibly lead to havoc, the government, at this writing, has plans for legislation that will create something similar to the Securities and Exchange Commission in the United States, this to be called the Securities and Investments Board.

The Paris Stock Exchange, or the Bourse de Paris, is a legal monopoly designed to facilitate the trading of securities. This privilege of monopoly covers both listed and unlisted securities. But in France, dual listings are not allowed. Every security may be listed on only one of the French exchanges. Trading

**Figure 4.** *Trading on the floor of the Paris Stock Exchange. (Courtesy Paris Stock Exchange.)*

occurs in the following fashion: Sworn officials appointed by the minister of the economy are responsible for the collection of all buy and sell orders; this collection they bring to the exchange to effect trades between brokers representing buyers and brokers representing sellers. These officials (agents de change) do not perform the same function as U.K. exchange jobbers or U.S. exchange specialists, but they may on occasion deal directly with clients after market hours as long as their dealings are based on closing prices and as long as they buy or sell as soon as possible—for, by law, they may not own securities professionally. Soon the Paris stock exchange will become internationalized; France plans to open the exchange's membership to outsiders. This means that soon any investor will be able to buy into a brokerage—if the Finance Ministry and stock market authorities approve. There are five different ways of stipulating prices on the exchange; these are similar to the ways of stipulating prices on all other exchanges:

1. *Au mieux* (at the market price). This means that the order will be executed at the market price if it is placed before the market opens, otherwise it is executed at the first price available following receipt of the order.

2. *Cours limite* (limit order). This means the buyer has specified the highest price he or she will pay; or the seller has specified the lowest price at which he or she will sell.

3. *Premier ou dernier cours* (opening or closing price). This means that the order will be executed at the opening price of the stock or at the closing price of the stock, depending upon which the buyer or seller has specified.

4. *Sans forcer ou soignant* (without forcing or carefully). This means the *agents de change* can spread the order out over the entire market session or over a number of market sessions because the market is too narrow for the entire order to be executed at once.

5. *Stop order.* This means that the buyer or seller has fixed the limits on the prices at which he or she wants to buy or sell.

Now, it must be re-emphasized that the exchanges listed in this chapter are not the only exchanges in U.S. and foreign markets, and they have not been selected for review because of their superiority to other exchanges. Rather, they have been selected to help familiarize the reader with the fact that there are many exchanges listing securities, and also to show how they may differ in organization, procedure, and size. For a listing of countries having one or more stock exchanges, see Table 1-3.

## Table 1.3
## Countries With More Than One Stock Exchange

| | | |
|---|---|---|
| Argentina | Canada | United States |
| India | Japan | Uruguay |
| Pakistan | Chile | France |
| Australia | Netherlands | Norway |
| Philippines | Switzerland | Venezuela |
| Belgium | Colombia | Germany (Fed. Rep.) |
| Italy | New Zealand | Hong Kong |
| Spain | Costa Rica | |
| Brazil | United Kingdom | |

## *Review Questions*

A. The statements below are either true or false; indicate which.

1. The stock market is that market for corporate stocks created by national and local exchanges around the world. _____

2. Since the 1700's, small, informal exchanges have existed in the United States. _____

3. In their early days, stock exchanges not only dealt in corporate stocks but also in the slave trade. _____

4. The first organized exchange in the United States was established in Philadelphia in the year 1790. _____

5. The New York Stock Exchange was originally called the New York Curb Exchange. _____

6. There is now only one exchange in the United States: The New York Stock Exchange. _____

7. Floor brokers conduct transactions for other members of the same exchange in return for a commission. _____

8. Registered brokers are members of an exchange who buy and sell securities for their account. _____

9. Odd-lot dealers are those exchange members who buy from, or sell to, customers of commission brokers dealing in fewer than 100 shares. _____

10. Block positioners usually handle trades of thousands of shares of stock. _____

B.   Fill in the correct answer.

11. A _____ is a marketplace for securities already in the hands of the public.

12. The largest regional stock exchange in the United States is the _____ Stock Exchange.

13. The _____ Market is the market for those securities not sold on any of the exchanges.

14. Through the creation of the National Association of Securities Dealers, the _____ Market has developed

into a well-organized electronic auction center representing millions of dollars in trades every day.

15. Another name for la Bourse de Montreal is the _____
_____ .

16. The _____ Stock Exchange is a legal monopoly in France created for the trading of securities.

17. A _____ order means the buyer has specified the highest price he or she is willing to pay.

18. Is it true that there are more than one hundred stock exchanges worldwide? _____

19. Are some stocks listed on more than one stock exchange?
_____

20. Are dual listings allowed on the Paris Bourse? _____

## CHAPTER 2

# Stock Quotations

More often than not, if you decide to buy or sell stock in a corporation you will do your business through a stockbroker who, in turn, will make the purchases or sales for you through one of the many organizations which make a market for corporate stocks. These organizations are exchanges like those discussed in Chapter One.

## Exchange Requirements

Each exchange has its own requirements for the stock which it is willing to list, and these requirements will vary widely. Just knowing what exchange a stock is listed on gives some seasoned investors an idea of its investment characteristics.

For instance, if an investor notes that a company's stock is listed on the New York Stock Exchange, he knows that:

1. the company has attracted a great deal of national interest;
2. the company has a relatively strong position, as well as stability, in its industry;
3. the company's market is an expanding one and it has the ability to expand right along with it.

He also knows that in all probability, the company has:

1. the capability of earning, in a competitive market, and before deductions for federal income taxes, at least $2.5 million; it also has recorded earnings in each of the past two years of at least $2 million before taxes;
2. at least $16 million in net tangible assets;

3. at least a million common shares held by the public;
4. at least two thousand stockholders owning 100 shares or more of its stock.

---

### Table 2.1
### Stock Market Quotations

| 52-Week High | Low | Stock | Div A | Yld %B | PE Ratio C | Sales 100s D | High | Low | Last | Chg. |
|---|---|---|---|---|---|---|---|---|---|---|
| 33 | 20⅛ | AAR s | .50 | 1.6 | 22 | 41 | 32⅜ | 31¾ | 31⅞− | ⅜ |
| 37 | 21⅞ | ADT | .92 | 2.6 | 20 | 240 | 34⅞ | 34⅝ | 34⅞+ | ¼ |
| 41½ | 23⅝ | AFG | .12e | .3 | 12 | 915 | 38¾ | 37½ | 38⅝+ | 1 |
| 40¼ | 16¾ | AGS | ... | ... | 22 | 222 | 37 | 36¾ | 37 | ... |
| 14⅞ | 6¾ | AMCA | ... | ... | ... | 110 | 8¾ | 8⅝ | 8¾+ | ¼ |
| 9⅜ | 4⅞ | AM Intl | ... | ... | ... | 853 | 9 | 8¾ | 8⅞ | ... |
| 33¾ | 24½ | AM Int pf | 2.00 | 6.1 | ... | 61 | 32¾ | 32¼ | 32¾+ | ¼ |
| 62⅛ | 47¼ | AMR | ... | ... | 12 | 10735 | 55¼ | 53¾ | 54⅛− | 1¼ |
| 12⅞ | 8 | ARX s | ... | ... | 13 | 196 | 10⅞ | 10⅝ | 10⅝− | ⅛ |
| 59⅝ | 28¾ | ASA | 2.00a | 3.3 | ... | 4646U | 62¼ | 60⅛ | 60¼+ | 1 |
| 17⅛ | 9¾ | AVX | ... | 1.9 | ... | 355 | 16¾ | 16½ | 16¾+ | ¼ |
| 32¾ | 26½ | AZP | 2.72 | 8.5 | 11 | 1417 | 32 | 31⅝ | 32 | ... |
| 67 | 39⅜ | AbtLb s | 1.00 | 1.5 | 28 | 5285 | 66¾ | 65⅜ | 65¾− | 1⅛ |
| 34 | 25 | AccoWd | .62 | 2.0 | 20 | x217 | 30¾ | 30⅜ | 30¾+ | ⅜ |
| 14⅛ | 9 | AcmeC | .40 | 3.2 | 23 | 175 | 12¾ | 12⅜ | 12⅝+ | ¼ |
| 8⅝ | 6⅛ | AcmeE | .32b | 4.1 | 27 | 15 | 8 | 7⅞ | 7⅞ | ... |

---

## Typical Quotations

Table 2.1 gives a partial listing of stock market quotations. Let's take a close look at these quotes in order to interpret some of the transactions which the listing shows have taken place.

But first note that the fractional parts of the quotations which are listed are in eighths, fourths, and halves of a dollar. We are, actually, counting by 12-½,

$$⅛ = 12\text{-}½ \text{ cents} \qquad ⅝ = 62\text{-}½ \text{ cents}$$
$$\tfrac{2}{8} (¼) = 25 \text{ cents} \qquad \tfrac{6}{8} (¾) = 75 \text{ cents}$$
$$⅜ = 37\text{-}½ \text{ cents} \qquad ⅞ = 87\text{-}½ \text{ cents}$$
$$\tfrac{4}{8} (½) = 50 \text{ cents}$$

Bearing this in mind, let's zero in on Figure 2.1 and check the action in Am International. Column by column now:

*52-Week High.* This price ($9.37½) represents the highest price at which the stock was sold during the past fifty-two weeks. That high, however, does not represent the present day's listing, so if AM International reached a new high today, it would not change the number in this column, not until the next day's listing.

*52-Week Low.* This price ($4.87½) represents the lowest price at which the stock was sold during the past fifty-two weeks. This low, however, does not represent the present day's listing, so if AM International reaches a new low today, it would not change the number in this column, not until the next day's listing.

*Stock.* In this column appears the name of the stock, which is usually abbreviated.

*Div (dividend).* This amount here indicates the total amount of dividends the company is expected to declare on each share of stock. As you can see, the common pays no dividend. But just below the common is the AM International preferred and this pays a dividend of 2.00 per share.

*Yld (yield)%.* This is the annual rate of return, expressed as a percentage, which the purchaser would receive if he purchased the stock at the present price. For example, if the preferred is paying out dividends of $2.00 per share per year and the closing price of the preferred stock is $32.75, then by dividing the 2.00 by the closing price, the yield (6.1%) is determined.

*P/E Ratio.* This is the price-earning ratio. It is determined by dividing the current market price of a share of stock by the earnings per share. Since the earnings per share are not listed in stock quotations, the P/E ratio listed in the quotations will help you determine what the earnings are. Simply divide the closing price of the stock by the P/E ratio; the result is the approximate earnings per share—"approximate" because the P/E ratio is given rounded to the nearest whole number.

*Sales 100s.* The number in this column represents how many hundreds of shares were traded for AM International on the day for which quotations are given. Thus, the 853 (for the common shares) in this column actually represents 85,300 (853 x 100) shares.

*High, Low, Last.* The dollar values in these columns represent the highest and lowest prices at which AM International traded for the day and the last price at which AM International traded.

*Chg. (Change).* The number in this-column represents the difference—plus, minus, or no change at all—between the last price quoted for the present day's listing and the last price quoted for the previous day's listing. For AM International common there was no change. The stock closed on this day at exactly the same price it closed the day before.

What do we know about AM International common stock? We know for the last fifty-two weeks it has been selling between $9.37½ and $4.87½ per share. We also know that if we had purchased it at its closing price for the day ($8.87½) we would be purchasing it close to its high for the year. We also know that it is a fairly active issue, having traded some 85,300 shares. But is the stock priced too high? Or is it at bargain prices? A lot more research is required before these questions can be answered. You would have to take a look at the stock's history, the present economic environment in general, the economic environment for those industries of which AM International is a part, and try to gather from your broker or some other analyst just what the projected earnings may be.

But even with all this information, you can't be guaranteed that your decision will be the correct one. You would also want to check investor interest in the stock, whether it's a takeover candidate, whether its management is strong or weak, what its financing needs may be in the future, what its book value is, what its balance sheet has to say. As you will realize from some of the sample transactions which are presented in Chapter 5, you do not buy or sell stocks when your entire research has been nothing more than a glance at the present day's listing. It is not that simple.

Stock quotations that we find in the financial sections of newspapers actually tell us a bit more than has been explained so far through the use of alphabetical symbols or abbreviations.

In the price columns there may be additional alphamerics (letters, numbers, other symbols, and marks) indicating that a price represents a high or a low trading price for the year. In the dividend column there may be footnotes representing extra payouts besides the regular dividend; additional stock dividends; liquidating dividends (dividends paid as a result of selling the assets of a company); dividends paid in some foreign currency.

## Sample Transactions

Let's take a look now at some transactions, just to get used to using the tables and working with fractions. We'll concentrate here on determining the cost to purchase stock (before commissions, which will be discussed later) and computing dividends.

***Example No. 1.*** You buy 200 shares of XYZ at the high ($35¼) of the day; (a) how much did the shares cost you and (b) what is the total amount of dividends you will receive based on a current payment of $2.24 per share per year.

a) 200 shares × $35-¼ =
   200 shares × $35.25 =
   $7,050 total cost.

b) 200 shares × $2.24 =
   $448.00 per year in dividends.

Regardless, then, of whether or not the value of the stock goes up or down, as long as there is no change in the dividend payout, you will receive $448.00 per year from this investment.

***Example No. 2.*** You buy 25 shares of ABC Corporation at the low ($16⅞) of the day; (a) how much did the shares cost you, and (b) what is the total amount of dividends you will receive based on the current payment of $1.24 per year per share?

a) 25 shares × $16-⅞
25 shares × shares = $16.87-½ =
25 shares × $16.875 =
$421.875 =
$421.88.

b) 25 shares × $1.24 =
$31.00 per year in dividends.

Once again, whether or not the value of the stock goes up or down, as long as there is no change in the dividend payout, you will receive $31.00 per year from this investment.

## Review Questions

Questions 1-3 are either true of false; indicate which.

1. The largest exchange in the United States is the New York Stock Exchange. _____

2. Yield is the annual (unless otherwise specified) rate of return. _____

3. PE ratio refers to the number of times by which the company's latest twelve month earnings must be multiplied to obtain the current stock price. _____

4. Convert the following fractions to parts of a dollar:

| a. ⅛ | d. ⅝ | a. _____ | d. _____ |
|---|---|---|---|
| b. ¼ | e. 1¼ | b. _____ | e. _____ |
| c. ⅜ | | c. _____ | |

5. You buy 200 shares of XYZ Corp. at $20½. The company pays an annual dividend of $.50 per share. How much in dividends will you receive each year from XYZ?

```
┌─────  CHAPTER  ─────┐
```
# 3

# Types of Stock

In Table 3.1, there is an additional listing of a few New York Stock Exchange issues and the usual market numbers that tell the investor what the trading range of the shares has been over the past twelve months, what is the dividend and current yield,

## Table 3.1

| 521Week High | Low | Stock | Div | Yld. | P/E | Shares | High | Low | Last | Chg. |
|---|---|---|---|---|---|---|---|---|---|---|
| 22³/₈ | 16 | PSvCol | 2.00 | 9.3 | 10 | 1487 | 21¹/₂ | 21¹/₈ | 21¹/₂+ | ³/₈ |
| 26 | 21¹/₄ | PSCol pf | 2.10 | 8.6 | ... | 3 | 24³/₈ | 24¹/₈ | 24³/₈+ | ¹/₄ |
| 18⁵/₈ | 10 | PSInd | | ... | 8 | 1731 | 16⁵/₈ | 16³/₈ | 16¹/₂− | ¹/₈ |
| 45³/₄ | 26 | PSIn pfA | 3.50 | 8.9 | ... | 100 | 39¹/₂ | 39¹/₂ | 39¹/₂ | ... |
| 15¹/₈ | 8¹/₂ | PSIn pfC | 1.08 | 8.6 | ... | 100 | 12¹/₂ | 12¹/₂ | 12¹/₂ | ... |
| 108 | 68 | PSIn pfG | 8.38 | 8.6 | ... | 950 | 97 | 97 | 97 | ... |
| 11³/₈ | 7³/₈ | PSvNH | | ... | 4 | 613 | 8¹/₂ | 8¹/₄ | 8¹/₄− | ¹/₈ |
| 23³/₄ | 17 | PSNH pf | | ... | ... | 2900 | 20 | 19¹/₂ | 19¹/₂− | 1¹/₈ |
| 25¹/₂ | 17 | PNH pfB | | ... | ... | 12 | 22⁵/₈ | 22⁵/₈ | 22⁵/₈ | ... |
| 33¹/₄ | 24 | PNH pfC | | ... | ... | 4 | 27¹/₂ | 27¹/₂ | 27¹/₂ | ... |
| 31¹/₄ | 21³/₄ | PNH pfD | | ... | ... | 7 | 25³/₈ | 25¹/₄ | 25¹/₄− | ¹/₂ |
| 27³/₄ | 18⁷/₈ | PNH pfF | | ... | ... | 14 | 22¹/₂ | 22¹/₂ | 22¹/₂− | ¹/₈ |
| 28⁷/₈ | 19¹/₈ | PNH pfG | | ... | ... | 45 | 24 | 23¹/₂ | 24  + | ¹/₈ |
| 39¹/₄ | 30¹/₂ | PSvNM | 2.92 | 7.7 | 11 | 228 | 37³/₄ | 37³/₈ | 37³/₄+ | ¹/₈ |
| 48¹/₄ | 34⁵/₈ | PSvEG | 2.96 | 7.2 | 15 | 1382 | 41¹/₂ | 40⁵/₈ | 41³/₈+ | ³/₄ |
| 26³/₈ | 23 | PSEG pf | 2.17 | 8.5 | ... | 5 | 25¹/₂ | 25¹/₂ | 25¹/₂ | ... |
| 91¹/₄ | 74 | PSEG pf | 6.80 | 7.6 | ... | 250 | 89¹/₂ | 89¹/₂ | 89¹/₂ | ... |
| 27⁵/₈ | 25 | PSEG pf | 2.43 | 9.5 | ... | 21 | 25¹/₂ | 25¹/₂ | 25¹/₂− | ¹/₄ |
| 101 | 83¹/₂ | PSEG pf | 7.70 | 7.9 | ... | 9500 | 98¹/₈ | 98 | 98  − | ¹/₂ |
| 101¹/₄ | 84¹/₄ | PSEG pf | 7.80 | 7.9 | ... | 5340 | 98⁷/₈ | 98³/₈ | 98⁷/₈+ | ¹/₈ |
| 93³/₄ | 81¹/₂ | PSEG pf | 8.08 | 8.7 | ... | 1590 | 93 | 92 | 93  + | ¹/₂ |

what is the ratio between the price of a share and the current earnings per share, how many issues were traded, what the day's trading range has been, and what is the difference between the day's closing price and the previous day's.

You will notice that some of the abbreviated names of the stocks are followed by the letters "pf," which indicates that the stocks are "preferred" issues. Generally, preferred stocks pay a higher dividend than common stocks and they generally have a narrower trading range — but not always.

When one purchases shares of stock strictly for income purposes he does not want to take a chance on highly volatile issues that may result in capital losses that completely offset accumulated dividend income.

Many companies offer only common stock. Some offer various classifications of common as well as many classifications of preferreds. What both common and preferred stocks mean to a corporation is a flexible method of financing.

Preferred stock issued by a corporation carries with it first rights over common stock in regard to dividend payments. In those cases where a corporation finds itself forced into bankruptcy or into some form of reorganization, preferred stockholders will, in almost all cases, have priority over common stockholders in the distribution of all assets. But whatever special treatment the preferred shareholder receives in these circumstances occurs only after the claims of bondholders and other creditors have been satisfied.

What claims the preferred stockholder can make on the corporation are generally limited to the liquidating par value of the stock. This is to say that if the par value of the preferred stock is $100, then its owner is entitled to a maximum of $100 in cash or other assets for each share that he owns.

That par value, by the way, is also used to calculate the dividend on each share. For example, if you own 100 shares of an 8% preferred stock, with a par value fixed at $100, your annual dividend will amount to $80. But this dividend is never guaranteed. At any time the corporate board can elect to postpone declaration of the dividend.

## Preferred Stock

Preferreds give a special kind of financial flexibility to the corporation. Owners of preferreds are considered stockholders but they have no rights to share in corporate profits as do common shareholders. And, to mention it once more for emphasis, in hard times the corporation can elect *not* to declare the dividend; would it were that they could cancel payments due their creditors with such ease! But preferred issues are not all benefit to the corporation, for the dividends paid to holders cannot be deducted for tax purposes as can dividend payments to common shareholders.

Preferred stocks are issued with varying rights and privileges but they generally fall under the following classifications:

- — callable;
- — cumulative;
- — participating;
- — convertible;
- — prior

A *callable* preferred stock is one that is redeemable on or after a specified date and at a stated price. Just about every preferred stock contains a call feature. This call feature is important to the issuing company. It is important because preferred stock is generally purchased for income purposes so its price will move in accordance with interest rates. When interest rates are low, the price of the preferred will be higher.

For example, a 6% preferred, $100 par value may very well sell near par when interest rates are low enough to make a 6% return attractive. However, if short-term interest rates skyrocket, it would be expected that the price of the preferred will come down so that the rate of return is substantially increased.* This is a bit tricky to understand if you are unfamiliar with the arithmetic associated with preferred.

But consider a 6% preferred stock, $100 par value. If you

---

*This is, of course, only one of the factors influencing the price of preferreds. Yields will vary depending also on the quality and stability of the corporation issuing the stock.

purchase it at $100 your annual dividend is $6 ($100 × .06). Bear this in mind: this dividend rate per share remains fixed. When declared it is 6% of the *par* value regardless of the market price of the stock.

If interest rates skyrocket, people will ignore a preferred paying only 6%. Thus the price of the stock will be bid down until the dividend represents a sufficient enough return to attract investors.

Consider, if you will, the same 6% preferred ($100 par) now selling at $50 per share. The dividend is still $6 but the price per share is half of what it had been. The return on investment, in this case, if the shares are purchased, is 12% ($6 divided by $50).

In the exercises which follow, see if you can determine what the annual dividend will be. The arithmetic is not complicated, for this is not a test of your ability to multiply or work with percentages, but rather to familiarize you with the relation between the par value of the preferred and the dividend rate.

| Preferred Stock Par Value | Dividend Rate | Annual Dividend |
|---|---|---|
| $100 | 7% | ? |
| 100 | 8% | ? |
| 50 | 9% | ? |
| 50 | 12% | ? |

The answers, which you would have been able to arrive at without pencil and paper or the aid of a calculator, are $7.00, $8.00, $4.50 and $6.00.

Do not, however, confuse the dividend rate with the rate of return, which must be determined by taking the annual dividend and dividing it by the price you paid for the stock. Try the brief exercises which follow to familiarize yourself with how the rate of return is arrived at. The arithmetic here is a bit more complicated than for the above exercises, but if you look closely you will see that a calculator or pencil and paper is not really required to perform the arithmetic.

| Preferred Stock<br>Market Price | Annual<br>Dividend | Rate of<br>Return |
|:---:|:---:|:---:|
| $90 | $6.00 | ? |
| 75 | 2.50 | ? |
| 50 | 5.00 | ? |
| 44 | 5.50 | ? |

As you will have noticed, the dividend rate for a preferred stock is based on the par value assigned to that stock; however, when you want to find the rate of return you will actually receive, the par value does not become a part of the arithmetical operations. The answers to the above, as you probably already know, are: 6.67%, 3 1/3%, 10% and 12 1/2%.

If, in the above examples, the par value for the preferred stock was $100 in every case, you can see how the reduction in market price increased the rate of return. A little arithmetic will reveal that, if indeed the par value was $100 in all cases, the dividend rates would have been, respectively: 6%, 2½%, 5%, and 5½%. So, if interest rates are high, the effect will be a downward slide in the price of the preferred until the rate of return available is competitive with those interest rates.

The reverse can also happen. Lower interest rates can put upward pressure on the price of the preferred.

With the more conventional types of long-term debt, a corporation can plan on the eventual retirement of the debt. For instance, it may issue a twenty-five-year bond on which it pays 8% per year in interest; at the end of the twenty-five years it can call in the bond at its face value. This call-in feature is not automatic in the case of preferred stock unless the preferred has been issued with a call feature. And without the call feature, the corporation might be forced into paying excessively high market prices to retire the issue.

*Cumulative* preferred stock contains provisions which bind the corporation to pay all dividends due preferred holders before dividends may be paid on common stocks. But here is the catch: If the corporation does not pay dividends on its common stock and has no plans to do so, the cumulative feature means nothing. By law, dividends on preferreds are cumulative unless otherwise stated.

In those circumstances wherein the corporation owes dividends to preferred shareholders yet wishes to declare a dividend on its common stock, it has the option of offering to convert the preferred issues to common. But before it can do so, the corporation must receive approval from stockholders.

Thus, if you were to invest in a preferred stock which, at the time of purchase, offered a 10% yield on your investment, you must be aware that unless the stock has a cumulative feature you have no guarantee of eventual compensation for skipped dividend payments. Even with the cumulative feature there is no guarantee of payment—except when there will be a dividend to common shareholders.

The dividend rate associated with each preferred means little unless the corporation has the financial muscle to back up its promise. This underscores the necessity of researching the fiscal, market, and management strength of the company in whose stocks you wish to invest.

Some preferred stock is issued with what is termed a *participating* feature. Owners of participating preferred are entitled not only to the stated dividend but also to special dividend payments after distributions to common stockholders. For example, suppose you are the owner of an 8%, $100 par, preferred and the provisions for participation take effect anytime common stock dividends exceed $8 per share. If the distribution to common shareholders is $10, then you will receive an extra $2 for each share of the participating preferred that you own.

Preferred stocks are also often issued with a *convertible* feature. This means that the preferred shareholder has the option of exchanging his preferred stock for common stock at a specific price. Note the word here: *conversion*. This means the preferred becomes common. In other words, the preferred is completely retired from the books.

The conditions under which the conversion takes place are specified by the corporation. Included in these conditions are the conversion rate and the conversion period, plus the call provisions. Corporations tend to favor convertible preferreds because of the way in which they affect earnings per share.

For example, consider that the current price for a share of XYZ common is $60. If the company wants to issue new stock it will do so through teams of underwriters.

These underwriters are individuals or firms who specialize in bringing securities to market. They, in effect, will guarantee XYZ that the shares they subscribe for will be brought to market. The profit to the underwriters will be the difference between what they pay for the shares and the price at which they finally sell them.

Because XYZ will deal with these underwriters instead of directly with the public (which would be cumbrous and expensive) they will discount the shares for the underwriters to, perhaps, $55 (probably much less, but this figure simplifies our arithmetic).

If the company needs to raise some $33 million dollars but can only sell the shares for $55, then it must issue 600,000 shares.

---

$$\$33,000,000 \text{ Divided by } \$55 = 600,000 \text{ Shares}$$

---

Now, those 600,000 shares will dilute the earnings per share and affect the market price accordingly. There are now 600,000 additional shares available over which earnings must be distributed. The company would be more to the wise if it found a means of obtaining the funds by issuing fewer shares. Thus, the advantage of the convertibles. The company need not discount the stock to bring it to market. It can easily bring the new issues to market at a higher price. When the market value of the underlying common shares increase, the convertible preferred will also increase in value and a profit can be made though conversion.

You will notice in scanning stock listings in the financial section of your newspaper that there are certain preferreds which have an unusually low dividend. These are very often the convertible preferreds. Because of the convertibility feature, the investor has the flexibility of switching to common to take advantage of capital gains during the market upswings or remaining with the fixed-income non-volatile preferred in slower times. Additionally, the preferred stock will generally move in the same direction as the common stock, and when that move is upwards, the preferred stockholder is in the comfortable position of having a "fixed-income" security providing good potential for capital gains.*

Some preferred stocks are also *prior* to other preferreds which means that they receive preferential treatment. No dividends can be distributed to other preferred holders until those holding the prior preferred stock receive their distributions.

It must be mentioned that certain preferred issues provide for what is called a *sinking fund,* although these types of securities seem to become more rare with each passing year.

A sinking fund is one which is established to assure the finalization of a debt. It is, briefly, a way of amortizing debt. The payments made into the sinking fund are usually in fixed sums during specified fiscal periods. At any time the accumulated funds may be used for open-market purchase of shares or to call in a percentage of those shares outstanding.

A glance down the daily listings for the New York Stock Exchange or the American Stock Exchange will indicate that there are relatively few corporations attempting to finance themselves with preferred stocks. The majority of corporations that are issuing preferreds are the public utilities like Public Service Gas & Electric, Detroit Edison, Cleveland Electric, etc.

The listings in the newspapers, however, do not detail the

---

*Interest rates, however, will change this scenario, for if interest rates go up, the convertible preferred *may* go down. The conversion price will also affect the relative movement of the cumulative preferred.

special provisions that go with preferred issues; it is necessary for the investor to contact his broker or the company to get the detail on the special rights and privileges that go with ownership.

## Advantages/Disadvantages of Preferred

The advantages to the corporation in the issuance of preferred stock may be seen as disadvantages to the investor.

—As there is no legal obligation in the case of dividends, the investor has no guarantee of income.

—Unless a preferred has a sinking fund provision, no eventual payment to the amount of the par value is required and the investor has not the market pressure, then, which will assure the full return of his principle.

—The corporation gives to the preferred shareholder no voting privileges. The preferred shareholder, therefore, has no way to participate in the management of the corporation through the election of representatives to the board — except under very unusual circumstances (as when successive dividend payments have been withheld).

—Unless a preferred stock is "participating," the shareholder cannot expect any income beyond the stated dividend rate (in relation to the par value).

## Common Stocks

Investment in common stocks represents a different ballgame than investments in preferred issues.

Common stock is the capital stock of a corporation and as such gives to its owner equity, or ownership, in the corporation. It brings to its holders certain legal rights, among which are the rights to:

—vote for members of the board of directors;
—receive dividends declared;
—receive proportionate ownership in the corporation.

In addition to these special rights, the common shareholder is in the comfortable position of knowing that, despite the fact that he is one of the owners of the corporation, his legal liability is strictly limited to the amount of his holdings.

But this is no argument for common stock, for common stock, despite its privileges, is far more risky than preferred. Prices can fluctuate considerably in short spans of time; common shareholders only receive dividends if there are any left after distributions to preferred shareholders; and in the event of liquidation, common shareholders are last on the list to get what is left of corporate assets.

The amount of authorized stock that may be made available is specified in a corporation's charter. Not all authorized stock may be issued at one time, as corporations often keep a certain amount of stock on reserve for stock options, stock dividends, or stock splits.

The term *authorized stock* is often confused with the terms *issued stock* and *outstanding stock;* but each of these terms have very different meanings. Authorized stock is simply the total amount of stock that may be issued by a corporation. Issued stock is that portion of authorized stock which is owned by stockholders or has been purchased by the corporation and is being held as treasury stock. Outstanding stock is that stock actually in the hands of the public.

---

| | |
|---|---|
| Authorized Stock: | Amount of stock that the corporation may actually issue. |
| Issued Stock: | A portion of, or all of, the authorized stock actually sold to the public or which has been purchased back by the corporation. |
| Outstanding Stock: | Stock actually in the hands of the public. |

---

Unlike preferred stock, common stock need not be issued with a par value. If you recall, in the case of the preferred issue, the par value has significance because preferred stock contains some of the provision of a debt instrument and therefore a par or face value plays its part when the stock is being recalled or retired. And, also, the par value becomes the muliplicand in the arithmetical operations to determine the dividend rate. In the case of common issues, however, the par value has no significance in fixing the dividend payment, as common stock dividends are declared and changed at the discretion of the board of directors. In fact, the par value assigned to common stock is simply contrived to facilitate bookkeeping efforts. But at whatever number this par value is fixed, it is usually a relatively low value. It is low in order that stockholders will not find themselves saddled with undue liabilities, which can happen if they acquire their shares at less than par (as they are liable for the difference to par).

In those cases when new common is authorized with no par, the stock is accounted for at whatever the price of the shares are currently selling for in the secondary markets created by the stock exchanges.

It is important to realize that the dividend on common stock remains the same regardless of the variation in the market price. In other words, if a dividend of $2 per share is declared on a stock currently selling for $20, the yield is 10%. Now, if the common stock increases any time after the declaration, the dividend still remains at $2 per share. If the stock goes to $40, then the new yield is 5%. The following exercise will help establish in your mind that the dividend yield in common stock is based

| Common Stock Priced | Annual Dividend | Dividend Yield |
|:---:|:---:|:---:|
| $ 5 | $1.00 | ? |
| 10 | 1.00 | ? |
| 15 | 1.00 | ? |
| 20 | 1.00 | ? |
| 25 | 1.00 | ? |
| 30 | 1.00 | ? |

not on any par value, but on the price at which you must pay for the stock.

The answers to the above, which you were probably able to arrive at quite easily, are: 20%, 10%, 6²/₃%, 5%, 4%, 3¹/₃%.

## Market Value of Common and Preferred

This market value at which common stock is currently valued is determined solely by the law of supply and demand and may possibly be unrelated to the current fiscal performance of the issuing corporation. It is possible, given the unpredictability of the stock market, that a corporation's stock may be declining in value at the same time that its earnings per share are increasing.

In the case of preferred issues, the market value will fluctuate in relationship to interest rates as well as with investor confidence in the corporation issuing the stock, as preferreds compete with fixed-income instruments. The price of common stock, however, will fluctuate mainly in relation to investor confidence in the issuing corporation or anticipation of positive market interest in the stock. Anything, however, can affect the movement of both preferreds and common, including wars, hurricanes, and just plain investment ignorance or incorrect financial reporting. One would expect, however, that common stock be priced in some relation to its book value, or even its liquidating value, but this is not always the case.

## Book Value

Book value is arrived at by finding the difference between assets and liabilities. If a corporation has assets of $2 million and liabilities of $1 million, its book value or net assets will come

---

Outstanding Shares:     100,000
Book Value:   $1,000,000

$1,000,000 Divided by 100,000  =  $10 per Share
Book Value

---

to, easy enough, $1 million. Corporations, however, generally calculate their book value in terms of each share of outstanding stock. This per-share figure is arrived at by dividing the total book value by the number of shares.

This book value must not be confused either with the liquidating value or with the par value of the shares. Many years ago in accounting there was indeed some relationship between book value and par value, but, today, par value, to emphasize the fact once more, has simply become an arbitrary assignment for bookkeeping purposes. Theoretically, book value and liquidating value should be coincident, but in the real marketplace it is impossible that they should be. There are certain costs associated with the liquidating process itself, and assets are never actually sold for what the accountant claims they should be worth. For companies, however, who by nature of their business (such as hotels or amusement parks) own a great deal of real estate, which is rarely accounted for at current market valuation, liquidation may result in per share income that exceeds the recorded book value.

But book value is still an important factor in stock selection. Analysts generally expect that a stock should be selling at least at book value and they use this as *one* of the many gauges in selecting stocks for further research and possible recommendation.

## Classes of Common

To this point, the discussion on common stock has proceeded as though there were only one class of common that may be issued. In fact, however, there are a number of classes of common stock that a corporation may bring to market. Each class is assigned special rights and privileges.

Generally, the distinction between the various classified common stocks that might be issued centers around voting privileges.

As a rule, common stockholders have the legal right to vote for the men and women who will serve on the board of directors. They have this right to vote as they are actually owners of the corporation, although the individual shares that they hold generally give each of them little control over the corporation unless they can join forces with other shareholders to accumulate votes. It is often possible for shareholders to do this — that is, band together to combine their votes in order to get representatives on the board who will steer the corporation in a direction which best benefits them.

Thus, the reason for the issuance of more than one class of common stock.

One class usually contains voting privileges and the other does not.* Upper management or special-interest groups will hold the stock with voting privileges, and the general public will be issued the stock without voting rights. In this way, the corporation may be run independently of the general stockholder.

In those cases wherein a common issue does not carry with it voting privileges, it is usually the case that the stock gives its owner the right to special claims on earnings or assets over and above voting common. In this way, it is made especially attractive to the public regardless of the loss of voting privileges.

Most stockholders care little about voting rights. Generally, their investment is relatively small and they are simply interested in dividend income and/or capital gains. They have their own careers to keep in place and have little desire to get involved in corporate politics. The majority do not even bother to attend annual meetings, and if they do cast a vote it is, more often than not, by proxy statement.

## Voting Rights

A proxy statement is actually a written power-of-attorney that a stockholder turns over to another to vote his corporate stock. In most cases, it is the executive group of the corporation that goes after the proxies, and they do this to assure that the votes cast support the viewpoint of the present board of directors. Proxies fall under the regulation of the Securities and Exchange Commission (SEC) when they are solicited by publicly held

---

*It is now becoming more popular for holders of one class to have multiple votes per share and/or the ability to convert to other classes of stock.

corporations. The main requirements of the SEC are that the proxy statement include:

—name of officers and directors,
—number of shares held by officers and directors,
—renumeration of officers and directors,
—any pension and retirement plans to be acted upon,
—provisions for the stockholder to vote against the board's directives,
—proposed amendments to the corporate charter or by-laws.

There are two methods by which stockholders may vote for their board of directors. These are the statutory method and the cumulative method.

In the statutory method, a majority vote is the determining factor. Each stockholder is entitled to one vote for each share of stock he owns. Thus, if a stockholder owns ten shares, he has ten votes; if he has a thousand shares he has a thousand votes.

It is important to underscore the fact that a majority of votes is required to elect a director, not merely a plurality.* For example, if the leading candidate receives 500 of 1000 votes, he cannot be elected. He needs 501 votes.

In the cumulative voting system, the math is a bit cumbrous. This is because in cumulative voting, a minority of stockholders, who ordinarily would automatically be at a disadvantage in a statutory vote, are given a special chance to elect their representatives to the board.

Bogen explains the mathematics in the following way:** "If a corporation has 300 shares of voting stock represented at the stockholders' meeting, there are five directors to be elected and the minority owns 148 shares, it would be entitled to 740 votes. If the minority wished to elect candidates, it would cast 370 votes for each. The majority interest owning 152 shares is entitled to 760 votes, so that if it spreads these votes over five candi-

---

*Bogen, Jules I., ed., *Financial Handbook*. New York: The Ronald Press, 1964, pp. 13-14.
**Ibid., pp. 13-15

dates each would receive 152 votes, and over four candidates 190 votes. Thus it is useless for the majority to spread its votes over more than three candidates who would be unopposed, as the minority would have no votes left after having used its voting power to assure the election of two directors."

The formula for determining how the shares are to be voted with cumulative voting is:

---

$$\text{Minimum Number of Shares Required} = \frac{\text{Shares Outstanding} \times \text{Number of Directors Desired}}{\text{Total Number of Directors To Be Elected}} + 1$$

---

Thus, to elect one director in a corporation with 300 shares outstanding, the minority shareholders would need 51 shares, with 255 votes, all which must be counted for the election of one director. Only a 17% representation of the voting stock, therefore, is necessary to achieve minority representation.*

## Review Questions

1. In stock listings "pf" identifies _____ stocks.

2. What is the yield on a stock selling for $40 and paying a $1.50 per year dividend? _____

3. What is the P/E ratio on a stock earning $2 per share and selling for $50? _____

4. Do preferred stocks carry first rights over common stock in regard to dividend payments? _____

---
*Ibid.

5. If you own 100 shares of 10% preferred stock with a par value of $50, what would be your annual dividends? _____

6. Are dividends on preferred stocks guaranteed? _____

7. _____ preferred stock is that which is redeemable on or after a specified date and at a specified price.

8. _____ preferred stock contains provisions which bind the corporation to pay all money due these preferred holders before dividends may be paid on common stock.

9. _____ preferred stock may be exchanged for common stock.

10. _____ preferred stockholders receive preferential treatment over other preferred holders much the same as preferred stockholders have preferential treatment over common stock holders.

11. Unless a preferred stock has a _____ _____ provision, no eventual payment to the amount of the par value is required from the issuing corporation.

12. Unless a preferred stock is a _____ preferred, the shareholders cannot expect any income beyond the fixed dividend of the security.

13. _____ stock is the capital stock of the corporation and gives the owners of the common equity, or ownership, in the corporation.

14. _____ stock is the amount of stock that a corporation may actually issue.

15. _____ stock is the authorized stock actually in the hands of the public.

16. _____ value is arrived at by finding the difference betwen assets and liabilities.

17. Analysts generally expect that a stock should be selling at least at its _____ value.

18. A _____ statement is a written power-of-attorney that a stockholder turns over to another to vote his corporate stock.

19. If a 6% preferred with a par value of $100 is selling at $80, what is the current yield? _____

20. If a 6% preferred with a par value of $100 is selling at $150, what is the current yield? _____

21. If a company needs to raise $1 million but can only expect to get $50 per share when it brings the stock to market, how many shares will it have to issue? _____

22. Does a new stock issue dilute or increase the value of your current holdings? _____

23. If there are 200,000 shares outstanding and the book value of the corporation is $1 million, what is the book value of each share of stock? _____

24. Will book value and liquidating value always be the same? _____

## CHAPTER 4

# Buying and Selling Stock

When you buy or sell stock through a stockbroker you must pay a commission (brokerage fee) each time you buy and each time you sell stock. The exact amount of the fee depends upon the number of shares that are bought and sold, whether the shares are traded in odd or round lots and upon the price of the stock. A round lot refers to multiples of 100 shares, and an odd lot is anything less than 100 shares.

## Brokerage Fees

Brokerage fees will vary considerably. In recent years there has been a proliferation of discount houses which offer bare-bones services and which charge their customers very low trading commissions. On the other end of the spectrum are the larger and more service-oriented brokerage houses which not only handle a customer's buy and sell orders but also publish and distribute a wealth of material to help in selecting stocks with strong potential.

In the examples of buy-and-sell transactions which will follow, the commission rates are arbitrarily selected, for we are not as concerned with the procedures for computing brokerage fees as we are in how those brokerage fees subtract from profits and add to losses in stock trades.

Brokerage firms charge a minimum fee for executing orders, usually from $35 to $40. Thus, on small odd-lot orders you will find yourself paying a rather high percentage in commissions. For example, if you were to sell 15 shares of stock at $25\frac{1}{8}$, the commission, based on one broker's schedule, would be about $35.00. That is over 9 percent in commissions. Under the same price structure you could sell 100 shares of stock at $11.00 and pay only about $35.00. In this last case the commission amounts to only about 3 percent.

Brokerage fees are always being revised, so it is very hard to talk in specifics. By the time this book gets into your hands there's no telling what the fees for executing your orders will be. The table on which we are basing brokerage fees for our examples may or may not be near the current averages. The important thing to remember is that these fees must be considered in determining where your break-even point will be in buy-and-sell transactions.

In the transactions and exercises which appear in this and following chapters, the brokerage commissions will be supplied. And for purposes of simplification, brokerage fees and other related costs will all be grouped together and referred to as "fees."

Having that fee schedule at hand before buying and selling is always a good idea. Without it you may decide to sell a stock at a price at which you believe you will achieve at least a marginal profit. But after all fees are deducted from or added to a transaction, you may very well find yourself with a loss rather than a gain.

If you buy 100 shares of stock at $12.00 per share, and one year later sell it at $12.50 per share, at first calculation it appears that you have made a $50.00 profit. But if the fees on both the buy and sell orders amounted to $78.00—zappo, you've a loss of $28.00 after tieing up your money for a year.

If you buy and sell securities fairly regularly, your annual costs for brokerage fees can well add up to thousands of dollars, and that of course reduces your profits considerably.

Savings in brokerage commissions can add to your profits; and brokerage information and research services can help you select the right stocks. So it pays to shop around for a broker who offers you exactly the right combination of price and services to help you win in the market.

## Investor Incentive

Investors will purchase stock for a number of reasons. But, of course, in the final analysis they've but one goal in mind, and that goal is to make as much money as they can. Many purchase stock for the purpose of selling it later at a higher price. Others purchase stock because they find the dividends being paid offer them a higher rate of return on their investment than they would receive in a bank savings account. Others will invest both for the profit they may receive on buy-and-sell transactions as well as for the rate of return they will receive on their money (via dividends) while they wait for the price of that stock to climb.

The money a bank distributes to its savings depositors is called "interest"; it is legally obligated to pay the declared interest rate. However, the share of profits that a bank, or any corporation, may distribute to its shareholders is called "dividends." But all stocks do not pay dividends and even if they have been paying dividends, there is no guarantee that they will continue to do so. The determining factors in whether or not a dividend will be paid are the issuing corporation's continued success and/or whether or not the board of directors decides to share profits with stockholders or just reinvest the money back into their corporation.

## Determining Yield on Investments

The dividend paid to the stockholder represents a return on his investment, and as such it is often expressed as a percent value, and referred to as the "rate of return." Another term for rate of return is "yield." The yield is determined by dividing the amount invested in a company's stock into the annual dividends. You've already read how this is done in Chapter Two under "Yield %," but for further clarification, here are some additional examples.

*Example No. 1.* You invest $1,000 in a stock that pays an annual dividend of $100.00 per year on your investment. What is your rate of return?

$$\$100.00 \div \$1,000 = .10 \text{ (or 10\%)}$$

**Example No. 2.** You purchase 100 shares of ACF Industries at $35.25 per share. Annual dividends are $2.24. What will be your rate of return?

$$\$2.24 \div \$35.25 = .064 \text{ (or } 6.4\%)^*$$

In each of the previous examples, the brokerage and other related fees have not been considered in the calculation. They usually are not until after the stock is sold and the investor is interested in determining what was his total return for the period in which he held the stock. But some investors will include the buy commissions in their calculations for a more accurate picture of their rate of return, and then recalculate again after the sale of the stock.

**Example No. 3.** You have purchased 100 shares of ACF at $35.25 per share. You receive four quarterly dividend payments totalling $224.00 and then sell the stock after thirteen months for a $100.00 profit. Brokerage and related fees come to $130.00. What was your true rate of return?

(100 shares × $35.25) + $130.00 = $3,655.00 total cost
$324.00 (total div. + profit**) ÷ $3,655.00 = .0886 (8.86%) rate of return

An interesting thing to note is that you do not have to own shares of stock for an entire quarter to receive dividends due for that period. Neither do you have to keep a stock for an entire year to be eligible for the annual payout. Very often you may own the stock for only a couple of weeks or even days and yet be eligible for the quarterly, semiannual, or annual payout. As long as you purchased the stock before the ex-dividend date. you are eligible for the coming dividend payment.

By "ex-dividend" is meant "without dividend." This is to say that a stock selling ex-dividend is being sold without the rights

---

*This is the way the operation would be preformed on a calculator.
**Bear in mind that profits from the sale of stock and dividends are treated differently for tax purposes.

to the coming dividend. For transfer and record purposes, every stock on which a dividend is declared will have an ex-dividend period. This is because provisions must be made to allow enough time for the delivery of the stock. Usually, the time allowed is four or five days.

For example, suppose a dividend is declared payable to holders of record listed on the company's books on, say, May 11. Since five days must be scheduled to allow for delivery of the stock, the stock would be declared ex-dividend beginning May 6. Anyone who purchases the stock after May 5 will not be entitled to the coming dividend.

Buyers of stocks usually make note of ex-dividend dates, for, generally, unless they are short-term speculators, they are interested in the yield—or total rate of return—they will receive from their investment.

Remember not to confuse the term "rate of return" with what is termed the "dividend rate." These terms mean two entirely different things, as you have learned in Chapter 3. But to thoroughly distinguish the terms, let's review the two kinds of stock a corporation will issue.

As explained in Chapter 3, there are many kinds of stock that a corporation issues; but, generally speaking, they may be divided into two classifications: common and preferred. In most cases, the preferred stockholder gets *preference* when corporate profits are distributed. Therefore, when dividends are declared they are distributed to preferred stockholders and then (if there are any left to be distributed) to common stockholders. The annual dividend paid on the preferreds is based on the par value of the stock, whereas in the case of common stock the remainder of the profits is simply divided evenly by share. Preferred stocks generally pay higher dividends, as illustrated in Table 4.1.

Remember, *par value* is an arbitrary value assigned to a share of stock by company directors. In the case of preferred issues, it becomes the muliplicand in the operation to establish the dollar return an investor can expect based on the preferred's rate. This is to say that if an investor owns 100 shares of an

8% preferred, *$100 par*, he may expect to receive up to $800.00 per year on his investment. We say "up to" because this return on investment can vary—depending upon decisions by the board of directors.

---

### Table 4.1
### Yields on Preferred
### and Common Stocks
### 1970-82

| Year | Preferred (10 stocks in % per year) | Common (in % per year) Composite (500 stocks) | Industrials (400 stocks) |
|------|------|------|------|
| 1970 | 7.22 | 3.83 | 3.62 |
| 1972 | 6.88 | 2.84 | 2.61 |
| 1973 | 7.23 | 3.06 | 2.79 |
| 1974 | 8.24 | 4.47 | 4.13 |
| 1975 | 8.36 | 4.31 | 3.96 |
| 1976 | 7.98 | 3.77 | 3.48 |
| 1977 | 7.61 | 4.62 | 4.43 |
| 1978 | 8.25 | 5.28 | 5.06 |
| 1979 | 9.11 | 5.47 | 5.20 |
| 1980 | 10.60 | 5.26 | 4.95 |
| 1981 | 12.36 | 5.20 | 5.81 |
| 1982 | 12.53 | 5.81 | 5.48 |
| 1983 | 11.02 | 4.40 | 4.04 |

From tables in the 1980 and 1985 *Statistical Abstract of the United States*, p. 545 and p. 507 respectively. Preferred stock yields are based on 10 stocks, 4 yields, with issues converted to a price equal to $100 par and a 7% annual dividend before averaging.

---

Common stocks need not be assigned a par value at authorization. When they are not, they are listed on the books at market value.

For both preferred and common stock, it is important to remember that the true value is what someone else is willing to pay for it—and, therefore, the true worth is whatever the quoted bid price is for a share of the stock.

If you purchase a 5% preferred stock which has a par value of $100.00, then your annual dividend on each share is $5.00. The 5% is your dividend rate (5% × $100.00 = $5.00) if you purchased the stock for $100. The value of the preferred in the market place may go way above or way below $100.00, but the dividend will always be $5.00. The dividend rate on the par value will always remain 5%; the true yield based on the present value of the stock, however, will change according to the ratio of the market value of stock to the dividend.

*Your* rate of return, then, is the annual dividend divided by what you actually paid for the stock in the market place. You see, although the preferred stock has a par value of $100.00, you may very well have purchased each share at an average of $95.00 per share. Therefore, while the dividend rate was 5% (of par value), your actual rate of return is $5.00 divided by $95.00, the result of which is .053 or 5.3%.

**Example No. 4.** You purchase 50 shares of a 6% preferred stock. Par value is $100.00. You paid a total of $5,150, including fees, to purchase the stock. What is your rate of return?

6% × $100.00    = $6.00 per share annual dividend
$6.00 × 50 shares = $300.00 total annual dividend
$300.00 ÷ $5,150 = .0582 or 5.82%*

**Example No. 5.** You purchase 100 shares of a 5% preferred stock. Par value is $25.00. You paid a total of $2,375, including fees, to purchase the stock. What is your rate of return?

5% × $25.00    = $1.25 per share dividend
$1.25 × 100 shares = $125.00 total annual dividend
$125.00 ÷ $2,375 = .0526 or 5.26%

As you have noticed, the procedures for determining the rate of return on preferred stock are to find the amount of the dividend, then divide that amount by the price of the stock.

---

*You may also simply divide the dividend per share by the cost per share, but this will give you a slightly inflated rate of return, since it does not include fees.

## Making and Losing Money

Believe it or not, you can play the market to go up or you can play it to go down.

When you play the market to go up, or you're expecting an individual stock to move higher, you are being "bullish." A "bull" takes what is called a "long" position in a stock. That means he has purchased a company's stock and his investment plan is to hold onto it until it increases to a certain value.

When you play the market to go down, or you're expecting an individual stock to move lower, you are being "bearish." A "bear" takes what is called a "short" position in a stock or decides not to purchase any. If he shorts the stock, this means he sells the stock before he buys it. How does he do this? First, he tells his broker that he wants to "sell short" on a particular stock and he places his order.* The broker, in turn, borrows the shares to be sold and holds them until the investor decides to buy them back. Now everything works in reverse. Each $1/8$ of a point that the stock goes up, the bear loses money. But each $1/8$ of a point that the stock goes down, the bear makes money.

Now, let's look at some hypothetical situations and see how money is made and lost in the market place. The first series of transactions presented will be bullish; this is to say that the investors will actually buy the shares in anticipation of their increasing in value. The next series of transactions will be bearish; that is, the investors will be playing certain stocks to go down in value so they will make a profit.

### ☐ *Mr. John Phelps* ☐

The first investor you must meet is Mr. John Phelps, a very thrifty young man. But he's dissatisfied with the interest his money has been earning in the local savings bank. He feels that if he were to invest his money *successfully* in the stock market, he could better keep up with inflation. The $6^{1}/_2$ percent he's getting on his savings just isn't enough. So he withdraws about $5,000 from his account and invests in the stock market.

---

*A margin account is required (see Chap. 6) and a bear is required to have in deposit in his account at least 50 percent of the value of the stock he has sold.

*Transaction No. 1.* On September 15, 1981, John Phelps takes his first shot at the market and buys 300 shares of stock in an aviation firm, which we will call Company A. His costs:

| | |
|---|---|
| 300 shares at $13.50 | = $4,050.00 |
| Fees | 97.00* |
| Total Cost | $4,147.00. |

Note that his actual cost per share was $13.82 ($4,147 divided by 300 shares) after commissions. But Phelps thought this all peanuts compared to what he would earn when the shares doubled in price.

*Transaction No. 2.* A little more than one month later, the shares of this same aviation company take a bit of a tumble and are now worth only $11.00. Phelps decides to sell out, fearing that the shares will depreciate even further. He sells at $11.00.

| | |
|---|---|
| 300 shares at $11.00 | = $3,300.00 |
| Fees | 90.00 |
| Amount Received | $3,210.00. |

After fees were deducted, Phelps actually had received only $10.70 for each share.

---

### SCOREBOARD

| | |
|---|---|
| Bought 300 shares of Company A at | $4,147 |
| Sold 300 shares of Company A at | 3,210 |
| *Total Loss* | $ 937 |

---

*Transaction No. 3.* The newspapers announce that a financial company wants to take over a publishing company and the talk on the street is that the publishing company's stock could very well double in just days. Phelps decides to take a chance and purchase stock in the publishing company, which we will

---

*Brokerage fees are arbitrary assignments in this and all other examples. In actuality, they will vary depending upon whether an investor uses a full-service or discount broker.

call Company B. He gets the shares at $31-¾ apiece.

| | | |
|---|---|---|
| 100 shares at $31-¾ | = | $3,175.00 |
| Fees | | 65.00 |
| Total Cost | | $3,240.00 |

**Transaction No. 4.** Negotiations between the two companies fell apart and the market place loses interest. The result is that the shares Phelps holds fall sharply. Phelps has held the stock long enough to collect 25 cents per share in dividends, but then finally bails out when the stock is at $25-¼.

| | | |
|---|---|---|
| 100 shares at $25-¼ | = | $2,525.00 |
| Fees | | 60.00 |
| Amount Received | | $2,465.00 |

---

### SCOREBOARD

| | |
|---|---|
| Bought 300 shares of Company A at | $4,147 |
| Sold 300 shares of Company A at | 3,210 |
| Loss | ($ 937.00) |

| | |
|---|---|
| Bought 100 shares of Company B at | $3,240 |
| Sold 100 shares of Company B at | 2,465 |
| Loss | ($ 775.00) |

| | |
|---|---|
| *Total Losses* | ($1,712.00) |
| Dividend Income (Company B) | 25.00 |
| Total Losses | ($1,687.00) |

---

Poor Mr. Phelps. He had been earning better than 6% on his money. Now he is losing hundreds. Well, if he is smart enought to pick a strong mover next time, he just might make up his losses or even turn a profit.

**Transaction No. 5.** Mr. Phelps now decides to buy 100 shares of stock in a retail store which, for convenience, we will refer to as Company C. He gets the shares for $17-⅝ per share.

| | |
|---|---|
| 100 shares at $17.625 | = $1,762.50 |
| Fees | 44.00 |
| Total Cost | $1,806.50 |

**Transaction No. 6.** After holding the shares for awhile, Mr. Phelps decided that his market timing was poor and Company C will not increase in share value for some time. He manages to sell the shares for exactly the same price at which he purchased them: $17-⅝.

| | |
|---|---|
| 100 shares at $17.625 | = $1,762.50 |
| Fees | 46.34* |
| Amount Received | $1,716.16 |

Despite the fact that he sold the shares at exactly the same market price at which he purchased them, thanks to commissions and sales tax, Mr. Phelps got back a lot less money than he paid out.

---

## SCOREBOARD

| | |
|---|---|
| Bought 300 shares of Company A at | $4,147.00 |
| Sold 300 shares of Company A at | 3,210.00 |
| Loss | ($ 937.00) |
| | |
| Bought 100 shares of Company B at | $3,240.00 |
| Sold 100 shares of Company B at | 2,465.00 |
| Loss | ($ 775.00) |
| | |
| Bought 100 shares of Company C at | $1,806.50 |
| Sold 100 shares of Company C at | 1,716.00 |
| Loss | ($ 90.34) |
| | |
| *Total Losses* | ($1,802.34) |
| Plus Dividend Income (Company B) | 25.00 |
| Total Losses | ($1,777.34) |

---

*Fees on sell transactions are slightly higher in these examples just to underscore that the investor may incur postal expenses for returning securities (usually by registered mail) and also for the S.E.C. tax (very minimal) associated with the sale of securities.

Mr. Phelps had to admit that making money in the stock market was not quite as easy as he had supposed. He withdrew $5,000 from his savings account, invested a good portion of it, made $25 in dividends but lost $1,802.34 in trading. Whew! He would have been better off had he left his money where it was. Now he must decide whether to throw in the towel or try to recoup his losses by reinvesting his money in the market.

## ☐ *Ms. Alexis Scott* ☐

Ms. Scott had dabbled in the stock market for more than ten years. For the most part, she had been very conservative, investing mainly in utilities which had been paying very high dividends. Now she has decided to become a little more aggressive in her investing techniques, and at the same time that Mr. Phelps was anticipating a bull market, she began to plan and prepare for a bear market. She sold some of her utility stock and decided to do some serious trading. As it turned out, she went after the same securities as Mr. Phelps, though she did not make her investments at exactly the same time or for the same reasons.

*Transaction No. 1.* Ms. Scott decides to take a short position in Company A. She calls her broker, tells him of her plans. The broker borrows the stock from another account so she can "sell" it at the market price of $13-1/2. She sells 300 shares.

| | |
|---|---|
| 300 shares at $13.50 | = $4,050.00 |
| Fees | 100.00 |
| To Be Received | $3,950.00 |

*Transaction No. 2.* The company's shares drop to a price of $11.00 and Ms. Scott decides that it is time to purchase the shares sold short; she calls her broker and he executes the order for her at $11.00 per share.

| | |
|---|---|
| 300 shares at $11.00 | = $3,300 |
| Fees | 83 |
| Total Cost | $3,383 |

---

### SCOREBOARD

Sold short 300 shares of Company A at $3,950.00
Bought 300 shares of Company A at   3,383.00
Profit                          $ 567.00

---

Ms. Scott made a tidy little profit for herself. On an investment of $3,950 she has made a profit of $567. That is a rate of return of almost 14.4 percent ($567 divided by $3,950). And as only two months elapsed between transactions, that's a 14.4 percent return in two *months*. Mr. Phelps, on the other hand, having played the stock in this same company to go up in price lost $937 on a $4,147 investment. He had a 22.6 percent loss in pretty much the same time that Ms. Scott made her 14.4 percent.

***Transaction No. 3.*** Ms. Scott had a feeling that the publishing industry was in for a time of it and she decided that the shares of Company B, then selling at $17-⅝ per share, were at an ideal level for a bear to make some money in a very short time. She instructed her broker to sell short at the market price.

200 shares at $17.625               = $3,525.00
Fees                                   89.10
To Be Received                   $3,435.90

***Transaction No. 4.*** The publishing company became, as we learned from Mr. Phelps' situation, a takeover candidate and the shares skyrocketed in price. Ms. Scott decided to wait out the news, since she believed the takeover attempt would fail—and it did—but the stock seemed to settle in the $24.00 to $26.00 range and Ms. Scott was advised that she ought to bail out. When the stock was at $25-¼ she decided to purchase those shares she had sold short.

200 shares at $25.25                = $5,050.00
Fees                                  110.00
Total Cost                          $5,160.00

---

### SCOREBOARD

| | |
|---|---:|
| Sold short 300 shares, Company A, at | $3,950.00 |
| Bought 300 shares of Company B at | $3,383.00 |
| Profit | $ 567.00 |

| | |
|---|---:|
| Sold short 200 shares, Company B, at | $3,435.90 |
| Bought 200 shares of Company B at | $5,160.00 |
| Loss | ($1,724.10) |
| *Total Losses* | ($1,157.10) |

---

As the scoreboard indicates, Ms. Scott, who had gains of $567.00 after her first short position is now in the red, with $1,157.10 in losses.

**Transaction No. 5.** Ms. Scott sells short Company C at $25-⅛. The transaction is for 100 shares.

| | |
|---|---:|
| 100 shares at $25.125 | = $2,512.50 |
| Fees | 60.30 |
| To Be Received | $2,452.11 |

Ms. Scott watches the movement of this stock quite carefully. Much to her dismay, the prices of the shares begin to climb in price. But she doesn't panic. And finally the market goes bearish; her stock declines.

**Transaction No. 6.** Ms. Scott purchases the shares sold short at $20-½.

| | |
|---|---:|
| 100 shares at $20.50 | = $2,050.00 |
| Fees | 51.95 |
| Total Cost | $2,101.95 |

Another gain! But, for Ms. Scott, two wins and one loss still add up to defeat, as the scoreboard shows:

---

### SCOREBOARD

Sold short 300 shares, Company A, at    $3,950.00
Bought 300 shares of Company A at    $3,383.00
Profit    $ 567.00

Sold short 200 shares, Company B, at    $3,435.90
Bought 200 shares of Company at    $5,160.00
Loss    ($1,724.10)

Sold short 100 shares, Company C, at    $2,452.11
Bought 100 shares of Company C at    $2,101.95
Profit    $ 350.16
*Total Losses*    ($ 806.94)

---

Once we look at the bottom line, it becomes pretty clear that both Mr. Phelps and Ms. Scott would have been much better off if they had left their money in their savings accounts. But they took their chances and learned at least one lesson: It's not that easy to make money in the stock market.

### ☐ *You* ☐

You, too, decide that, what with inflation and the possibility of exceptional rewards, the stock market might be the place for your money. You would like to try a few trades. But you know Mr. Phelps and Ms. Scott rather personally, and they've confided to you that it would certainly have been better if their money were left locked tight in the bank. But you decide to give it a try anyway. There are a couple of stocks you've had your eye on and you are going to try and play them for all they are worth—or what you think, or have been told, they are worth.

**Transaction No. 1.** You take a long position in a well-known drug chain, Company A. You buy 100 shares at $26-½.

| | |
|---|---|
| 100 shares at $26.50 | = $2,650.00 |
| Fees | 59.00 |
| Total Cost | $2,709.00 |

**Transaction No. 2.** Two months later you sell your holdings in the company for $33½.

| | |
|---|---|
| 100 shares at $33.50 | = $3,350.00 |
| Fees | 63.00 |
| Profit | $3,287.00 |

---

### SCOREBOARD

| | |
|---|---|
| Bought 100 shares of Company A at | $2,709.00 |
| Sold 100 shares of Company B at | $3,287.00 |
| Profit | $ 578.00 |

---

**Transaction No. 3.** You not only felt that the shares in the drug chain Company A would increase no further in share value, but you decided that the stock would now begin to depreciate, so a couple of weeks later you sell short 300 shares at the market price of $30-½.

| | |
|---|---|
| 100 shares at $30.50 | = $3,050.00 |
| Fees | 63.00 |
| To Be Received | $2,987.00 |

**Transaction No. 4.** As you predicted, the price of the stock declined and you decided to cover your short position by buying the shares at $20.00.

| | |
|---|---|
| 100 shares at $20.00 | = $2,000.00 |
| Fees | 50.00 |
| Amount Paid | $2,050.00 |

---

## SCOREBOARD

| | | |
|---|---|---|
| Bought 100 shares of Company A at | $2,709.00 | |
| Sold 100 shares of Company A at | $3,287.00 | |
| Profit | | $ 578.00 |
| | | |
| Sold short 100 shares, Company A, at | $2,987.00 | |
| Bought 100 shares of Company A at | $2,050.00 | |
| Profit | | $ 937.00 |
| Total Profits | | $1,515.00 |

---

As the scoreboard indicates, you have played the shares in the company to go up, and then later you played them to go down. Good thinking! Of course, this strategy doesn't always work; just think of what would happen if after you sold short the shares and the company continued to go up.

***Transaction No. 5.*** You purchase 100 shares of a preferred stock in a major airline, Company B. The stock cost $20.00 per share but was paying a $1.87 dividend.

| | |
|---|---|
| 100 shares at $20.00 | = $2,000.00 |
| Fees | 48.00 |
| Total Cost | $2,048.00 |

***Transaction No. 6.*** One year later you sell your holdings in the airline at $21.00 per share.

| | |
|---|---|
| 100 shares at $21.00 | = $2,100.00 |
| Fees | 52.00 |
| Total Received | $2,048.00 |

But you also received three dividend payments. If the dividend payout was $1.87 per share on an annual basis, then if you had your stock for four quarterly payments, you would have received $187.00 ($1.87 × 100 shares) in dividends. But, in fact, you didn't hold the stock long enough to receive four dividend payments. You actually only received three-fourths of the annual payout. The amount of dividends you received, then, was $140.25 ($187.00 × .75).

The above is only one method of determining the amount of dividends received. Another method would be to divide the annual dividend by 4 to determine the quarterly payout per share. Once that figure is determined, multiply it by 3 for the case above to determine the total amount received for each share. Then mulitply the result by 100 (number of shares).

You did well. A sum of $578.00 from selling long on Company A and then $937.00 from selling the same stock short. You broke even in the third transaction but at least received a total of $140.25 in dividends. Total return on your three transactions was $1,655.25. Congratulations.

---

### SCOREBOARD

| | | |
|---|---|---|
| Bought 100 shares of Company A at | $2,709.00 | |
| Sold 100 shares of Company A at | $3,287.00 | |
| Profit | | $ 578.00 |
| | | |
| Sold short 100 shares, Company A, at | $2,987.00 | |
| Bought 100 shares of Company A at | $2,050.00 | |
| Profit | | $ 937.00 |
| | | |
| Bought 100 shares, Company B, at | $2,048.00 | |
| Sold 100 shares, Company B at | $2,048.00 | |
| *Total Profits* | | $1,515.00 |
| Plus Dividend Income (Major Airline) | | 140.25 |
| *Total Profits* | | $1,655.25 |

---

## Dollar-Cost Averaging

Through payroll or broker plans, some investors take a dollar-cost averaging approach to investing. What they do is put an equal amount of money into the same stock, regardless of its current price, at equal calendar intervals—every week, month, quarter, six months, etc.

This represents a fairly safe approach to investing, but it is hardly foolproof. (No investment plan is.) Two major considerations are your willingness to stick to your plan and your selection of a good stock.

Where's the advantage in dollar-cost averaging? The advantage is that you buy more shares of stock while the stock is in a low trading range than you do when the stock is in a higher trading range. Meanwhile, as the stock increases in value, you make a profit on those shares you purchased at the lower price.

Suppose, for instance, you feel, after a great deal of research, that over the long term, stock in the Gyro Corporation is a very worthwhile investment. However, you haven't a lot of money to commit at one time and, if you did, you probably wouldn't take

## Table 4.2
## Dollar-Cost Averaging*

| Date | Cost Per Share | No. Bought | Purchase Price | Total Shares | Total Invest. | Total Mkt. Value |
|------|----------------|------------|----------------|--------------|---------------|------------------|
| 5/86 | $10 | 50 | $500 | 50 | $ 500 | $ 500 |
| 6/86 | 12 | 41 | 492 | 91 | 992 | 1,092 |
| 7/86 | 11 | 45 | 495 | 135 | 1,487 | 1,496 |
| 8/86 | 10 | 50 | 500 | 186 | 1,987 | 1,860 |
| 9/86 | 8 | 62 | 496 | 248 | 2,483 | 1,984 |
| 10/86 | 9 | 55 | 495 | 303 | 2,978 | 2,272 |
| 11/86 | 10 | 50 | 500 | 353 | 3,478 | 3,530 |
| 12/86 | 12 | 41 | 492 | 394 | 3,970 | 4,728 |
| 1/87 | 15 | 33 | 495 | 528 | 4,465 | 7,920 |
| 2/87 | 16 | 31 | 496 | 559 | 4,961 | 8,944 |
| 3/87 | 17 | 29 | 493 | 588 | 5,454 | 9,996 |
| 4/87 | 18 | 27 | 486 | 615 | 5,940 | 11,070 |
| 5/87 | 19 | 26 | 494 | 641 | 6,343 | 12,179 |
| 6/87 | 20 | 25 | 500 | 666 | 6,934 | 13,320 |

*Broker- and corporate-sponsored programs offer plans whereby fractional shares may be purchased and the same exact amount of money can therefore be invested each time.

a chance on putting it all in one investment. So you decide to invest about $500.00 per month in the shares.

As you will notice by reviewing Table 7.1, you are not always in a position to realize a profit (before fees). In fact, from July '86 until October '86 if you sold all your shares, you would lose money. In November, however, you were at a break-even point (remember commissions). After November '86 you were in the black (which is to say, you were making a profit).

Market value was determined by multiplying per share price times the total number of shares purchased. The amount of profit or loss may be determined by finding the difference between total investment and market value.

The market value of the shares of stock are rarely on a one way trip north or south. Prices fluctuate—today up, tomorrow down; the day after, up again, etc. If you play the game of dollar-cost averaging, you need to pick a stock that will be bullish on the long-term—and you've got to stick to your game plan!

## Review Questions

1. If you buy 100 shares of stock for $10.00 per share and sell it six months later for $10-1/4 per share, what is your profit before commissions? _____

2. If you buy 100 shares of stock for $10.00 per share and sell it five months later for $10-1/2 per share, how much is your profit (or loss) if your buy and sell commissions total $65.00? _____

3. About where would your break-even point be if you purchased 200 shares of stock at $9.00 per share and the buy-and-sell commissions were $53.00? (Remember to approximate fees for the sell transaction.) _____

4. Will savings in brokerage commissions really enhance your profits if you trade frequently? _____

5. Must you pay a brokerage commission even if you take a loss on a stock transaction? _____

6. Determine the rate of return for each transaction below, each of which represents a common stock purchase.

| Cost of Shares | Annual Dividends | Rate of Return |
|---|---|---|
| $950.00 | $45.00 | ? |
| $2,500 | $125.00 | ? |
| $6,000 | $295.00 | ? |

7. Determine the rate of return for each of the transactions below, each of which represents a preferred stock purchase of 100 shares.

| Cost of Shares | Par Value | Dividend Rate | Rate of Return |
|---|---|---|---|
| $9,100 | $100.00 | 4½% | ? |
| $5,000 | $50.00 | 5% | ? |
| $6,200 | $50.00 | 6% | ? |

8. You buy 100 shares of AT&T at $55.00 per share, and 200 shares of PSE&G at $18.00 per share. Each stock declined by 10%. You decide you need the money elsewhere and sell all your holdings. What is your profit or loss?

_____

9. You buy 200 shares of AM International at $15-1/8. You sell it six months later at $15-3/4. Buy commissions are $30.00 and sell commissions $32.50. What is your total profit or loss?

_____

10. You purchase 100 shares of Litton Industries at $75.00, 200 shares of Mobil at $30-5/8, and 300 shares of IT&T at $30-7/8. What is your total cost before commissions? _____

11. You sell the 100 shares of Litton purchased in Question no. 10 above at $86-1/4 per share. What is your profit if buy-and-sell commissions total $165.00? _____

12. You sell 200 shares of Mobil purchased in Question no. 10 above at \$31-1/4 per share. What is your profit or loss if buy-and-sell commissions total \$150.00? _____

13. Refer to Table 4. What is your total profit before commission if you add your holdings after the June '86 purchase? _____

14. Refer to Table 4.1. Would you have a profit if you had sold all your holdings after the August '86 purchase? Before commissions? After commissions? _____

15. Refer to Table 4.2. Would you have a profit if you sold your holdings after the October '86 purchase? _____

16. What is the advantage of dollar-cost averaging? _____

17. True or false? If you play the game of dollar-cost averaging, you need to pick a stock that will be bullish on the long-term—and you've got to stick to your game plan.

## CHAPTER □ 5

# Opportunity Cost

More likely than not, the common or preferred stocks in which you will invest are those listed on one of the registered exchanges in the United States. But you are by no means limited to these markets and may very well find yourself some day trading in securities listed on any of the more than one hundred exchanges worldwide, from the exchange in Buenos Aires to the exchange in Salisburg, Zimbabwe.

But before we take a closer look at stock investing for the purpose of developing a practical perspective, there is an important concept to which you should be introduced. This is the concept of *opportunity cost.*

### A Definition and Example

In a strictly economic sense, opportunity costs represent the dollar value of the resources used to develop and market one product or service instead of another. Put another way, opportunity costs represent the value of that which must be disregarded because some other good or service is to be produced.

Perhaps the most simple example is that of a farmer who decides to plant and husband corn which he expects will bring him $100,000 in the marketplace. If, however, he were to use his land to produce a completely different crop that he could sell for $120,000, then the opportunity cost involved in growing corn is $20,000 ($120,000 - $100,000). The opportunity cost represents how much more he could have made if he chose to invest his time, money, capital, and labor in this other product.

Just as the farmer must, so must every other businessman weigh all the alternatives available before he decides to invest his capital, labor, or land to produce some product or service. He must always be aware of the investment that will provide him the best return.

## Considerations for the Stock Investor

Now, the stock investor must weigh his alternatives just as the farmer and businessman must. As a point of fact, the stock investor is a businessman, although his business from a legal and tax accounting perspective is only a single proprietorship under his own rather than an assumed name. And it may very well be only a part-time and, at that, a very occasional business, but it is a business nonetheless. His market is the securities market. He buys stocks or bonds or other investments which he assumes will assure him a greater return *plus* some level of safety than he may find in other investment opportunities. In terms of stock selection, the decision is never an easy one because so many variables must be weighed and there literally are thousands of securities from which to choose. The research is too much for any one individual and that's the reason many investors depend, at least to some degree, on the research services that brokers and independent investment advisors provide.

To further drive home the idea of considering opportunity costs before making any investment decision, consider the following hypothetical situation.

You invest $12,000 in 600 shares of American Telephone and Telegraph paying a $1.20 dividend per share per year. This means that in the next twelve months you will receive $720.00 in dividend income.

There are higher paying securities available to be sure, but you feel the dividend is secure and the price of the shares will remain stable and probably increase.

Now, assume also that you can expect an average 14% (annualized) return if you take out a 12-month bank certificate for the same period.

Fourteen percent of $10,000 is $1,400. This $1,400 represents $680 more than you would receive in dividends from your investment in AT&T shares. *Your opportunity cost is $680.*

See if you can determine the opportunity cost in the following exercises, assuming you could have received an average of 8% per year from your local credit union and that you held each of the following stocks for one year.

| Cost of Stock | Proceeds from Sale of Stock | Buy/Sell Commissions | Opportunity Cost |
|---|---|---|---|
| $ 700 | $ 800 | $ 60 | ? |
| 1,200 | 1,300 | 66 | ? |
| 1,500 | 800 | 90 | ? |
| 2,000 | 1,000 | 100 | ? |
| 2,500 | 2,500 | 125 | ? |

You would have received from the credit union $56, $96, $120, $160, and $200 respectively. Subtracting the buy/sell commissions from the profits you received, or adding those commissions to the losses you received give you the total profit or loss from the stock transactions. Finding the difference between the profit or loss and the interest you would have received from the credit union gives you the following opportunity costs: $16, $62, $910, $1260, and $325.

You may, of course, argue that the stock may well go up in price so that on top of the dividend income you will also receive some profit. But there is no guarantee that the shares will indeed go up in price for the same period, and if they should, they must increase about 4 ½ to 5 points in order to compensate for the opportunity from other investments and the buy and sell commissions you must pay to the broker. And, remember, the market price of the shares can very easily decrease.

The point of the matter is that you, as an investor, must realize the importance of approaching the market with the same awareness that any businessman approaches his investment decisions.

## Return on Investment (ROI)

What every investor wants is the best return possible on his or her investment. But the stock market offers no guarantees. Stocks can go down quite as easily as they can go up, and from a purely arithmetical perspective. Too, dividends may be cancelled at any time, for a company is under no legal obligation to pay dividends, not even on preferred issues.

Because of the uncertainty with which the stock investor must always deal, he or she should always approach the market realizing that he must be compensated for that uncertainty. Thus, he should have no interest in putting his money into securities which offer him a total return not much above what he can get from a certificate of deposit.

Let's get personal and consider *you* as an investor who must determine what rate of return would make a certain gamble worthwhile. Certainly, this is never an easy decision if you are tempted to take the gamble in the first place. Many people would reply that no investment is worth risking their hard-earned money. You, of course, would agree with them but you like the attractiveness of securities offering 50% or 100% return over the long term. You are willing to keep your eyes and ears open for potential big winners. Besides, its not only the chance of winning big that excites you; it is the very game itself. The entrepreneur in you leads you to search for a good corporate common. So, you begin that search for the right stock, that search for the gamble that is worth taking.

Suppose, for instance, that your research efforts, or the investment newsletters to which you subscribe, indicate that the stock in XYZ Corporation is a worthwhile investment over the long term. It does not pay a dividend, but it is selling below book value, market forecasts for the company are good, and the stock has the potential to double in price.

That all reads quite invitingly. But when will the stock double in price? And what is the downside risk? If in the past five years the share price has ranged from $10 to $60 and the stock is now priced at $30, you know it is a highly volatile issue. There is great risk here. Is a 100% return worth the gamble when you can possibly lose everything? Or if there is a good chance that you may possibly tie up your money for fifteen years before you realize your goals?

If you were to invest in this stock of such high promise and after three years it registers only a 15% increase in price, you will realize, after tying up your money, a profit of only $1,500 before commissions and other fees are considered.

---

$10,000 Original Investment x 15% Capital Gain
= $1,500

---

If you had, instead, simply put your money in a savings account at 6% interest and compounded quarterly (possibly a no-risk situation, as most savings accounts are insured) you would have after that same three-year period $11,956.18 instead of $10,500.00.

In this particular example, the opportunity cost is minimal ($11,956.18 - $11,500.00 = $496.18); however, there was a great deal of risk undertaken in the purchase of the stock only to finally result in less money for you than a savings account would have paid. Not only that, but you also bought *The Wall Street Journal* every so often and then sat on the edge of your chair as you checked the stock listings to see if your investment was paying off. . .a lot of sweat for a small return on your investment.

---

### COMPOUND INTEREST CALCULATION
P = Original Principle; i = Interest; n = Number of Interest (or Conversion) Periods; S = Compound Amount of P.

$$S = P (1 = i)^n$$
$$S = \$10,000 (1 + .015)^{12}$$
$$S = \$11,956.18$$

---

Consider now the possibility that over that same three-year period you wound up taking a 20% loss from your stock investment at the same time that you could have invested in certificates of deposits averaging 12% over the same period. How are you going to explain to your wife or husband about that trip you *could have* taken?

It is incredibly difficult to pinpoint either the amount of return or the time of the return on stock investments. This is especially true in the case of common stocks which are generally much more volatile than the preferreds. But preferreds fluctuate also. The investor needs to keep this in mind at all times, and before he invests one single penny in the market he must be sufficiently convinced that his expected return makes the gamble worthwhile.

Actually, risk-taking should always be kept to a minimum. In fact, the best advice that can be given in terms of investing one's hard-earned money is that whatever vehicles he or she does invest in should have a very high degree of safety as well as a very high rate of return. Financial advisors may argue that this is a contradiction, but it is, nonetheless, important to research as thoroughly as possible to find such a contradiction. If you cannot find a safe stock promising a high rate of return (through some combination of dividend income and price appreciation) put your money in the bank, in real estate mortgages, or even government savings bonds.

There is no denying that any investment brings with it a certain degree of risk. But the real question is *how much risk?* And, considering the possible rate of return, *is the risk worth it?* Every dollar lost is compounded by the opportunity cost from other possible investments.

As for the rate of return—well, this is the major consideration of every stockholder. Every investor wants the highest possible return he can get on his money. He would like high dividends and extraordinary capital gains. He can most often have only one or the other; often he winds up with neither!

### Review Questions

1. _____ _____ represents the value of that which must be disregarded because some other good or service is to be produced.

2. You invest $5,000 in 100 shares of American Telephone paying $3 per share in dividends per year. For the same annual period, you could have put your money in certificates that would have paid you 10% in interest. What was your opportunity cost?

3. ROI is the abbreviation for _____ _____ _____ .

4. Determine the ROI in each of the following:

| Cost of Stock | Buy/Sell Commissions | Capital Gain | ROI |
|---|---|---|---|
| $ 9,600 | $400 | $1,200 | ? |
| 920 | 80 | 900 | ? |
| 14,700 | 300 | 500 | ? |
| 3,850 | 150 | 100 | ? |
| 2,380 | 120 | 750 | ? |

5. Assuming semi-annual compounding, what would be the amount of your principal after a one-year period for each of the following situations:

| Original Principal | Interest | Balance |
|---|---|---|
| $1,000 | 8% | ? |
| 1,000 | 9% | ? |
| 1,000 | 10% | ? |
| 2,500 | 8% | ? |
| 2,500 | 9% | ? |
| 2,500 | 10% | ? |

6. True or false? It is easy to pinpoint the amount of return and the time of that return for stock investments. _____

7. True or false? It is worth any amount of money to purchase a stock that can triple in ten years. _____

8. True or false? Risk-taking should always be kept to a minimum. _____

9. You buy 100 shares of XYZ stock at $1,000. The yield at the time is 8%. You receive seven quarterly dividend payments before you sell the stock for a $200 loss. How much did you gain or lose from holding the stock for that period? _____

10. You buy 100 shares of XYZ stock selling at $25.00. Quarterly dividends are 50 cents per share and you receive eight dividends before you sell the stock for a $220 gain. Commissions on the buy and sell transaction s were $60 and $65 respectively. Would you have been smarter to have purchased a certificate paying 9% interest compounded semi-annually? _____

## CHAPTER 6

# Margin Accounts: Making and Losing More

Investors are constantly on the lookout for ways in which they can make a small amount of money do the work of a large amount of money. If you had $1,000 to invest in a stock that you believed would double in value, wouldn't you like to find a way to make that money triple when the stock doubled?

One way to do this is to set up a "margin" account with your broker. A margin account is one which allows you to borrow the money needed to purchase additional securities from your broker. And it is all done automatically once the account is set up; there is none of the usual hassle the average consumer must go through when he wants to borrow money. There are, of course, restrictions and, depending upon the law at any given time, the amount which you may be allowed to borrow will vary.

You must pay interest on the money you borrow, but this is usually a relatively low rate—*but not always.* The borrowed money in each stock purchase gives you the kind of leverage you need to greatly increase your profit or your income. However, it is also the kind of tool that can work against you—it can greatly increase your losses.

Let's take a brief look at the mathematics. You have $1,000 to invest in a stock and so does your friend, Mr. Phelps. You both believe the stock has a chance of doubling in value in a very short time, so you are both quite bullish.

Mr. Phelps invests his $1,000. One month later the stock doubles and Mr. Phelps sells out. His return on investment before commissions and sales tax is 100%, for he has made $1,000.

You, however, decide to buy the stock on margin. This means you can actually purchase $2,000 worth of stock. The stock, of course, doubles and you sell out at the same time as Mr. Phelps, then pay the broker back the money you borrowed. Your return on investment before commissions and interest charges is 300%. Your $1,000 has become $3,000. Let's look at how this was accomplished.

1. You had $1,000 to invest in a stock.
2. You borrowed $1,000 from your broker and now had $2,000 to invest.
3. The stock doubled and you sold it. Amount received on the sale was $4,000 ($2,000 × 2).
4. You paid back the $1,000 you borrowed from the broker. You now have in your account $3,000 ($4,000 − $1,000).
5. $3,000 is three times the amount you started with. That is a tripling of your money.

With his $1,000, Mr. Phelps made another $1,000. With your $1,000 you made another $2,000. You tripled your money while Phelps only doubled his. You made $1,000 more than he with the same exact investment!

But if the stock went south instead of north (which is to say that if the price of the stock declined instead of increased), you would have wished that you were as conservative in your investment policies as Mr. Phelps.

For example, this time assume that instead of doubling in price the stock decreased so that on selling out, Mr. Phelps, before commissions, was left with only $500.00. (Stock decreases 50%—50% × $1,000 investment = $500.00).

You however, would be left with nothing if you sold out when the stock had declined 50%. Why? Well, look closely:

1. You had $1,000 to invest in a stock.
2. You borrowed $1,000 from your broker and now had $2,000 to invest.

3. This stock declined 50% in price and so did your investment. Amount received on sale, then, was $1,000 ($2,000 × 50%).
4. But you owe the broker $1,000. You pay him back and you are left with . . . nothing.

Mr. Phelps still has $500.00. You have nothing. Both of you started out with $1,000. He lost half of his money. You lost all of yours.

You see, margin gives a lot of leverage to an investor. Wow! can it increase profits. But, wow! can it accelerate losses!

Once you have opened that margin account, you only have to advise your broker that you are making a purchase "on margin," and the broker automatically puts up his part of the money. How much he puts up depends upon what the current ruling from the Federal Reserve is. Federal Reserve regulations will change from time to time. Margin requirements are tied in with other economic controls. At the time of the stock market crash in 1929, investors were only required to put up 10% of the money required for purchases. At other times, investors were not required to put up anything at all; all money could be borrowed from the broker.

In opening a margin account, the investor is required to sign, logically enough, a margin agreement. Some of the main points in the agreement are:

1. The broker will use the stock purchased as collateral for the loan from the broker.
2. The broker has the right (though he seldom exercises it) to sell the securities without notice to assure that the money due him will be paid.
3. Balance of all money borrowed will be charged interest by the broker.

## Margin Requirements

Initial margin requirements are set by the Federal Reserve Board. The actual margin requirement will change from time to time in accordance with general economic policy. But let's assume for simplification that margin requirements are 50%, which means that if you purchase stock on margin, you must put up 50% of the money.

There is one special caveat here, however, and that is that initial deposits are required on all margin accounts; at the present time the requirement is a $2,000 deposit. Thus, if you purchase $2,000 worth of stock on margin, the broker will put up nothing. If you purchase $4,000 worth of stock, however, you need put up only $2,000, although you always have the option of putting up the full amount.

Now, there is another type of margin requirement and this is called *equity* margin. It is usually set by an exchange and/or the broker. It varies from exchange to exchange and broker to broker. At the present time it is generally 35% on two-position accounts and 50% on one-position accounts. It is computed in the following way:

1. Subtract the debit balance in the margin account from the market value of the security purchased.
2. Divide the result by whatever is the market value of the collateral.
3. If the result in number 2 is below the equity margin requirement, then the account must deposit additional funds.

Let's put the formula to work. Suppose you have purchased two or more securities and their total value is $5,000. As you have purchased them "on margin" you need only put up $2,500.

That's easy enough!

But now suppose that the market value of your holdings decreases by 40%. The result is that your equity in the account is now 16 2/3%. That means if you were to sell all your holdings, only 16 2/3% of the proceeds will actually be yours.

In this instance, your equity has been reduced to below 35%, and your broker is sure to send you a notice indicating that you must deposit enough money in your account to bring the balance up to the margin requirement. He has the right to sell stock

60% x $5,000 = $3,000 (The new market value of your stock)
$3,000 - $2,500 (the money borrowed) = $ 500
(your equity)
$ 500 divided by $3,000 = 16²/₃% (your equity margin)

in your account if you do not respond to his request by depositing money or additional securities in your account.

## Two Types of Margin

Thus, there has come to be two types of margin, the first being
the *initial* margin required by the Federal Reserve and the second being the *equity* margin required to maintain the account.

The Federal Reserve regulates only the margin required on
initial purchases. It does not require any maintenance deposits.
It is generally the stock exchanges that set the maintenance
requirements—and/or individual brokerage houses. For instance, the New York Stock Exchange requires 25% deposits
on all "long" accounts but its member brokers generally require
35%. The Boston Stock Exchange, however, sets no *equity*
margin requirements although its members will generally adhere to the 35% rule.

Purchasing stock on margin is very risky business, although it
can be highly profitable.

Most brokers will generally advise investors to limit their use
of margin. But many speculators will try to take full advantage
of the leverage that margin provides. If they can make $5,000
do the work of $10,000, then they will try to do just that. But so
often investors get caught in a sliding market, wind up with
those margin calls, and are forced to dig into their pockets for
extra money or else sell their stock to cover themselves and
maintain their credit rating with their broker.

Some investors will even double or triple the risk by borrow-
ing money from a bank and using that borrowed money to
make margin purchases. Here is a case of borrowed money on

top of borrowed money to gamble on the market. Of course, if the selected stock goes north, the profit is considerable; but if the stock goes south, the losses are just as considerable.

## Short Sales

There is something which is called a *short* sale in which the investor sells a stock he does not own in anticipation of buying it back later at a lower price. His profit is the difference between the selling price and the buying price as it would be in any stock transaction, only the sequence is reversed.

Margin requirements of the Federal Reserve also apply to short sales. The following arithmetical procedures are used to determine the percentage margin:

1. Add the net proceeds of the short sale to the initial margin.
2. Take the sum arrived at (in No. 1 above) and divide it by the current market price of the stock.
3. Subtract 1 from the result obtained in No. 2 above.

To put it another way:

$$\frac{\text{Net Proceeds (Short Sale)} + \text{Initial Margin}}{\text{Market Value (Current) of the Stock}} - 1$$

Through the initial margin requirements of the Federal Reserve apply to short sales just as they do to regular stock transactions, maintenance margin requirements are somewhat more strict on short sales. As these can change from time to time, it is well that you consult your broker before trading.

## *Review Questions*

1. A _____ account is one which allows the investor to borrow money from his broker to help finance the purchase of securities.

2. Initial margin requirements are set by the _____  _____.

3. Assume that the equity margin requirement is 35%. You have just purchased two or more securities having a total value of $10,000. Declines in the price of the securities result in paper losses to you of $3,000. Will you be required by your broker to deposit additional funds in your account? _____

4. True or false? Short selling is a sure way to profit because stocks always eventually go down. _____

5. True or false? A margin account is required before an investor may sell short on a stock. _____

## CHAPTER 7

# Dividends

Dividends are payments, usually in cash, that a corporation makes to its stockholders. The dividend represents the stockholders' share of profits which the board of directors decides to distribute. However, even when the corporations incur losses, they may pay dividends in order to impress stockholders or would-be investors in their commitment to an uninterrupted schedule of dividend payments.

From a strictly accounting perspective, a dividend is an appropriation of either accumulated or current earnings. But sometimes dividends represent no more than a return of invested capital.

### Types of Dividends

Dividends are a complex subject. Basically, they are the net earnings of a corporation distributed to stockholders. From an accounting perspective, dividends actually reduce the value of each share of stock. So, in effect, the stockholder is simply being presented with a payment of some dollar value which represents exactly the resulting depreciation in the value of each share.*

There are two main types of dividend payments: cash and stock. Cash dividends are by far the more prevalent type. And regardless of the accounting transactions which actually reduce assets to allow the payment, in practice these payments, when consistent and possibly increasing, tend to make the shares so

---

*This does not mean, however, that the market value of the shares will *necessarily* depreciate. There are always a number of factors affecting market price.

much more attractive in the marketplace. Investors seem to be generally disinterested in the debate on the relevance of dividends. They like to see their assets converted to at least some cash on a regular basis. So what if the dividend reduces their equity? They may appreciate that it at least provides some liquidity.

## Stock Dividends

Stock dividends are a bookkeeping game. They appear to be ranked second to cash dividends in terms of importance to investors. But what is a stock dividend, anyway?

A stock dividend consists of the authorized but unissued shares of stock that are paid to stockholders in lieu of cash. From a strictly financial perspective, what happens is that the corporation's capital structure is revised because the stock dividend has reduced the earnings surplus by exactly the same amount that the capital stock has been increased.

Observe:

---

A. Capital Account *Before* 50% Stock Dividend:
   Capital Stock = $500,000 (100,000 Shares at $5 per Share)

   Retained Earnings: $500,000

B. Capital Account *After* 50% Stock Dividend:
   Capital Stock = $750,000 (150,000 Shares at $5 per Share)

   Retained Earnings: $250,000.

---

The stockholders in the corporation now have the superficial satisfaction of owning a greater number of shares than before. However, the book value per share is now lower:

Formula: Book Value = Capital Stock + Returned Earnings
Divided by Number of Shares

A. Book Value Before Split:
$500,000 + $500,000 Divided by 100,000
= $10 per share

B. Book Value After Split:
$750,000 + $250,000 Divided by 150,000
= $6.67 per share

If the book value has been reduced by one-third, then the market value of the stock will reflect the depreciation.

The stockholder has, in effect, received no immediate gain from the stock dividend. However, he does have a tax advantage in that the stock dividend is not taxable as ordinary income but as capital gains and if he holds the shares long enough before selling, might wind up with the tax advantage of a long-term capital gain. And, if cash dividends are paid at some future date, the extra shares will mean extra income.

The corporation has benefited because it has given the stockholder something (potential for profit) without having to give up cash. If the cash dividend remains the same or is to be increased, the effect on the market value of the stock will be very positive.

## The Stock Split

There is another type of stock distribution called the stock split. Like the stock dividend, the stock split does not change the proportionate ownership of the stockholder in the corporation.

If we take a look at the mathematics of a stock split we would immediately observe that, unlike in the case of the stock dividend, the par value of the shares is reduced. Net worth, however, remains unchanged.

If you were originally holding 1,000 shares, you would be holding 2,000 after a *2 for 1* stock split. This holds true for every other shareholder as well—that is, after the *2 for 1* split, they all have twice the amount of shares they previously had—but, of course, each individual share is worth half as much.

---

A . Before the split:
   You own 1,000 shares at $20 par value ($20,000).

B . After a *2 for 1* split:
   You own 2,000 shares at $10 par value ($20,000).

---

The main purpose of the stock split is to increase market interest in the stock; it is expected that the lower price will result in higher trading activity. This increased interest in the stock should exert upward pressure on the price. Thus, one of the advantages to the stockholders is the potential extra profits that each advance in the stock can mean after the split. If dividends are maintained at the same dollar value per share—a rare occasion—the stockholders can also benefit by increased income (if one considers a cash dividend something extra). If there is an increase in the dividend payment with each share, then the stockholders benefit handsomely.

---

Before 2 for 1 Split: Dividend = $2 per share.
After 2 for 1 Split:   Dividend = $1 per share.

If there is a 10% increase in the dividend (to $1.10 per share), the stockholder has twice the number of shares earning an extra 10 cents.

---

## Reverse Splits

Reverse splits occasionally occur. This is to say that instead of a 2 for 1 split, a company may very well declare a 1 for 2 split. In this case, everything happens in reverse of what was described previously. The par value of the stock is doubled, but the stockholder has half as many shares as before. Again, his proportionate ownership remains unchanged. The reason for reverse splits is to increase the market value of each share. It's a play at investor psychology. If the price of a stock is too low, investors may pass it by as an investment that appears too risky. For instance, when a stock is at $10 per share, every one dollar decrease in market value represents a 10% loss to an investor; but at $20 per share, each one dollar change represents only a 5% loss. But reverse splits are rare as most boards of directors realize that a reverse split might rightly or wrongly suggest financial difficulties; therefore, directors tend to shy away from the idea.

## Scrip and Bond Dividends

Besides cash and stock dividends, a company may also issue scrip dividends or bond dividends, though these are generally unusual forms of dividend payments—unusual because stockholders are generally wary about their corporation going into debt to pay dividends.

The scrip dividend comes in the form of a note which may be payable at any future time or which may be payable in specific installments at fixed intervals of time. This allows a corporation to continue its uninterrupted schedule of dividend payments without having to deplete its cash account. If scrip dividends are issued they are generally interest-paying notes. From a corporate accounting perspective they are recorded as current liabilities.

Bond dividends are actually a form of scrip dividend, but as bonds generally have a rather extended maturity date, what the investor is saddled with is a long-term obligation due him by the corporation. From both a corporate financial perspective as well as an investor's perspective, bond dividends, as well as scrip dividends, result in something akin to fiscal nonsense. This is because the corporation is incurring unnecessary debt simply to have something to give the stockholders, and when one considers that it is actually the stockholders who are incurring the debt, what are they getting?

There is another type of dividend that can possibly be declared. It is called a property dividend and it is paid out of corporate earnings or, generally, as the result of one form of liquidation or another. Usually it is a distribution of the holdings of a corporation in other concerns or various debt instruments in which the corporation has invested.

### Dividend Schedule

In terms of the schedules in which dividends may be paid, dividends can be classified as:

—regular dividends;
—extra dividends;
—extraordinary dividends;
—cumulative dividends;
—liquidating dividends;
—interim dividends.

—*Regular dividends* are the cash dividends that are paid on shares of stock, generally on a quarterly or semiannual basis. These payments are made at the discretion of the board of directors and may be cancelled or postponed at any time.

—*Extra dividends* are those declared in addition to what may be termed the regular dividend. For instance, XYZ Corporation may generally pay a 25-cent dividend each quarter on each share of stock. Each fourth quarter—or at any other time—it may pay an additional 40 cents per share so that the total payout is 65 cents *at this time.*

—*Extraordinary dividends* are those paid as a result of annual profits on the part of the corporation. Often referred to as "special" dividends, these dividends are paid with the understanding that they are a non-repeatable payment and the stockholders cannot anticipate similar returns in the future.

—*Cumulative dividends* are those which are in arrears on certain preferred stocks. For instance, you may own an 8% preferred ($100 par) on which the last two quarterly payments of $2 per share were not declared. On the next quarter, if the dividend is paid you will receive $2 per share plus the $4 per share you are owed. Interest does not accrue on the unpaid dividends.

—*Liquidating dividends* are actually capital distributions and, as such, they are not taxable. They do not represent a distribution from earnings but rather a refund of original investment. Each payment will result in a reduction of the value of each share.

—*Interim dividends* refer to partial payments to stockholders from corporate profits during any given fiscal period.

Many companies, it must be noted, do not have a regular dividend policy but prefer to declare dividends only when the board of directors is so moved. Companies adopting such a policy are said to have an **irregular** dividend policy.

It must also be noted that many corporations have no dividend policy whatsoever. They prefer to simply reinvest their earnings, thereby increasing the net worth of the stock. Investors in such companies cannot rely on any periodic income—which dividends represent—and must be satisfied with an investment program with capital gains as the sole objective.

What determines a corporation's policy on dividend payments are a number of factors:

—legal factors which may inhibit or limit a corporation's right to pay dividends;
—financial considerations;
—management considerations.

The legal factors affecting a corporation's dividend policies have to do with its financial stability. If a company in poor shape decides to pay a dividend without amending its current corporate charter by reducing the recorded value of its capital, it is at once cheating both its creditors and its stockholders. The capital position of the company is the basis for credit, and a company in debt has no right to arbitrarily reduce its recorded capitals to "appease" stockholders. The stockholders are doubly cheated because they may not be aware of the basis for the dividend, a basis which will ultimately wind up reducing the market value of their holdings.

Financing considerations have to do with the corporate tax on undistributed earnings, the treatment of dividends as ordinary income (which is to the disadvantage of higher tax-bracketed stockholders) and the loss of possibly needed investment capital that money used for dividend payments can represent.

Management considerations encompass all of the preceding points covered, plus the marketing aspects of selling a corporation to the public, maintaining the value of the stock in the secondary market so that if new shares are issued they can be issued successfully, and in-market penetration or organization. This last means the corporation may need to use its earnings for expansion, mergers, or takeovers.

Dividend decisions are not decided by the vote of stockholders, except perhaps in some very closely held corporations. They are, rather, declared by the board of directors who determine the amount that shall be paid, which classes of stock shall be paid, which classes of stock shall receive the payments, and the date on which the dividend will actually be paid.

The dividend is not paid on the date it is declared, but at some future date to stockholders of record (that is, stockholders of a specific date).

### Review Questions

1. _____ are payments that a corporation makes to its stockholders.

2. A _____ _____ consists of authorized but unissued shares of stock that are paid to stockholders in lieu of cash.

3. Determine the book value for each share of stock before and after the indicated stock dividends:

| Capital Stock | Retained Earnings | Book Value | Stock Dividend | New Book Value After Stock Dividend |
|---|---|---|---|---|
| $500,000 | $500,000 | $10 | 50% | ? |
| 100,000 | 50,000 | 6 | 20% | ? |
| 100,000 | 100,000 | 10 | 10% | ? |

4. If you are holding 1,000 shares of XYZ before a 3 for 1 split, how many shares will you own after the split? _____

5. If you have $5,000 worth of stock in XYZ Corporation, how much money will you have in XYZ stock after a 3 for 1 split? _____

6. If you own 1,000 shares of stock in XYZ before a 1 for 2 reverse split, how much stock will you own after the split? _____

7. If you have $5,000 in XYZ stock, what will be the dollar value of your holdings after a 1 for 2 reverse split? _____

8. _____ dividends are the cash payments that are paid on shares of stock at the discretion of the board of directors.

9. _____ dividends are those declared in addition to what may be termed the regular dividends.

10. _____ dividends are those paid as a result of annual profits.

11. _____ dividends are those which are in arrears on preferred stocks.

12. _____ dividends are actually capital distributions and, as such, are not taxable.

13. _____ dividends are partial payments to stockholders from corporate profits.

14. _____ dividends come in the form of notes which may be payable at any future time or which may be payable in specific installments at fixed intervals of time.

15. True or false? All stockholders are entitled to receive dividend payments. _____

┌─────── CHAPTER ───────┐

**8**

# Considerations in the Quest for Profit

In the abbreviated listings in Table 5.1 we note the highest and lowest prices at which shares for the three corporations sold during the past year as well as the highest and lowest prices at which shares traded yesterday. The "change" column represents the difference from the last price quoted on the previous day's trading.

---

### Table 5.1

| 52-Week High | Low | Stock | Div. | High | Low | Last | Chg. |
|---|---|---|---|---|---|---|---|
| 39⅞ | 26⅝ | ADT | 1.52 | 36⅛ | 36¼ | 36¼ | + ⅝ |
| 18⅝ | 15¾ | AELPw | 2.26 | 16¾ | 16⅜ | 16⅝ | + ¼ |
| 51¼ | 36⅜ | AMExp | 2.20 | 39¾ | 38½ | 39 | + ½ |

---

The annual "high" and "low" cannot be used to gauge the current direction of the stock because there is no way of knowing, for example, if ADT began the period at $39⅞, fell to $26⅝, and has since climbed to $36¼ where it is at present—or the movement has been exactly the reverse, and therefore it started the period at $26⅝.

### Determining Profit and Loss

Assume that you purchased 100 shares of ADT at $26⅝ ($26.625), and sold those shares at $39⅞ ($39.785). You will have had capital gains of $1,325.00.

---

Bought 100 Shares at $26⅝ = $2,662.50
Sold 100 Shares at $39⅞ = $3,987.50
Profit = $1,325.00

---

If, on the other hand, you had purchased the stock at $39⅞, and later sold at $26⅝, you will have had a loss of $1,325.00 instead of a gain.

Any dividends received while the shares were held would increase the return, or reduce the loss, but the dividends are not treated as capital gains; they are treated as ordinary income.

There is never any guarantee that a stock will increase in price. Thus the necessity for a great deal of research before making any investment.

### The Necessity of Playing for Profit

But should someone who buys stock simply for dividend income be concerned with profit? Most assuredly. Sooner or later the stock must be sold, either for you personally or for your heirs, and you will want the stock to have appreciated in value and at a rate at least equal to the rate of inflation for the period in which you owned it.

But if stocks can be so volatile that their depreciation completely offsets dividend income, why buy stocks?

People buy stocks when they feel that such investment will give them a higher *rate of return* than other financial instruments. They may choose to invest in a security paying 6% interest because it also appears capable of realizing for them capital gains of 50%. Such a total return on investment makes the security much more preferable.

Thus, while dividend income is certainly important to stockholders, capital gains are an absolute necessity.

Stock traders quite readily fall into two categories: that of *investor* and that of *speculator.*

The difference between the investor and the speculator is primarily one of perspective, but also includes the frequency with which they conduct their trading activities. One would generally categorize the *investor* as the man or woman seeking long-term capital gains by investment in the stock of Blue Chip or other financially sound corporations that have been around for a long time. One would categorize the speculator as the man or woman trading extensively in short periods of time (sometimes frequently in one day), hoping to use part of immediate capital gains as current income and part for reinvestment. Often speculators buy and sell on margin.

This is not to say that the investor might not seek to take short-term capital gains or might not trade heavily during certain periods. He or she must always be ready to buy or sell whenever market activity or economic news deems it necessary. But generally the investor takes a position in a security with the *intention* of long-term capital gains, although he may very well sell out tomorrow.

But, as there is never any guarantee of profits or dividends from investments in stock, the argument could be well taken that anyone investing in the market is a speculator.

Thus, whether one invests on a short-term or long-term basis, he or she must be prepared to engage in stock analysis with as much sophistication as can possibly be mustered. Otherwise one must find someone to do his or her research or else depend upon broker or security research firms for recommendations. But regardless of one's expertise in the stock market, regardless of the money earned by buying and selling securities, no one is right all the time in picking stocks for investment or speculation.

## The P/E Ratio

In considering the stocks that will bring the highest return on investment, stock traders generally look at projected earnings per share and the price-to-earnings ratio at which the same stock is traditionally sold.

Future earnings per share are an important consideration because fundamentally an investment in stock is an investment in the future of a corporation. What stock was worth yesterday is unimportant; no one buys the past. What stock is worth tomorrow is what makes the current price attractive or not.

Of course, past and present fiscal performance cannot be completely ignored, for they must be seen as indicators of the strength and foresight of management. A comparison of past and present performance of the stock in relation to overall market movement and other economic indicators also helps the investor formulate some projection of what the stock may do in the future.

If the growth rate of a company has been consistent and market forecasts are favorable, investors and speculators will be interested. If, however, the corporate performance, as reflected by the stock price history, has been cyclical, showing extreme highs and lows, then only the speculator might be interested — and his or her timing will be of the utmost importance, as one would not want to buy or sell at the wrong periods in the cycle.

Thus the importance, as minimal as it may be, of the price-earnings ratio — it helps gauge the relative position of the stock. The ratio is determined by dividing the current market price of the shares by the annual earnings per share. Thus, if a stock is selling at $80 per share and its earnings per share are $10, then the P/E ratio is 8 ($80 divided by $10).

While the P/E ratio is a handy tool, it guarantees nothing. Taken by itself it is not the basis for any decision to buy or sell stock. But it does give an historic perspective for the relationship between earnings and selling price.

In the exercises below, see if you can determine the P/E ratio or the earnings per share, depending upon which is required.

| Stock Price | Earnings per Share | P/E Ratio |
|:---:|:---:|:---:|
| $12.25 | 1.75 | ? |
| 15.75 | 2.10 | ? |
| 26.00 | 3.25 | ? |
| 29.75 | 3.50 | ? |
| 24.05 | 3.70 | ? |
| 24.80 | ? | 6.2 |
| 40.50 | ? | 9.0 |
| 44.10 | ? | 9.8 |
| 60.00 | ? | 12.0 |
| 78.75 | ? | 15.0 |

The answers for the P/E ratio are: 7.0, 7.5, 8.0, 8.5, 6.5. The answers for the earnings per share are: $4.00, $4.50, $4.50, $5.00, and $5.25. As you can see, the P/E ratios were arrived at by dividing the earnings per share into the stock price, and the earnings per share were determined by dividing the P/E ratio into the stock price.

If, historically, the stock for XYZ Company sells for 7 to 10 times earnings, then if you project that earnings will reach $10 per share three years hence, you might assume that the stock will be worth $70 to $100 per share. If it is currently selling at $35 per share, you have some potential of doubling your money in three years. Note, however, that we speak here in terms of *potential*. Whether or not you will actually realize such an increase in share value, or can depend upon a constant P/E ratio, will depend upon any number of circumstances that can occur and that might not even be directly related to the fiscal performance of the stock: political upheavals, wars, national monetary policy.

The P/E ratio when compared to past trends for the stock can be a buy or sell signal. If a P/E ratio is relatively high, then one realizes the possibility that projected growth is already reflected in the price of the stock. If the ratio is low, it may be reflecting investor anticipation of earnings trouble—or simply an oversight by the investment community; if this last is the case, it could be a valuable investment.

There is no standard formula for determining what may or may not be a satisfactory P/E ratio. One cannot easily state that a high P/E ratio indicates investor confidence or that a low one does not. Each stock must be evaluated in terms of its past history in relation to its own activity, activity within its group, and activity in relation to the market as a whole.

One aspect of the subject of earnings that often catches stock investors by surprise is their representation. Now, corporations do not deliberately try to mislead the financial community, but accounting practices differ markedly in many instances. Accounting is by no means a total science or even near to becoming one. A lot of interpretation goes with recording numbers and preparing financial reports. Two CPAs can tell two different stories with the same accounting data.

In scanning financial reports, stockholders should pay attention to R&D outlays. By R&D is meant "research and development." Heavy expenditures here may diminish current earnings, but at the same time point to increased or new market penetration and, therefore, high sales in the future. Stockholders should also pay attention to depreciation deduction that, in effect, create cash for the internal financing of expansion programs or create cash for reducing current debts.

## Tell-tale Ratios

Financial reports can be highly confusing to the investor. Not everyone has a background in accounting that enables them to read the stories P&L statements and balance sheets tell. But by zeroing in on some important ratios, one has the advantage of quickly putting together important indicators of a corporation's health.

Even if one prefers to buy and sell stock on the advice of his broker or other investment counselor, it is important to have some knowledge of finance that can help you zero in on the best choice of recommended stock selections. One does not guarantee himself capital gains simply by selecting stocks by the throw of a dart at daily listings or by blindly following an advisor's advice.

Every investor should well seek to understand, besides the P/E ratio, the following ratios:

—current ratio,
—quick ratio,
—debt-to-equity ratio,
—operating ratio,
—shareholder's equity ratio.

The *current ratio* is found by totalling the current assets and dividing that total by the current liabilities. It is a measure of liquidity.

---

Current Ratio = Current Assets Divided by Current Liabilities

---

Thus, if XYZ Company has current assets of $10 million and current liabilities of $5 million, the *current ratio* is 2 to 1. This means the corporation has available $1 for every $1 of current liabilities. It can quite easily meet its short-term obligations. If, however, the current ratio were 1 to 2, the company would be in a rather shaky financial position.*

The *quick ratio* is found in almost the same way as the current ratio except that in this case inventory is not calculated along with the current assets. Current assets are generally made up of cash, accounts receivable, and inventories. But inventory may include unsaleable items so it is hard to determine its true value (quick ratio is sometimes called *acid test* ratio).

---

Quick Ratio = Current Assets (Less Inventory) Divided by
Current Liabilities

---

*A 2 to 1 ratio is usually the rule of thumb for credit applications. But exceptions are almost always made, for there are other factors to be considered; such as type of business, merchandise turnover, seasonal influences, etc.

Thus, if XYZ Company has current assets of $10 million (less $2.5 million in inventory) and current liabilities of $5 million, its quick ratio is 1.5 to 1. This is to say that there is $1.50 available for every $1.00 in liabilities. If XYZ were forced to cover its debts immediately, but could not unload its inventory, it would still *not be* in trouble. However, if the quick ratio were 1 to 1.5, this would indicate excessive liabilities and possible problems in meeting its debts.

The debt-to-equity ratio is the relationship between stockholders' liabilities and total assets. If owners' equity is $2 million and total assets are $1 million, then we can be sure that the corporation's financial picture is relatively attractive, for this is a 2 to 1 equity ratio and the higher the stockholders' equity in relation to total assets, the stronger the corporation.*

---

Debt-to-Equity Ratio = Owners' Liabilities Divided by
Stockholders' Equity

---

An impressive debt-to-equity ratio means less need for credit, and indicates that the corporation's finances are in shape for long-term commitments.

The *operating ratio* is found by taking the total operating expenses and dividing that total by net sales. By total operating expenses is meant all but finance and tax-related expenses.

---

Operating Ratio = Total Operating Expenses
Divided by Net Sales

---

This ratio indicates net profit. The relationship between the ratio and the net profit it represents is opposite what you would expect. The lower the ratio, the higher the profit. Thus, if total

---

*There are actually a number of debt-to-equity ratios. Two other common types are the relationship between long term debt and capitalization, and between total liabilities and stockholders' equity.

operating expenses are $4 million and total sales $10 million, the operating ratio would be 40% ($4 million divided by $10 million). Subtracting the operating ratio (40%) from 100% gives the operating income.

*Return on shareholders' equity* is another ratio that is expressed in percentage points. It is often referred to as *return on investment* (ROI) or sometimes as *return on shareholders'* investment. It is determined by dividing net income by shareholders' equity.

---

Return on Shareholders' Equity = Net Income Divided by
Shareholders' Equity

---

Thus, if net income for any fiscal period is $100 thousand and shareholders' equity is $1 million, then the return on shareholders' equity is 10% ($100 thousand divided by $1 million). If current interest available from certificates is about 14%, then a 10% return on investment is hardly worth the gamble, especially considering the risk inherent in any stock investment.

To test your skill at determing the various ratios discussed in this subsection, try the following exercises. The values are rounded off to numbers that are easily divisible so that you can immediately see relationships without getting too involved in the arithmetic. The important thing is recognizing and applying the formula.

1. Find the current ratio for each of the following:

| Current Assets | Current Liabilities | Current Ratio |
|---|---|---|
| $1,000,000 | $500,000 | ? |
| 1,500,000 | 500,000 | ? |
| 250,000 | 500,000 | ? |
| 725,000 | 725,000 | ? |

The answers are found by dividing the current assets by the current liabilities and are: 2 to 1, 3 to 1, 1 to 2, and 1 to 1.

2. Find the quick ratio for each of the following:

| Current Assets | Inventory | Current Liabilities | Quick Ratio |
|---|---|---|---|
| $ 500,000 | $100,000 | $ 200,000 | ? |
| 750,000 | 500,000 | 250,000 | ? |
| 1,000,000 | 100,000 | 400,000 | ? |
| 1,000,000 | 100,000 | 1,900,000 | |

The answers are found by subtracting the inventory from the current assets and dividing the result by the current liabilities: 3 to 1, 1 to 1, 2 to 1, 1 to 2.

3. Find the debt-to-equity ratio for each of the following:

| Owner's Liabilities | Stockholders' Equity | Debt-to-Equity Ratio |
|---|---|---|
| $2,000,000 | $1,000,000 | ? |
| 1,000,000 | 2,000,000 | ? |
| 250,000 | 750,000 | ? |
| 1,000,000 | 400,000 | ? |

The answers are found by dividing owner's equity by total assets: 2 to 1, 1 to 2, 1 to 3, and 2.5 to 1.

4. Find the operating ratio (and express it in percent) for each of the following:

| Total Operating Expenses | Net Sales | Operating Ratio |
|---|---|---|
| $ 50,000 | $ 150,000 | ? |
| 250,000 | 1,000,000 | ? |
| 500,000 | 5,000,000 | ? |
| 500,000 | 1,500,000 | ? |

The answers are found by dividing total operating expenses by net sales: 33⅓%, 25%, 10%, and 33⅓%.

5. Find the return on shareholders' equity for each of the following:

| Net Income | Shareholder's Equity | Return on Shareholder's Equity |
|---|---|---|
| $1,000,000 | $ 100,000 | ? |
| 3,500,000 | 700,000 | ? |
| 4,000,000 | 200,000 | ? |
| 5,000,000 | 1,250,000 | ? |

The answers are found by dividing the net income by the shareholders' equity: 10%, 20%, 5%, 25%.

## Market Forces

Now, the ratios discussed here are by no means the only ratios examined by financial analysts. But they are a starting point for the investor with little or no background in accounting and finance. But there is, necessarily, a caveat. All the ratios can point to financial stability and a good return on investment, but you may still wind up losing money.

How can this happen? Well, one must remember that there is a distinct difference between a corporation's business performance and the performance of its stock. The value of a corporation's stock is determined strictly by the law of supply and demand, and the value of that stock need not reflect corporate performance. People buy or sell stock on the basis of what they expect others will be willing to pay for it in the future. A corporation, therefore, may be doing extremely well, but investors may feel its future unpredicatable and thereby shy away from it, bringing down the market value of each individual share. In this case, the company is doing well but investors' fears, real or imagined, are bringing down the value of the stock. (Or, a company may be doing poorly but its stock is on the rise. In this case, investors anticipate a turn-around situation and bid up the price of the stock. Now the corporation is doing poorly but the stock is on the rise!!) Thus, regardless of how sound a company may appear, one must be certain that its stock is not overpriced—unless she is planning to sell short. This is where the P/E ratio comes in; it helps to determine what the possible selling price of the stock will be in relation to earnings *if its history is any prediction of the future.*

Stock market prices move up or down depending upon the demand for individual stocks at any given time. Fiscal performance, interest rates, market trends—all add to the level of demand, but are not the only influences on stock performance.

Many readers may have noticed that newspapers or broadcasts will headline on any single day that the *market is up* or that the *market is down.* There are thousands of stocks listed on the U.S. exchanges and in the over-the-counter market. Everyone realizes that the chance of their prices falling or rising in unison is just about impossible. So what do these headlines and announcements mean when they indicate the up or down of the market?

What is meant when it is stated that the market is up or down is that certain indexes which are generally representative of overall market activity are up or down. Many stocks move independently of these indexes. These indexes, then, can only measure *general movement.* And they are not forecasts, though too often they do become the catalysts for bullish or bearish short-term phases in the market.

For instance, suppose you are considering purchasing 100 shares of XYZ Company at $20 per share with the anticipation of selling them later at $30 per share. This would represent—if it came to pass—a $1000 profit or a 150% return on investment.

However, if at the time you are considering the investment, you hear that the "market is down," you may decide to wait a little longer before making the purchase—hoping that the price will decline even further. Suppose now that every other investor is of the same mind. In this case, the result would be very little demand for the supply of stock available. When supply exceeds demand, the result is eventual downward pressure on prices.

You may, on the other hand, hear that the market is up and,

therefore, decide, like many other investors to buy those shares in XYZ before the stock increases. This will put upward pressure on stock prices because everyone will be scrambling for available shares before the price goes up beyond their reach. Instead of placing a limit order (as "100 shares at $100"), you place a market order ("buy at the current market price"). The result is that you get the stock at whatever the current market price is when your order is executed. Conceivably, you might get the stock at a price ½ point or more beyond the ask-price prevailing when you placed the order.

## Indices

The most frequently quoted index is the Dow Jones Industrial Average which has been a reference for investors since 1896. When it was first compiled, it consisted of only a dozen stocks, the activity of which was said to reflect the general price movement of all corporate stocks. Today it consists of thirty stocks. The stocks which make up this list are occasionally changed to reflect changing economic patterns in corporate America. Below is a list of the stocks which make up the list as of this writing. Current listings may be found by checking *The Wall Street Journal* every Monday, *Barron's* on the weekend, or other financial newspapers.

### THE DOW JONES INDUSTRIALS

| | | |
|---|---|---|
| Allied-Signal | Gen Electric | Owens-Illinois |
| Aluminum Co. | Gen Motors | Philip Morris |
| Amer Can | Goodyear | Procter & Gamb |
| Amer Express | IBM | Sears Roebuck |
| AT&T | Inco | Texaco |
| Beth Steel | Int'l Paper | Union Carbide |
| Chevron | McDonalds | USX Corp. |
| DuPont | Merck & Co. | Utd Technol. |
| East Kodak | Minn. M & M | Westinghouse |
| Exxon | Navistar | Woolworth |

The Dow Jones Industrial Average is generally used in conjunction with two other Dow Jones indexes: the Transporation and Utility Averages. The stocks which are used to make up these averages will change from time to time, just as will the individual stocks that make up the Industrials.

Again, the listing of stocks given are for those which make up the averages at this writing. Current listings may be found in the same papers that list the Industrials.

## DOW JONES TRANSPORTATION STOCKS

| | |
|---|---|
| AMR Corp | Leaseway Tr |
| Amer President | Norfolk Southn |
| Burlington Nth | NWA Inc. |
| Canadian Pac. | Overnite Transp |
| Carolina Frt | Pan Am Corp. |
| Consol Freight | Sante Fe Sothn |
| CSX Corp | Trans World Air |
| Delta Air | UAL Inc. |
| Eastern Air | Union Pacific |
| Fed Express | USAir Group |

## DOW JONES UTILITY STOCKS

| | |
|---|---|
| American Electric Power | Niagara Mohawk Power |
| Centerior | Pacific Gas & Electric |
| Columbia Gas Systems | Panhandle Eastern |
| Commonwealth Edison | People's Energy |
| Consolidated Edison | Philadelphia Electric |
| Consolidated Natural Gas | Public Service Entrp. |
| Detroit Edison | Southern California Edison |
| Houston Industries | |

According to the Dow Theory, the market is governed by three major types of price movement: daily fluctuations, short-term changes, and long-term trends. Dow theorists, therefore, use all three averages discussed above to forecast *changes* in the market trend.

If all three averages are higher than they were on the previous day, then this should indicate an upward trend in prices.

The Dow Jones Averages are so widely quoted that one becomes brainwashed with their significance. But some basic math should indicate the relative extent of their true value. They represent an infinitesimal percentage of the stocks actually traded on all exchanges, and less than one-fourth of the total *value* of all New York Stock Exchange stocks. Like eveything else that has to do with the stock market, these averages can sometimes be depended upon, sometimes they cannot.

There are a number of other widely-used indexes, but none appear to be quite as popular as the Dow Jones Averages—except, perhaps, for Standard and Poor's 500. This is a broadly based index popular with industrial investors; it is popular because its sample is so extensive.

But whether one looks at the S&P 500, the DJ Industrials, or other indices such as Moody's, the New York Stock Exchange, the New York Times, Value Line, etc., what is important is that you see them in perspective.

They are not always dependable indices and one often contradicts the other. This is to say that if the indicators point to an upward trend, that does not mean that the stock you buy will go up. The DJ Averages can increase twenty days in a row, and the stock you own can decrease in value during that same period!!

### Why Buy?
Well, now you are confused.

— All the ratios can point to a strong and healthy company, but the stock can still decline in price, and it will do so because it obeys its own law: the law of supply and demand.

— The indices can indicate an upward turn in the market, but the stock you buy can still go down.

"The ratios can say the company issuing the stock is healthy and a worthwhile investment. The indicators can point to a healthy market on an upswing. And I can still lose money?!!"

Yes.

So, you may ask, why buy stock?

That's no easy question to address, and the answer which

follows, you must understand is only one man's opinion.

Buying stock is risky business. Even the pros lose a lot. Some financial advisors and stock analysts never buy stock for themselves. They know there is more money in writing about stocks and the stock market, or in researching stocks for others—and a lot less risk, unless, of course, one has a sadistic client bent on evening the score at any cost.

So, again, why buy stock?

We all hear many answers to this question, from "having a piece of America," to "getting higher yields," and "tax advantages," to "making a big killing." But, having a piece of America can wipe you out, higher yields can be cancelled by capital losses, many people lose more money trying to save on taxes then they would if they just paid them, and it takes a lot of money to make a lot of money.

So, one last time, why buy stock?

In this author's opinion there is only one reason to buy stock and that has to do with one's inner nature. If there is a bit of the entrepreneur in you, the gambler, if you enjoy trying to earn more than you can from some savings bank, if you enjoy knowing that the potential for large capital gains is there regardless of their probability, and you enjoy the challenge of picking the right stock—then the stock market is the place for *some* of your money (perhaps 10% of it).

## Ten Commandments for Investors

While this text is in no way intended to lead you into or away from the market, it would be inappropriate to end this chapter without laying down some considerations for would-be investors. Certainly no one would find fault with the following ten guidelines, although they might want to add to them or change the priorities.

Thus:

1. Be sure you have a basic understanding of economics, particularly the effects of inflation and unemployment on the na-

tional economy; and that you have an understanding of business cycles.

2. Study the fundamentals of business finance so that you learn how to read corporate reports, particularly a stockholders' report.

3. Know the basic arithmetic of investment.

4. Never select a stock entirely on your own. Subscribe to one or two investment newsletters. Very often their contrary opinions will confuse you enough to dampen your enthusiasm, the kind of enthusiasm that often leads an investor into a poorly timed investment. The stock you finally select should have *at least* three recommendations: one from your market newsletter, one from your stockbroker or another professional, and one from—you.

5. Determine your investment goals and select your stocks accordingly. If you are looking mainly for income and long-range capital gains, you do not invest in a penny stock. And if you are in a rather high-income tax bracket, care little about dividends, and want the tax advantage of long-term capital gains, you do not want to put your money in Public Service Gas and Electric.

6. Invest in stocks of strong companies that have been around for awhile. The stock may fluctuate according to market forces, but over the long-term your investment will be relatively safe. For a start, stick to Standard & Poor's 500 stocks.

7. Keep tabs on your stock and the economic forces that can affect it. Do not be afraid to bail out if that becomes the most practical thing to do.

8. Do not put all your money in one stock. Diversify. But do not spread your investments so thinly that you cancel out the advantage of being in the market in the first place.

9. Do not buy on impulse. Research your intended investment as thoroughly as possible. It is better to miss a one- or two-point advance than rush into a one- or two-point decline.

10. Read the financial papers. Become interested in the world. Become a part of the investment community through your studies and reading. Learn market terminology.

## Review Questions

1. If you purchased 100 shares of Con Edison stock at $26⅝ per share, and later sold them for $27⅜ per share, what would be your profit before commission? _____

2. If you purchased 500 shares of International Aluminum at $15, and later sold them for $12¾, what would be your total loss? _____

3. If you sold short 100 shares of Apache Corporation at $10⅜ per share, and later "purchased" the shares for $8⅞ each, what would be your profit or loss? _____

4. True or false? If you hold a stock long enough, you will always realize a profit. _____

5. If a stock selling at $80 has a P/E ratio of $10, what are its earnings per share? _____

6. True or false? The P/E ratio is all you need to know to decide whether or not to purchase a stock. _____

7. Current assets divided by current liabilities = _____
_____ .

8. Current assets (less inventory) divided by current liabilities = the _____ _____ .

9. Owners' liabilities divided by stockholders equity = the _____ _____ .

10. Total operating expenses divided by net sales = the _____ _____ .

11. Net income divided by shareholders' equity = _____ .

12. True or false? The price of your stock will always go in the direction of the market in general. _____

13. True or false? The most frequently quoted stock index is the Dow Jones Industrial Average. _____

14. True or false? The closing price of a stock, when compared to its opening price for the same day, is a dependable indicator of which way the stock will move at the beinnning of the next day's trading. _____

15. True or false? Never put all your investment money in one security. _____

# CHAPTER 9

# Puts and Calls

Buying and selling options has become a popular activity with many investors because, with options contracts they can:

— Get a relatively high return from what is, when compared to an investment in most securities, a relatively small amount of money,

— Diversify their portfolios, because the low price of options allows their money to be distributed over many contracts or some combination of stock, bond, warrant, and option purchases,

— Be assured that their losses will be no more than what they had to put up for the option, plus any broker commission.

Options are risky business, nonetheless, and certainly not for everyone. They are also confusing business to investors used to buying and selling only corporate stocks. They are risky business partly because of the time limitations attached to each contract, as well as the fact that an investor must be able to predict what direction the price of the underlying security will take during the term of the contract; after the expiration date of a contract, a stock option is worthless. They are confusing business because of the very different terminology associated with options trading.

There are basically two types of options, though they may be used in combinations which allow the investor greater flexibility. These are *call* options and *put* options.

*Call Option.* An option which gives legal right to the buyer to purchase the underlying security at a fixed price until the expiration date of the call. You may be either the buyer or the seller of a call.

*Put Option.* An option which gives legal right to the buyer to sell the underlying security at a fixed price until the expiration date of the put. You may be either the buyer or the seller of a put.

## Contract Terminology

Puts and calls are already defined. But there are some other terms with which you must become thoroughly familiar. Someday an English major will rise to the top of the ranks in the investment community and, quite wisely, revise stock option nomenclature, which, although quite appropriate, is nevertheless quite confusing to the beginner.

To begin with, there is something called the *premium.* When you buy an option you give to the seller (also known as the writer) an agreed upon sum of money. You give him, say, $100 for the privilege of buying a put or call. *Or,* now taking the role of an option writer, you receive $100 from the buyer of the option you have to sell. That $100 is the *premium;* it is the money that the writer of the option gets to keep under any circumstance. That $100 has not purchased any stock for the option buyer; it has simply purchased the *rights* granted under the option contract.

The premium earned by you as the option writer, or paid by you as the option buyer, is generally the fee for the right to buy 100 shares of some corporation's stock, say, the stock of that well-known corporation, XYZ. This stock is now the *underlying security* upon which the option contract is based. But remember, the premium of $100 paid to the writer does not buy one single share of XYZ; it only buys the right to purchase or sell 100 shares of XYZ at some agreed upon price during the term of the option contract.

In this contract for which a premium of $100 was paid, it will have been stipulated that the buyer of the contract must exercise his option (buy or sell XYZ at $50 per share) within a certain time. The very last day on which the option may be exercised is called the *expiration date*. The writer (or seller) of the option keeps the $100 premium whether or not the buyer exercises his option.

If the buyer of the contract does decide to exercise his right under the contract and does buy XYZ, the price he pays is called the *striking* price—or the *exercise* price.

Let's sumarize:

> *Premium.* Money paid by the buyer of an option to the seller of the option.

> *Underlying Security.* The stock on which the contract is based.

> *Expiration Date.* The last date on which the buyer has the right to exercise his option.

> *Striking Price.* Also known as the exercise price, it is the fixed price for which a stock can be purchased or sold.

> *Writer.* The seller of a put option or a call option contract.

## Option Listings

If you were to turn to the financial pages in any large newspaper you would come across a section titled "Option Trading" where the prices and expiration dates of options offered on various exchanges are listed. Table 9.1 is a section from a typical listing, this one from *The Wall Street Journal.* Let's zero in on the column headings and one listing. The particular listing to which reference is being made is of options on the Chicago Board Options Exchange. Note that the last three columns relate to prices for put options.

> *Month (Mar, June, Sept).*These are the expiration months for the various contracts offered. Options listed in Table 9.1 expire in March, June, and September. There will be separate listings for options expiring in other months.

*Option & N.Y. Close.* Here is listed the underyling security and the price at which the stock closed for the day. Referencing the first listing, you can see that Apache *stock* closed on the New York Stock Exchange at a price of $12.75 per share.

---

### Table 9.1.
### The Wall Street Journal listing of some options available on the Chicago Board Options Exchange.

| Option & NY Close | Strike Price | Calls—Last | | | Puts—Last | | |
|---|---|---|---|---|---|---|---|
| | | Mar | Jun | Sep | Mar | Jun | Sep |
| Apache | ..10 | 2½ | 3 | 3¼ | r | 3-16 | r |
| 12¾ | ... 15 | r | 7-16 | ¾ | 2½ | r | r |
| BrisMy | ..35 | 8½ | r | r | r | ⅛ | r |
| 44½ | ... 40 | 4⅜ | 5½ | r | r | ½ | 1⅛ |
| 44½ | ... 45 | ⅛ | 2 | 2⅞ | ⅝ | 2½ | r |
| 44½ | ... 50 | r | 7-16 | 1 | r | r | r |
| Bruns | . 17½ | r | 8½ | s | r | 1-16 | s |
| 25⅜ | . 22½ | 3⅛ | r | s | r | r | s |
| 25⅜ | . 27½ | r | 1¼ | s | 2 | r | s |
| 25⅜ | ... 25 | 15-16 | 2 5-16 | 3½ | ¼ | 1½ | 2⅛ |
| 25⅜ | ... 30 | r | 11-16 | r | 4½ | r | r |
| Celan | ....60 | 8¾ | s | s | r | s | s |
| 69½ | ... 65 | r | r | r | r | 2 | r |
| 69½ | ... 70 | ¼ | 2¼ | r | ⅞ | r | r |
| Chamln | . 25 | r | 1⅛ | r | 1½ | 2⅜ | 2⅞ |
| CompSc | . 15 | 1-16 | ⅞ | r | r | r | 1¾ |
| 13¾ | ... 20 | 1-16 | ¼ | ⅝ | r | r | r |
| Dow Ch | . 25 | s | 4⅝ | r | s | r | r |
| 29¼ | ... 30 | ¼ | 1 5-16 | 2 3-16 | ⅝ | 1¾ | 2⅝ |
| 29¼ | ... 35 | 1-16 | 5-16 | ⅝ | 5½ | r | r |
| Esmark | 37½ | 2½ | r | s | r | r | s |
| 40½ | . 42½ | 1-16 | r | s | r | r | s |
| 40½ | ... 35 | r | r | r | 1-16 | ½ | r |
| 40½ | ... 40 | r | 3¼ | r | 9-16 | 2¾ | r |
| 40½ | ... 45 | 1-16 | r | r | r | r | r |
| F Bost | ... 35 | r | 5 | r | r | r | r |
| 39⅝ | ... 40 | ¼ | 2¾ | r | 1 | 2½ | 3¾ |
| Ford o | .33⅜ | 4⅝ | s | s | r | s | s |
| 38⅛ | . 36⅝ | 1¾ | r | s | 5-16 | r | s |
| 38⅛ | ... 40 | ⅛ | 2⅛ | s | 2 | r | s |
| Ford | .... 30 | s | 8½ | r | s | 5-16 | r |
| 38⅛ | ... 35 | 3 | 4⅞ | 6¼ | 1-16 | 1⅛ | 1⅝ |
| 38⅛ | ... 40 | 3-16 | 2⅛ | 3⅝ | 2⅛ | 3½ | 4 |
| 38⅛ | ... 45 | 1-16 | 13-16 | 1¾ | r | r | r |
| 38⅛ | ... 50 | r | 5-16 | r | r | r | r |
| Gen El | ..45 | 4⅞ | 5½ | 7 | 1-16 | 7-16 | r |
| 50⅝ | ... 50 | 13-16 | 2⅞ | 4½ | ⅜ | 1¾ | 2½ |
| 50⅝ | ... 55 | 1-16 | 1 | 2 1-16 | 5 | 5¼ | 5½ |
| 50⅝ | ... 60 | 1-16 | ⅜ | 1 | 10¼ | r | r |
| G M | .....65 | 2⅛ | 4⅞ | 6¼ | ⅛ | 2 | 2⅞ |
| 67⅜ | ... 70 | ⅛ | 2 7-16 | 4⅛ | 3 | 4⅜ | 5¼ |
| 67⅜ | ... 75 | 1-16 | 1 1-16 | 2⅜ | 7⅝ | 8 | r |
| 67⅜ | ... 80 | 1-16 | ½ | 1½ | r | r | r |
| 67⅜ | ... 85 | 1-16 | ⅛ | ¾ | r | r | 13 |

*Strike Price.* Here is the price, $10, at which the option buyer can *purchase* the stock from the writer of the *call*—or at which the option buyer may *sell* the stock to the writer of the *put.*

*Calls-Last.* Here is the price of the option—in option language, the premium that was last paid for the option. For Apache, we see that the price for calls expiring in March are $2.50, those expiring in June are $3, and those expiring in September are $3.25. As option contracts are almost always for 100 shares of stocks, the actual cost for the March, June, and September options are, respectively, $250, $300, and $325. In the case of put options on Apache, we see that there are no March and September contracts being offered, but there is one for June.

But understanding how to read the listings does not mean that you have the information available to make a decision to buy or sell an option or to even consider getting involved. First you have to have the money to play with. Then, you must be prepared to do a great deal of homework on options trading as well as on the stock market in general. But, let's continue on this complicated topic, not to make you an expert or even to prepare you to make your first purchase, but rather, to help you understand what option trading is all about. Then, when you are ready, if you ever are, to look seriously into opening an account, you will at least understand the fundamental arithmetic and some of the basic terminology.

## Call Options

Call options are defined as those which give legal right to the buyer to purchase the underlying security at a fixed price until the option contract expires. As an option trader, you may either buy or sell (write) calls.

When the price of a stock goes up, the premium for the related call may also go up. Buyers of call options, therefore, hope to resell the contracts at a higher price. They will buy a call if they anticipate strong performance by the stock of the underlying corporation.

*Example No. 1.** You have purchased a call on XYZ Corporation for $3 per share; the cost to you is $300. XYZ is selling at this time at $20 per share. Before the expiration date of the call contract, XYZ common climbs to $25 per share and the premium for the call is now $6. If you decide to sell your contract right now, you can realize a profit of $300. You will have doubled your money.

It is easy to see how option trading can provide a great deal of leverage for investors. With a relatively small amount of money, they can reap substantial profits. To deal in the underlying stock referenced in the above example, you would have needed $2,000 to purchase the 100 shares. The $5 increase in the stock would mean a $500 gain for you, but that would represent only a 25% gain. Imagine if your investment in calls was equal to what might have been invested in the stock—your profit could have been much more.

*Example No. 2.* You have purchased a call on XYZ Corporation for $3 per share; the cost to you is $300. The value of the stock when you purchased the call was $20. Before the expiration date of the contract, XYZ falls to $10 per share and the premium on the call is $1.50. You are afraid the option may be worth even less as the expiration date draws near, so you decide to sell the contract for $1.50 per share. Your loss on the trade is $150.

The most you could have lost, before any broker fee is taken into account, is $300. If you invested in the stock itself and purchased 100 shares, there is always the chance that it will be worth nothing and your possible losses could equal $2,000, which represents your entire investment before commissions.

---

*Values assigned are to simplify the math and do not represent typical relationships between premiums and types of calls (or puts). How a put or call will actually move in relation to the underlying stock depends on those factors mentioned in the subsection on "Premiums."

But in dealing in the stock rather than the option, you are not pressured into selling by any contract expiration date, and can possibly take advantage of any upswing in the stock, should such an upswing occur. Of course, you always have the option, when dealing in calls, of purchasing the stock so that instead of maintaining the call, you now have a position in the underlying security and can take advantage of that upswing in per share price. But this may not always be practical because of the relationship of the stock price to the striking price.

Every buyer of a call may be looking for other advantages besides turning a profit on the contract itself. In Examples 1 and 2 above, you were attempting to buy the contract low and sell it high, succeeding in Example 1 but failing in Example 2. In either case, you always had that opportunity of exercising your option and *calling* for delivery of the stock though it would be impractical in Example 2. This you would accomplish by calling your broker and saying something to this effect:

"I wish to exercise my March call on XYZ, Mr. Broker. What is the cost to purchase the stock when your commissions are included?"

Sometimes an investor is interested in purchasing a security, but does not have the money required to buy immediately. He does, however, have the money to pick up an option to buy within a certain period of time, before the end of which he expects to have the required funds. In this case, he may decide to purchase a call on the stock. This way, if there is a sudden upswing in the price of the stock before he has the money, the call has insured that he can get the stock at the lower price.

Calls, it must be noted, are generally referred to as being *in-the-money*, *out-of-the-money*, or *at-the-money*. The first will demand a higher premium, the second, the least. The definitions are given below; examples are given in Table 9.2.

*In-the-money call.* A call having an exercise price below the current quote of the underlying stock.

*Out-of-the-money call* A call having an exercise price above the current quote of the underlying stock.

*At-the-money-call.* A call having an exercise price
equal to the current quote of the underlying stock.

Buyers of calls are attracted to the contracts because of the
substantial return they can get from a relatively small investment
and the limited risk which an option contract affords. Sellers
(writers) of calls are interested in the income the premium affords, and the "insurance" the contract gives against declines
in the underlying security.

## Table 9.2
## Types of Calls.

| Stock | Current Quote | Exercise Price | Call |
|-------|---------------|----------------|------|
| Apache | 12¾ | 10 | In-the-money |
| Bristol Meyers | 44½ | 35 | In-the-money |
| Brunswick | 25⅜ | 27½ | Out-of-the-money |
| Dow Chemical | 29¼ | 30 | Out-of-the-money |
| Esmark | 40½ | 42½ | Out-of-the-money |
| Ford | 38⅛ | 45 | Out-of-the-money |
| General Electric | 50⅝ | 60 | Out-of-the-money |
| General Electric | 67⅜ | 65 | In-the-money |
| General Motors | 60 | 60 | At-the-money |

If you decide to become a writer rather than a buyer of a call,
you must realize that you will be obligating yourself to deliver
100 shares of the underlying security anytime the buyer decides
to exercise his option.

In the previous examples, you were the buyer of a call. At
anytime you felt it to your advantage to do so, you could have
exercised your option and demanded the shares of the underlying security be sold to you at the exercise price. But in the examples which follow, you are now the writer of calls. The buyer
of your call can demand delivery of the underlying security from

you at the exercise price anytime prior to the contract's expiration.

You can always avoid your obligation to deliver the underlying security at the exercise price by becoming the buyer of another call equal to the one you have written.*

There are two types of calls which can be written. These are termed covered and uncovered (naked) calls. If you write a call on a security which you already own, then you are writing a covered option. If, however, you are writing the option against a security which you do not own, you are writing an uncovered option.

The regulations governing the writing of uncovered options are strict, as they must be to insure the safety of individual contracts as well as the integrity of the options market. If you want to write a naked call, you must set up a margin account with your broker and maintain the margin necessary to assure that you can actually buy the required amount of shares in the underlying security should the buyer decide to exercise his option. There are tremendous risks involved in writing uncovered calls, for the writer may at any time be forced to put up additional funds to cover his position. At this time, to write either uncovered calls or uncovered puts, the investor is required to have from $10,000 to $25,000 in equity in his account.

*Example No. 3.* You own 100 shares of XYZ stock for which you paid $100 per share. You expect that on the short term the stock will remain at that price or go lower; yet you feel the long term possibilities make holding onto the stock worthwhile. Therefore, you write a call against the stock, receiving in return a $10 per share premium, or $1,000. The stock declines to $95 per share and remains at that level until the contract expires. The stock declined $5 per share, or $500; yet, during that

---

* The writer of a call is never obligated to deliver the original shares of the underlying security. He is only obligated to deliver a similar amount of stock in the same corporations and, therefore, always has the option of purchasing new stock to meet his obligation.

same interval, you had a gain of $1,000 from the premium for the call (assume the call is at-the-money.)

The higher the premium you are able to get, the greater the protection against declines in the underlying security. At the $10 per share premium used in Example 1, you, in effect, were insured against a stock price drop to $90 per share. Nonetheless, even if the stock went down to $80 per share, as long as it eventually went back over $90 before you sold out, you would reap some profit, not counting broker fees.

**Example No. 4.** You own 100 shares of XYZ stock for which you paid $100 per share. You expect that on the short term the stock will remain at that price or go lower; yet you want to hold onto the stock for the long term. Therefore, you write a call with an exercise price of $100, receiving in return a $10 per share premium, or $1,000. The stock increases in value to $120 per share. The buyer of your call decides to exercise his option and wants the stock for $100 per share. *You must sell the stock at $100 per share.*

As you can calculate, you are unable to profit from the increase in the price of the shares you own and you must sell your holdings. But you did earn $1,000, on the call.

A call (or put, for that matter) may or may not move point-for-point along with the underlying stock, depending upon whether the option is in, at, or out-of, the money, and the time remaining until the expiration date of the contract.

There is, as you may have deducted, a lot to buying and writing calls. It's a stock market game, so to speak, that must be played under time constraints. Call contracts, like put contracts, have expiration dates, and you must exercise your options or make your money before contract expiration.

This subsection has only been concerned with the fundamental arithmetic of buying and selling calls; its objective has not been to teach you how and when to buy calls. For call option strategy and tax consideration refer to the texts listed under "stock options" in the dictionary.

## Put Contracts

Investors buy puts because they expect the underlying security to depreciate in value, thereby putting upward pressure on the value of the premium.

The put buyer has the same perspective that the short-seller in the stock market may have, only the put buyer is not dealing directly in the underlying security, but rather in an option contract. He may, at any time to his advantage, decide to exercise his option and then deal in the underlying security, but generally it is much more to his advantage to just buy and sell the put.

Someone selling a security short runs a tremendous risk. For instance, if he sells Apache short at $10, expecting that it will decline to $5, at which price he plans to buy it back, he may find that, while on some tropical isle with his favorite companion, the stock has doubled instead of declining. . .or, worse, has quadrupled, and he owes his broker a lot of money. If he had purchased a put instead of short selling the stock, he would only lose what he paid in premiums for the put.

*Example No. 5.* * Assume that on March 1 the stock of XYZ is selling at $100 per share. You anticipate a decline in the price of the stock because you have judged it to be overpriced. You decide to purchase an XYZ at-the-money put option at a price of $10 per share. The cost to you is $1,000, as puts are generally for 100 shares of the underlying stock. Before expiration of the contract, XYZ stock declines to $85. At the same time the put has become more valuable and is now selling at $20 per share. The put contract purchased at $1,000 can now be sold for $2,000—resulting in a $1,000 gain, or the doubling of your money, before commissions.

---

*Values assigned are to simplify the math, and do not represent any typical relationship between the premium, exercise price and market value of the stock. However, with at-the-money or in-the-money puts, we will assume, for purposes of simplication, that the price of the option will move close to a point or better with each one point movement in the stock. However, it is important to note, that put premiums rarely expand as fast as call premiums.

The put allows you some advantages that selling short will not:

— You have lower transaction costs because buying and selling option contracts is generally cheaper than buying and selling stock.
— You can lose no more than the cost of the premium.
— You are required to put up less money because of the low cost of options.
— You have no liability regarding dividends as would the short seller.

In those cases where the option buyer owns the underlying stock, the usual purpose for the put is to "insure" the stock owner's position. Incentive for dealing in the put may be the result of any number of factors, including wanting to maintain a position in a stock expected to decline, yet realize a short-term profit.

*Example No. 6.* You own 100 shares of XYZ stock; the market forecasts are mixed and you fear the stock might decline in price. The current market value is $50 per share, and the put is selling at a premium of $4 a share with an exercise of $48. You buy the put. Before expiration of the contract, the stock declines in price to $35 per share. The put goes in the opposite direction, as expected, and increases to $20 per share. You sell the put for a gain of $16 per share, or $1600. You had paper losses of $1500, but an actual gain of $1600 before the broker's fee. The gain on the put covered the downslide in the price of the stock.*

One can easily grasp the advantage of buying puts on highly speculative issues which have tremendous upside potential in the long term, but possible downslide slips for the short or intermediate term. By buying the stock long and buying a put contract at the same time, the investor hedges his investment. The

---

*But you are, of course, at a tax disadvantage because you cannot write-off the paper loss and must pay taxes on the $1,600 cash profit.

put protects his position on any downslide. If the stock should head north, never allowing the possibility of realizing a profit on the put, the cost of the put will reduce the investor's profit by the cost per share of the premium paid for the option. This is to say that if the eventual profit on the sale of stock is $30 per share and the cost of the put if $4 per share, the true profit is only $26 per share before commissions are taken into account. But the protection in case of downslide is sometimes worth the reduction in profits.

Like call options, put options may be *in-the-money* or *out-of-the-money*. The definitions are given below; examples are given in Table 9.3. Note that the definitions are reverse what they are for calls.

> *In-the-money put.* A put having an exercise price above the current price of the underlying stock.

> *Out-of-the-money put.* A put having an exercise price below the current quote of the underlying stock.

> *At-the-money put.* A put having an exercise price equal to the current quote of the underlying stock.

---

### Table 9.3
### Types of Puts

| *Stock* | *Current Quote* | *Exercise Price* | *Put* |
|---|---|---|---|
| Apache | 12¾ | 15 | In-the-money |
| Bristol Meyers | 45 | 44½ | Out-of-the-money |
| CompuScan | 13¾ | 15 | In-the-money |
| Esmark | 40½ | 37½ | Out-of-the-money |
| Ford | 38 | 30 | Out-of-the-money |
| General Electric | 50 | 55 | In-the-money |
| General Electric | 67⅜ | 65 | Out-of-the-money |
| General Motors | 60 | 60 | At-the-money |

Now, if you were to change direction and decide to become a writer of a put, instead of a buyer, you would generally be after the income the premium affords. But, as a put writer, you must operate under the same restraints imposed upon writers of uncovered calls, meaning that you are required to have a margin account and sufficient funds on hand to cover your position. At the present time, writers of uncovered puts or uncovered calls must meet stringent margin requirements. Few individuals have the cash or securities to play with uncovered puts (or uncovered calls). But having the financial muscle to play the game is only part of the prerequisites; one must also have the knowledge, discipline, patience, and other characteristics it takes to play for what can become high stakes. An introduction to some of the basic arithmetic involved in writing puts follows; knowledge of how to select options and when to buy or write a contract must come from extensive study and practice.*

*Example No. 7.* You write an at-the-money put with an exercise price of $100 per share, and receive a premium of $10 per share. Through the expiration date, the underlying stock always remains above $100 per share, meaning that there is no possibility of the buyer exercising his option. You, therefore, have made $1,000 by writing the put.

As the writer of a put, you must realize that you will incur the cost of maintaining the margin required on your account during the term of the contract, so the $1,000 indicated above is your profit before the margin expense is calculated.

*Example No. 8.* You write a put with an exercise price of $100 per share, and receive a premium of $10 per share. The

---

*The game can always be played on paper before you ever actually invest. Just select a half-dozen or so puts and/or calls, and jot them down on paper with an explanation of why you selected them. Then watch the daily listings. Decide when you would want to sell if you did own them, and watch what happens to each selection until the contracts expire.

stock at this time is selling for $100. Before contract expiration, the stock falls below $100, and the buyer exercises his option. *You are obligated to buy the stock to cover your position.*

In dealing with puts as well as calls, an investor is, in effect, developing a very dynamic investment strategy. She is able to set herself up to possibly take advantage of temporary upswings or declines in the price of a specific security, or to squeeze extra income from her portfolio.

When an investor begins to deal in uncovered calls and puts, she must remember that she is taking high risk, chancing every single dollar of her investment. Once contracts expire, the put, or call, contract is worthless. Thus, when dealing with uncovered options, she should try to protect her investment by buying some combination of puts and calls. The extra investment and commissions this necessitates will make the return less impressive but will reduce the chance of total loss. However, puts-plus-calls strategies are no guarantee of success.

As with calls, put contracts will increase in value relative to expiration dates, underlying stock movement and interest rates, etc. But this relative movement may vary considerably for in-the-money, out-of-the-money and at-the-money contracts on the same underlying security.

In every way, options contracts are for the more experienced investors, and it is highly recommended that before anyone takes the gamble, he or she reads extensively on the subject and seeks the guidance of an experienced professional.

## Premiums (The Prices for the Option Contracts)

The premium placed on an option is what stirs trading interest and keeps the market in motion. Just as the majority of stock investors look to buy a security at a much lower price than it might be trading months later, so does the buyer of an option look for a premium that is much lower than it might be worth up to nine months later. The real trick is in determining which options will be worth more and which will be worth less.

Some buyers of options are more interested in the option contract in the traditional sense, as previous examples have illustrated, for they are not as interested in buying and selling contracts as they may be in actually acquiring the underlying security. In this case, the buyer of an option continually monitors the current market price of the underlying security and compares it with the exercise price of the option. When there is enough of a difference between the stock price and the option's exercise price, the buyer will exercise his option. Whether he wants that stock's price to be higher or lower than the exercise price depends upon whether he is the buyer of a call or put.

*If he is the buyer of a call,* he will want the price of the stock to advance high enough above the exercise price to allow him to realize a profit after the premium and all brokerage commissions are taken into account. *If he is the buyer of a put,* he must also calculate his break-even point after the premium and commissions, but now he wants the stock price to fall below the exercise price.

Whether or not that premium makes the option contract worthwhile depends, then, upon what will happen to the underlying security. In the case of Apache Corporation, selling at $10 per share, it is clear that if someone paid $250 for the March call, plus $30 in commission to his broker, Apache stock must climb a bit higher before the call buyer can realize a profit. The option would have cost her, actually, $280, and for that money *the buyer of the call* will have received the right to purchase 100 shares of Apache at $10 per share.

To give one example, if the buyer of the call decides to exercise her rights and buy 100 shares of Apache stock, she must pay a commission on the stock purchase. Should she then sell the stock immediately or on the short term, she must also estimate the sell commissions to determine her break-even point. For the sake of simplicity, let's estimate that the total fees paid to the broker for purchasing the call and buying and selling the stock will be $90.

| Premium | $ 250.00 |
|---|---|
| Brokerage Fees | 90.00 |
| Cost of Stock | 1,000.00 |
| Total Cost | $1,340.00 |

Thus, to realize a profit from the sale of the stock, *the call buyer* must sell it at $13.40 per share, or, roughly, $13½. If the price of the stock should rise to $20 per share, basic arithmetic reveals the impressive return on investment the buyer will realize.

But as Apache stock increases in price, so will the value of the call. The investor will soon realize that instead of becoming involved in the underlying security, she is better off just selling her option, for the premium for the call would have increased at a higher percent than the price of the stock. If she is not interested in accumulating the stock, she is generally much smarter to be dealing only in the option, the perspective on which this chapter focuses.

What about the writer of the call? What is in it for him or her?

The option writer wants that premium. He or she feels that Apache Corporation will probably decline in price, or else advance so slightly that the buyer has no advantage in exercising the option. The writer, therefore, earns the extra income the premium brings, and may also get to keep the underlying security.

Once the buyer has the option, he or she can sell it anytime prior to the expiration date. Just as the buyer may sell at anytime, so can the writer of an option buy his contract back any time before expiration. *A writer can sell an option, then buy it back*, something he or she will do whenever it is to his or her advantage. In this way, the writer can reverse his position to realize a profit or cut a loss.

But what about that premium? What actually makes it increase or decrease?

This is another way of asking, What is the value of a particular option? An option's worth is determined by its profit potential, or what may be called its intrinsic value, *and* its time value. The intrinsic value is determined by the amount by which the put or the call happens to be in-the-money. If it does not appear the put or the call can be exercised to the benefit of the owner, it is understandably a poor investment risk, and this will be reflected in the price of the premium. The time value is the value the investor puts on a premium in addition to its intrinsic value. He or she determines that it will remain in the money through expiration date, and by how much, and so, therefore, is willing to pay a higher or lesser premium.

The length of time remaining until expiration has a great deal to do with the value of a particular option. Who wants to chance holding a worthless contract? Or holding one that is worth less than before? The value of an option decreases as the expiration date approaches, so even an in-the-money option may not move point-for-point along with the underlying stock days or weeks before expiration.

Investors also consider the volatility of the underlying security in determining the value of any contract. Thus, a stock which has wide swings on the short term will generally command higher premiums for related options contracts. And, of course, investors also weigh interest rates, which, if they are on the increase, will put upward pressure on premiums.

## Complex Strategies

As this chapter has presented an introduction to options trading, the examples on the previous pages illustrated the most basic strategies. When the options game is played by the more sophisticated investor, he may use a number of highly complex strategies. These include dealing in double options, consisting of a single put and a single call which, though they may be exercised at different times, are sold as a single package; dealing in two calls and one put at the same time; and/or dealing in two puts and one call at the same time. Which strategy he or she uses will depend upon his or her objectives, tax situation, and evaluation of the underlying security in regard to the market in general. But these strategies are for the highly advanced trader, and will not be treated in this text.

## Review Questions

1. A _____ is an option which gives legal right to the buyer to purchase the underlying security at a fixed price until the expiration date of the call.

2. A _____ is an option which gives legal right to the buyer to sell the underlying security at a fixed price until expiration date of the contract.

3. A _____ is the money paid by the buyer of an option to the seller (writer) of the option.

4. The stock on which an option contract is based is called the _____ .

5. The _____ is the last date on which the buyer still has the right to exercise his option.

6. The _____ also known as the exercise price, is the price at which the option buyer exercises his rights.

7. _____ of call options hope to resell their contracts at a higher price.

8. Define an in-the-money-call. _____

_____

9. Define an in-the-money put. _____

_____

10. Define an out-of-the-money call. _____
_____

11. Define an out-of-the-money put. _____
_____

12. True or false? Stock option trading is a sure way to make money. _____

## CHAPTER 10

# Warrants and Rights

There are two additional types of "options" available to stock-holders. These go under the names of stock-purchase (or option) warrants and something called stock rights. Both are entitlements to the stockholder to purchase additional shares. But warrants and rights are very different.

## Warrants

There are two types of warrants available to stockholders. One is called a subscription warrant, and the other a stock-purchase warrant.

Subscription warrants are tied in with special subscriptions to new common stock issues. These special subscriptions are made available to current stockholders by the issuing corporation. They are rights to the stockholders to subscribe to a new issue in the same proportion as their current ownership in corporate common. The actual number of rights to which each individual stockholder will be entitled is represented by a *subscription warrant* which gives them legal right to act on their option.

Stock purchase warrants are often considered equity privileges and, therefore, are very often made available only to holders of certain corporate securities. But stock purchase warrants may also be issued separately for purchase by the public. Each warrant entitles the owner to purchase X amount of shares in the underlying stock for a certain period of time. There are exceptions to the time factor, however, for some warrants are what is called "perpetual"; that is, they are issued without any expiration date.

Two of the important terms associated with warrant trading you will already be familiar with from your knowledge of option trading. These are *exercise price* and *expiration date*.

Just as with stock options, the exercise price is the price which the owner of the warrant must pay to take ownership of the underlying security. The exercise price of a newly issued warrant will almost always exceed the current market price of the underlying security. For instance, if XYZ is selling at $20 per share, the warrants issued will have an exercise price above $20. If you should buy the warrants and the stock never reaches the exercise price before expiration, you stand to lose everything you paid for the warrant. If, however, the stock of XYZ exceeds the exercise price, you have the right to purchase shares at $20; and then you can turn around and sell the stock at the higher market price.

As the holder of a warrant, you must realize that your position is similar to that of the holder of the stock option—you own the warrant, not the stock. The warrant only gives you the right to purchase the stock before the warrant expires. When dividends are declared on the stock, you receive nothing because you are owner of the warrant not owner of the stock.

The basic value of a warrant is related to the current value of the stock for which it has been issued. To determine the value of a warrant, follow these instructions:

1. Subtract the exercise price of the warrant from the current market price of the common stock for which it was issued.

2. Take the answer from No. 1 above and multiply it times the number of shares the warrant entitles you to purchase. You answer is the theoretical value of the warrant. (See Table 10.1.)

*Example No. 1* You purchase newly issued warrants for XYZ stock. The stock is selling for $20 and the exercise price of the warrant is $25. The cost for each warrant is $5 and each warrant entitles you to purchase 2 shares of XYZ. You do not have to do any arithmetic to realize that you've got a worthless piece of paper, but let's do it anyway. Subtract $25 from $20. Your answer is less than zero, but just write down zero. Multiply zero times the 2 shares each warrant entitles you to buy: $2 \times 0 = 0$.

Why did you buy the warrant in the first place? You are bullish on the stock and anticipate that the price of the warrant will follow the stock price when it heads north.

***Example No. 2*** XYZ stock increases in value to $30 per share, which is a 50% increase in value. Meanwhile the warrants have increased in value to $10, an increase of 100%. You can make a lot more by selling your warrants than in exercising your rights and buying and selling the XYZ stock.

Why did the warrant increase so markedly in value compared to the stock. If we take the two arithmetical steps given on the previous page and formularize them, the answer becomes apparent.

| Stock Price | − | Exercise Price | × | Shares per Warrant | = | Warrant Value |
|---|---|---|---|---|---|---|
| $30 | − | $25 | × | $2 | = | $10 |

This is, of course, all theoretical and there will be some discrepancy between what the formula says the value of the warrant will be and what the marketplace is willing to accept as a good trading price. In the case of warrants, the price may skyrocket above and beyond the theoretical value by speculative forces highly bullish on the related stock. Investors expecting large gains in the market price of XYZ might be willing to drive the price of the warrant further north than good sense would ordinarily allow.

Corporations generally turn to the issuance of warrants when it is not within their means or plans to take on the fiscal burdens associated with the issuance of bonds or preferred stocks, for on these they are required to pay interest or dividends. The warrants provide a relatively painless way of raising necessary capital in a short amount of time. If the warrants are never exercised, the corporation stands to benefit handsomely. However, if the warrants are exercised, stockholders' equity will be diluted accordingly. Those additional shares that must now be issued to the holders of the warrants means the corporation must spread earnings over a greater number of shares—and dividends, also, when these are distributed.

Stock option warrants should not be confused with subscription warrants or stock rights.

The number of shares that each current stockholder is entitled to purchase is indicated on the subscription warrants that are sent to the stockholder *before* the new stock is made available. The certificates serve as documented proof that the holder is entitled to the stock. The proportion of new stock to which each warrant holder is entitled will be equivalent to the proportion of total corporate stock they owned at the time the warrants were distributed.

## Stock Rights

Stock rights are also privileges to stockholders to purchase additional shares of stock but, unlike warrants, stock rights usually carry an exercise price which is below the current market value of the related stock. For example, suppose a corporation decides to issue an additional 100,000 shares of stock. It has the option to sell them on the open market or to negotiate with investment banking concerns to move the shares at or close to the current market value. But the corporation may prefer to raise whatever capital is needed from existing shareholders, so the board of directors decides to offer special rights, and these rights will allow a discount (possibly) to those shareholders who participate. If the stock is selling for $10 per share, the rights may be to purchase the stock at $8 per share.

Whether or not the stockholders will be able to profit from the rights depends upon what happens to the market price of the stock during the subscription offer. It can very well happen that the price of the shares falls to below $8 and remains there; and the stockholders, if they want to buy additional shares, realize they are smarter to buy them on the open market than from the corporation through the rights offering. The result is chaos for the issuing corporation. The board of directors antici- pated $800,000 for the offering (100,000 shares at $8 each), but are unable to move even one share of the new stock. Instead of $800,000, they make zero dollars—unless they have made provisions for special underwriting efforts in the case of failure in the rights offering.

---

To determine the value of any rights offering:

$$\frac{A - B}{1 + C}$$

where
A = market price of the old stock,
B = the subscription price of the new stock guaranteed by the rights,
C = rights required for each new share offered.

---

In the case of the 100,000 share offering discussed in the previous example, one would determine the value of each right in the following manner:

1. Take the subscription price of the new stock ($8) and sub- tract it from the market price of the old stock ($10). The answer, of course, is $2.

2. Take the number of rights required to buy 1 new share (assume it is 4) and add one. The answer here is 5.

3. Divide $2 by 5. The answer is 40 cents. Each right is worth 40 cents.

On the day the new stock is issued, the stock is traded with- out privilege to the rights, or what is called ex-rights. The value of each right now is determined by the following formula:

$$\frac{A - B}{C}$$

where
A = market price of the old stock,
B = the subscription price of the new stock guaranteed by the rights,
C = rights required for each new share offered.

1. Take the subscription price of the new stock ($8) and subtract it from the market price of the old stock ($10). The answer, of course, is $2.

2. Take the number of rights required to buy 1 new share (assume it is 4) and divide that number into the difference arrived at in No. 1 above. The answer is 50 cents.

Thus, if you have 1000 rights of XYZ common, those rights are worth $50 to you.

### Table 10.1
### Comparison of stock/warrant values

| Stock Price | − | Exercise Price | × | Shares per Warrant | = | Warrant Value |
|---|---|---|---|---|---|---|
| $25 | − | $25 | × | $2 | = | $ 0 |
| 26 | − | 25 | × | 2 | = | 2 |
| 27 | − | 25 | × | 2 | = | 4 |
| 28 | − | 25 | × | 2 | = | 6 |
| 29 | − | 25 | × | 2 | = | 8 |
| 30 | − | 25 | × | 2 | = | 10 |
| 31 | − | 25 | × | 2 | = | 12 |
| 32 | − | 25 | × | 2 | = | 14 |
| 33 | − | 25 | × | 2 | = | 16 |
| 34 | − | 25 | × | 2 | = | 18 |
| 35 | − | 25 | × | 2 | = | 20 |

## Review Questions

1. Determine the value for each of the following warrants.

| Exercise Price | Warrant | Shares Per Warrant Value | Stock Price |
|---|---|---|---|
| $20 | $18 | 5 | ? |
| 20 | 16 | 5 | ? |
| 20 | 18 | 4 | ? |
| 20 | 18 | 3 | ? |
| 18 | 16 | 5 | ? |
| 16 | 16 | 5 | ? |
| 16 | 15 | 4 | ? |

2. When warrants are exercised, will stockholders' equity increase or decrease in value? _____

3. Do stock rights have exercise prices above or below the current market value of the underlying stock? _____

4. What is the value of each newly issued right having a subscription price of $5 on a stock with a market value of $10 per share? Each right entitles you to the purchase of 2 shares.

_____

5. Can stock rights be sold? _____

# CHAPTER 11

# Common Misconceptions

There are a few misconceptions that often get in the way of a new investor's attempts to turn a profit on stock trades. Those that relate to some of the material covered in previous chapters follow.

*A first misconception is that only stocks on the larger exchanges represent safe investments.* It is true that the larger exchanges, like the New York and American stock exchanges, have stringent requirements for the corporate stocks that they list, but good investment opportunities can be found on any of the regional exchanges, in the OTC market, and on many of the foreign exchanges. Additionally, the fact that a security is listed on, say, the New York Stock Exchange, is by no means an indication that it should be purchased without further research. You and I can wind up investing in losers on any exchange. There is no guarantee that comes with any stock purchase beyond ownership rights. The law of supply and demand governs prices for securities, and these prices will fluctuate considerably for many securities. Stock prices go up, stock prices come down; and there is always too great a chance that our investment timing will be unskilled enough to bring us into a stock high and out of it low. And, buying high and selling low is a loser's game.

*A second misconception is that trading volume alone is an indication of a stock's eventual direction.* Prices can go up or down on either high volume or low volume trading. Market watchers will monitor stock trading activities in an attempt to get some indication of where lies investor interest, thereby creating potential demand. But by no means can anyone assume that, because volume has been increasing in a given stock, the price of the stock is due to head north or, if already heading north, will there reside for any length of time. Remembering the old saying that "what goes up must come down," will help you develop a sensible perspective about stock prices. Being able to predict how much they will go up or down and for how long is what separates the winners from the losers in the stock market game. But heavy volume is only a flag that a particular stock might be worth investigating. The majority of investors rushing into one security can be, and often are, on many, many occasions quite wrong; and one very, very rich man or institution buying a great many shares can also be very, very wrong. There is no single indicator that can be relied upon for stock predictions. Volume shows investor interest; whether or not that interest is well-founded is another matter entirely.

*A third misconception is that a stock selling at its low for the year has only one way to go and that is up.* In the case of a stock at its new low, the only thing that can be certain is that a lot of people have already lost a great deal of money. They may lose much more. The value of stock can always go lower. The corporation issuing the stock can always go out of business, thereby making the stock worthless unless there is something to be gained from the liquidation effort. If the stock is selling at its low for the year, one might take that as a signal to look into the *possibility* of the stock's turnaround, but to accept the *new low* as an automatic signal to buy is absolutely unwarranted.

*A fourth misconception is that a stock closing at its high for the day will continue to climb in price on the next day.* The stock can quite easily open on the very next morning at a lower price. A *high close* is no indication that a stock's price is on a northbound tour. Again, there is no single indicator that anyone can seize upon and use as a crystal ball. And the daily closing prices of stocks represent little more than part of the history of the day's trading activity and some measure of the level of investor interest. If there is an impressive spread between the low and high of the day for a given issue, however, one might want to do some quick but thorough investigation to determine if they should chance buying in, or if already in, start getting out of the stock.

*A fifth misconception is that a stock with a low P/E ratio is a good buy and one with a high P/E ratio is not.* The price-to-earning ratio for a given stock can be used to develop a history of the trading pattern and may on occasion signal a worthwhile security for additional research. But stocks do not trade at the same ratios. For instance, utility stocks may have a lower P/E ratio than industrial stocks. A relatively high P/E ratio for one stock may be a relatively low one for another. There is an easy danger lying at the bottom of P/E arithmetic. Take, for example, the case of make-believe XYZ stock which is selling at 5 times earnings. The stock is listed for $10, and the earnings per share is $2.

---

| | |
|---|---|
| Market Price: | $10 |
| Earnings per Share: | $ 2 |
| P/E Ratio: | 5 |

---

The stock may ordinarily sell at $15 per share and a P/E ratio of 7½. The new and lower P/E ratio may quite simply indicate that the marketplace is wary of XYZ and investors are beginning to lose interest or are unsure of XYZ's future. The change in the P/E ratio may understandably excite investor interest, but a high or a low P/E ratio in itself is not an indication of anything more than the immediate relationship between the price of each share of stock and the earnings for each share of stock.

*A sixth misconception is that preferred stock rarely fluctuates, and so there is little chance for large capital losses.* Anyone believing this need only check the fifty-two week highs and lows for preferred issues on the New York and American stock exchanges. In times of greatly varying interest rates, which have a strong influence on preferred stock prices or poor corporate performance, which might threaten dividend distributions, preferred issues will fluctuate greatly. The dividend rate on each share of preferred is fixed unless it is a participating preferred. If that dividend rate offers a return in excess of what current interest rates are, there will usually be upward pressure on the stock. If interest rates, however, should rise high enough to make it advantageous to investors to sell out of the preferred and reinvest in interest-bearing instruments, the market value of the preferred will drop until the ratio between the dividend payment and the market price of the stock is competitive to interest rates.

A *seventh misconception is that preferred dividends are guaranteed.* The truth of the matter is that a corporation has no legal obligation to pay dividends. It is advantageous to a corporation to issue preferred stock instead of taking on other kinds of debt. If a comapny borrowed a million dollars from banks at 10% interest, it would be legally required to meet its obligations. But in the case of the preferred stock, if things get tough, the corporation can always decide not to declare a dividend. It is only obligated to pay a dividend if it declares a dividend; it, however, is never legally bound to declare a dividend. Corporations, however, realize the necessity of maintaining the integrity of their securities, and generally do not cancel dividend declarations on preferred issues unless it is absolutely essential that they do so.

An *eighth misconception is that a 2-for-1 stock split doubles the stockholder's money.* The stock split only gives the stockholder the potential of doubling his or her money while, at the same time, giving him or her the potential of losing all twice as quickly. If the stockholder owns 100 shares of stock having a par value of $50 per share, after the split he or she has twice as many shares, but each share is worth half what it was before the split.

Before split: 100 shares worth $50 each = $5,000
After split: 200 shares worth $25 each = $5,000

The result is the same: the stockholder still has $5,000 worth of stock. Now, of course, with each $1 increase in the price per share, the stockholder stands to gain $200 instead of $100; but she stands to lose twice as much with each drop in price.

*A ninth misconception is that book value and par value are the same thing.* The par value assigned to a stock is an arbitrary value for bookkeeping purposes. The book value is the basic value of the stock, obtained from the following formula:

$$\frac{\text{Capital Stock} + \text{Retained Earnings}}{\text{Number of Shares}}$$

Decreases or increases in the *book value* of the stock will generally be reflected in the market price. Once *par value* is assigned, however, it is not changed, and it would be a rare occassion, indeed, if the par value indicated the true worth of the stock.

*A tenth misconception is that an option holder actually owns the underlying security.* All the option holder has is a contract which says that he can buy or sell the underlying security at a certain price during a period of time indicated in the contract. Until he decides to exercise that option and actually place an order to buy the underlying security, he *only owns the right to* exercise his option, not any part of the underlying security.

*An eleventh misconception is that there are no brokerage commissions when stocks are sold; only the buyer pays commissions.* When you buy and sell securities through a broker, you must pay a commission when you buy the stock and pay a commission again when you sell the stock. In some unusual circumstances, the commission will be waived; this may occur as an adjustment for an incorrect charge against a previous order, or to compensate for a trading error on the part of the broker.

*A twelfth misconception is that the stock listings in The Wall Street Journal, Barron's, or any other financial newspaper or financial section of a newspaper offer sufficient information on which to make decisions to buy or sell stocks.* Stock tables listing prices, highs and lows, and dividend and earnings information are simply fact sheets which show the daily or annual statistics for listed issues. The information therein may help an investor spot an issue worth investigating, but there is certainly not enough information contained in any stock listing to enable a researcher to make a final decision about buying into or getting out of security.

## Review Questions

True or false.

1. Any stock listed on the New York Stock Exchange is a sure winner. _____

2. A 30% increase in trading volume from one day to the next indicates that a stock is a sure winner. _____

3. Always buy a stock selling at its yearly low. It is sure to go up. _____

4. A stock closing at its high for the day will continue to climb in price on the next day. _____

5. Stocks with low P/E ratios are always better buys than stocks with high P/E ratios. _____

6. Dividends on preferred stocks are guaranteed. _____

7. A stock split doubles the stockholder's money. _____

8. Book value and par value are the same thing. _____

9. There is little risk with stock options. _____

10. Everybody makes money in the stock market. _____

## CHAPTER 12

# Summary

## Exchanges

A stock exchange is a marketplace for securities. Many exchanges, and all those in the United States, are associations formed to facilitate the business activities of their membership. Stock exchanges do not engage in stock trading. They are not primary markets in that they have no involvement in new or additional corporate offerings. In the United States there are nine stock exchanges which are registered under the Securities and Exchange Act. Included among these are the two largest exchanges in the United States, the New York and American stock exchanges. In addition to these U.S. exchanges, there are exchanges located in over sixty other countries around the world. Many stocks are not listed on exchanges, but these may be purchased on the over-the-counter (OTC) market.

## Preferred Stock

As a stock investor, you will be purchasing either common or preferred stock. Many companies offer only common stock with various levels of classification; others offer both preferred and common; some only offer preferred.

Holders of preferred stock have the privilege of first rights to any dividend distributions. And in most cases, when a corporation moves into bankruptcy proceedings, preferred stockholders will, in the majority of situations, have priority during the distribution of assets. Preferred stockholders, however, while taking frontseat to common stockholders, take a backseat to bondholders and creditors; the claims of these last must always be satisfied before the claims of preferred stockholders will be honored. The claims that a preferred stockholder can make on the corporation are almost always limited strictly to the par value of the stock which they own.

There are many kinds of preferred stock: *callable, cumulative, participating, convertible, prior.* Almost all preferred issues are *callable;* this means that the stock is redeemable on or after a specified date and at a stated price. *Cumulative* preferred stock contains provisions which bind the corporation to pay all money owed on them before any dividends may be distributed to the holders of common stock; but, if the corporation does not pay dividends on its common stock and has no plans to do so, the cumulative feature becomes worthless.

*Participating* preferreds entitle holders not only to the stated dividend, but also to any special distributions that may be made to common stockholders. *Convertible* stocks give the holders the option of converting their preferred shares for common stock. *Prior* preferred stock provide that payments be made to no other preferred stockholders unless they are first made to the holders of prior preferred stock. Some preferred stocks provide for a sinking fund to help finalize debt; the sinking fund is simply a way of amortizing debt.

There are many advantages to a corporation in the issuing of preferred stock. In tough times, they need not pay the dividend; unless there is a sinking fund provision to the preferred, the corporation is not obligated to the extent of the par value. Unless there is a participating feature, the corporation need not worry about making special distributions already provided to common shareholders. And, of course, preferred stockholders have no voting privileges.

## Common Stock

Common stock is the capital stock of a corporation and as such gives to its owner equity, or ownership, in the corporation. It also gives the holder certain legal rights among which are the right to receive declared dividends and vote for members of the board of directors. In addition to these special rights, the common shareholder has the satisfaction of knowing that, while he is indeed one of the owners of the corporation, his legal liability is limited to the amount of his holdings.

The amount of authorized stock that may be made available is specified in a corporation's charter. By *authorized stock* is meant the total amount of stock that may be issued by the corporation. *Issued stock* is a percentage of, or all of the authorized stock actually sold to the public or which has been purchased by the corporation. Issued stock should not become confused with outstanding stock; *outstanding stock* is stock that is actually in the hands of the public.

## Book Value

Book value is the difference between assets and liabilities. The book value of each individual share of stock is arrived at by taking the number of outstanding shares and dividing that by the book value.

---

Book Value per Share = Book Value
Divided by Shares Outstanding

---

Book value of a common share is an important factor in stock selection. Analysts expect that stock should eventually sell at its book value.

## Opportunity Cost

One of the important concepts that stock investors must understand is that called *opportunity cost*. It represents the value of that which must be disregarded because some other goods or service is to be produced. To a stock investor, it has this significance: If he invests in a stock which winds up losing for him $1,000, when he could have put his money in the bank for the same period and earned $100, his opportunity cost was

$1,100. He lost $1,000 when he had the opportunity to keep that $1,000 and make an additional $100 besides.

## Return on Investment

Clearly, then, what every investor has to be on the watch for is the best place to put his money. Banks are a relatively sure thing; the stock market never is. Stocks go up; stocks go down; dividends may be cancelled at any time. Because of this uncertainty, the stock investor should have no interest in putting his or her money into securities which offer a total return not much above what is available from totally safe instruments. If you were to invest in a stock that returned only 15% on your original investment after three years, you would understandably have been a lot better off putting your money in a savings account that seemed unattractive because it was only paying 6% compounded quarterly at the time you invested in the stock.

Consider, on the other hand, the possibility that instead of seeing a 15% return on his investment from the stock, the investor realized a 20% loss. That little 6% savings account would seem an even greater opportunity than ever before. No wonder stock investors are often banging their heads against a wall.

It is considerably difficult to determine the expected return on stock investments. This is especially true of common stock investments which are, for the most part, highly volatile. But preferred stocks will also fluctuate considerably at times. Every investor needs to be aware of the unpredictability of stocks and, before he or she even invests that penny, must be convinced that the expected return makes the gamble worthwhile.

## Dividends

Many arguments are put forth about the relevance of dividends. Dividend payments actually reduce the value of a stockholder's holdings so, when those dividends are paid, what is the stockholder getting?

There are two main types of dividend payments, cash and stock.

Cash dividends are by far the most common, and are popular with investors and stockholders alike, who seem generally disinterested in the debate over the relevance of dividends. They like to see their assets converted to cash and returned to them on occasion; they evidently like the liquidity that dividend payments provide, and are not much bothered by the fact that the dividends are taxed as ordinary income.

Stock dividends are also popular with investors and stockholders. Stock dividends consist of authorized, but unissued, shares of stock paid in the place of cash to stockholders. Stock dividends necessitate revision of a corporation's financial structure because the stock dividend has a direct effect on the earnings surplus. A 50% stock dividend will have the following effect on the book value of each share, given that the value of the capital stock is $500,000 and retained earnings are $500,000.

---

Formula: Book Value per Share = Capital Stock + Retained Earnings Divided by Number of Shares

A. Book Value per Share Before Stock Dividend
$500,000 + $500,000 Divided by $100,000 =
$10 per share

B. Book Value per Share After Stock Dividend
$750,000 + $250,000 Divided by $150,000 = $6.67

---

The stockholder receives no immediate gain from the stock dividend, but has a tax advantage because the dividend is not taxable as ordinary income until he sells his holdings. If cash dividends are paid at some future date, the extra shares will mean additional dividend income.

Another type of dividend is a stock split; it does not change the proportionate ownership of the stockholders. The main purpose of the stock split is to increase market interest in the security as the lower price should attract investor interest thereby creating the kind of demand that gives upward momentum to stock prices. Thus, one of the advantages to the stockholder is the potential for extra profits on each increase in the value of the shares, for now the stockholder is holding twice as many shares as before. Losses on a downslide, however, are also greater as the stockholder has twice as many shares losing money as before.

Reverse splits are occasionally declared by corporations. In this case the par value of the stock is doubled but the stockholder winds up with half as many shares. His or her proportionate ownership in the corporation, however, remains unchanged. Reverse splits are rare, as most corporations realize such splits may rightly or wrongly suggest financial difficulty.

Besides cash and stock dividends, there are also scrip and bond dividends, though these forms of distributions to stockholders are rarely used. The scrip dividend is a note payable at some future date or in fixed installments. Bond dividends are a form of scrip dividend, but as bonds have an extended maturity date, the notes are generally unattractive to the stockholder. Besides, what the stockholder becomes is both an owner and lender to the corporation, a rather confusing position to most stockholders. More sophisticated investors see immediately that, in the case of scrip or bond dividends, what the corporation is actually doing is creating new debt simply to have something to pay out to the stockholder.

Dividends may be classified as *regular, extra, extraordinary, cumulative, liquidating,* or *interim.* Regular dividends are in cash and on a fixed schedule. Extra dividends are paid in addition to the regular dividends. Extraordinary dividends result from a corporation's decision to share extra profits with stockholders. Cumulative dividends are those which are in arrears on cumulative preferred stock. Liquidating dividends are non-taxable capital distributions. Interim dividends are partial payments to stockholders based on profits during some fiscal period.

## Ratios

In considering stocks that will bring a high rate of return on the original investment, stock traders generally look at projected earnings per share and the P/E ratio history and projection for the selected stock. When the growth rate of the company has been consistent and market forecasts are favorable, investors and speculators will be interested in the stock. Thus the reliance on the P/E ratio; it helps to gauge the relative position of the stock in terms of what price it may be able to demand in the marketplace. While the P/E ratio is a handy tool, it guarantees nothing. Taken by itself it can never be the basis for any buy or sell decision. But it does give an historic perspective for those trying to evaluate how investors will respond to the earnings record of the corporation.

There are other ratios that investors might observe before deciding upon whether or not to purchase a particular security. These are the *current*, *quick*, *debt-to-equity*, *operating*, and *shareholder's equity* ratios. These ratios may be found by using the following formulas:

> ***Current Ratio*** = current assets divided by current liabilities
>
> ***Quick Ratio*** = current assets (less inventory) divided by current liabilities
>
> ***Debt-to-Equity Ratio*** = owners' liabilities divided by stockholders' equity
>
> ***Operating Ratio*** = total operating expenses divided by net sales
>
> ***Return on Holder's Equity*** = net income divided by stockholder's equity

## Selecting Stocks

Every broker, financial advisor, and financial writer has a list of commandments to which an investor should adhere: Understand the subject of economics so that you can understand how fiscal and monetary policy will effect your investments; Study the fundamentals of business finance—understand the corporation's perspective; Know the basic arithmetic of investment; Never select a stock entirely on your own—get professional advice; Determine your investment goals and select your stocks accordingly; Invest in stocks of strong companies that have been around for awhile; Keep tabs on your stock and the economic forces that can affect it; Do not put all your money in one stock; Do not buy on impulse; Read the financial papers and keep up on the news.

## Margin Accounts

Initial margin requirements are set by the Federal Reserve Board. Equity margin requirements are set by stock exchanges and/or brokers. At most firms, it is 35% on two position accounts and 50% on one-position accounts. Equity margin is computed in the following way: Subtract the debit balance in the margin account from the market value of the security purchased. Divide the result by whatever is the market value of the collateral. If the result is below the equity margin requirement, then the stockholder must deposit additional funds or securities into his account.

If an investor wishes to sell short on any given stock, he absolutely must have a margin account. Margin requirements of the Federal Reserve also apply to short sales. Investors, however, will find that maintenance margin requirements for short-selling are somewhat more stringent than for margin accounts buying long. And, as these can change from time to time, it is well to consult your broker before selling short.

## Stock Options

Stock options are becoming more and more popular with investors. They offer a high return on a relatively small investment; they allow investors to diversify their portfolios even if their investment money is minimal; they limit the amount of money that may be lost from a bad transaction. But options are risky business nonetheless.

There are basically two types of options: *puts* and *calls*. A *put* option is one that gives legal right to the *buyer* to *sell* the underlying security at a fixed price until the expiration date of the put. A *call* option is one that gives legal right to the *buyer* to *purchase* the underlying security at a fixed price until the expiration date of the call.

Buyers of calls are interested in the substantial return they can get from a relatively small investment, and the limited risk which the contract affords. Sellers (writers) of calls are interested in the income the premium affords and the "insurance" the contract gives against declines in the underlying security. The writer of the call, it should be noted, is never obligated to deliver the original shares of the underlying security. He is only obligated to deliver a similar amount of stock in the same corporation and, therefore, always has the option of purchasing new stock to meet his obligation.

There are two types of calls which can be written: covered and uncovered (naked). Covered calls are written against stock you own; naked calls are written against stock you do not own. Regulations governing the writing of uncovered options are strict, as they must be to insure the integrity of the market. There are tremendous risks in writing uncovered calls; this is underscored by broker requirements that the investor have substantial equity in his or her account before he or she can write an uncovered call. Writers of puts must also meet strict margin requirements.

*Buyers of calls* want the price of the underlying stock to increase in value because this increase places greater value on the contracts they had originally planned to buy low and sell high. *Buyers of puts* want the price of the underlying stock to decline because this decline in value places greater value on the contracts they had originally planned to buy low and sell high.

## Warrants

There are two types of warrants: subscription warrants and stock purchase warrants. Subscription warrants are tied to new issues. Their purpose is to give existing stockholders first privilege of subscribing to any new issue of common stock. Stock purchase warrants are equity privileges and generally made available only to holders of certain corporate securities. But stock purchase warrants are often issued separately.

The basic value of a warrant is related to the current value of the stock for which it has been issued. To determine the value of warrant, all that is necessary is some simple arithmetic: Subtract the exercise price of the warrant from the current market price of the common stock for which it has been issued; then multiply the result times the number of shares the warrant entitles you to purchase.

For a corporation, warrants provide a relatively painless way of raising necessary capital in a short amount of time—particularly if the warrants are ever exercised. If the warrants are exercised, stockholders' equity is diluted.

## Stock Rights

Stock rights are also privileges to buy additional shares of stock, but stock rights usually carry an exercise price below the current market value of the underlying security, thus giving them immediate value—unless, of course, the price of the stock drops below the exercise price of the rights by the time the rights are issued.

As stock rights are transferable, the original holders may sell them to others if they so decide. The value of each right before issue is determined by the following formula:

$$\frac{A - B}{1 + C}$$

where A is the market price of the old stock, B is the subscription price of the new stock guaranteed by the rights, and C is the number of rights required for each new share offered. Once the rights are actually distributed to the shareholders the stock is traded *ex-rights*, and the rights themselves have an additional value which may be determined by the following formula:

$$\frac{A - B}{C}$$

where A is the market price of the old stock, B is the subscription price of the new stock guaranteed by the rights, and C is the number of rights required for each new share offered.

## Caveats

Investors often have some preconceived and very unfounded ideas or prejudices related to stock investing. Sometimes it takes a long time to jog their minds back to a more appropriate perspective. Following is a list of "do-not's" that will prevent you from falling into the same trap:

1.  Do not believe that the larger exchanges are the only markets for worthwhile investments.
2.  Do not believe that trading volume alone is an indication of a stock's eventual direction.
3.  Do not believe that a stock selling at its low for the year has only one way to go and that is up.
4.  Do not believe that a stock closing at its high for the day has to continue to climb in price on the next day.
5.  Do not believe that a stock with a low P/E ratio must necessarily be a better buy than a stock with a high P/E ratio.
6.  Do not believe that preferred stocks do not fluctuate in price.
7.  Do not believe that preferred dividends are guaranteed.
8.  Do not believe that a stock split doubles your money.
9.  Do not confuse book value and par value.
10. Do not confuse having an option to buy a security with actually owning the security.
11. Do not believe that brokerage commissions only apply to buy transactions.
12. Do not believe that stock listings present all the data you need to know to make a stock transaction.

## *Review Questions*

1. Determine the annual and quarterly dividends that will be paid on each of the following preferred shares:

| Par Value | Dividend Rate | Annual Dividend | Quarterly Dividend |
|---|---|---|---|
| $100 | 11% | $11.00 | ? |
| 100 | 5% | 5.00 | ? |
| 50 | 11% | 5.50 | ? |
| 50 | 5% | 2.50 | ? |

2. Determine the current yield on the following preferred stocks:

| Market Value | Par Value | Dividend Rate | Current Yield |
|---|---|---|---|
| $ 55.00 | $100.00 | 11% | ? |
| 110.00 | 100.00 | 11% | ? |
| 25.00 | 50.00 | 11% | ? |
| 100.00 | 50.00 | 11% | ? |

3. Determine the P/E ratio for each of the following:

| Market Value | Per Share Earnings | P/E Ratio |
|---|---|---|
| $24.00 | $2.00 | ? |
| 32.50 | 6.50 | ? |
| 48.750 | 7.50 | ? |
| 16.625 | 2.50 | ? |

4. Determine the earnings per share in each of the following:

| Market Value | P/E Ratio | Earnings per Share |
|---|---|---|
| $12.50 | 2 | ? |
| 24.00 | 5 | ? |
| 48.75 | 2.5 | ? |
| 50.00 | 5 | ? |

5. Determine the number of shares that must be issued in each of the following:

| Money Required | Market Value of Stock | Shares to be Issued |
|---|---|---|
| $12,000,000 | $60.00 | ? |
| 3,500,000 | 25.00 | ? |
| 1,000,000 | 10.00 | ? |
| 500,000 | 40.00 | ? |

6. Determine the book value for each of the following:

| Corporate Assets | Corporate Liabilities | Book Value |
|---|---|---|
| $2,200,000 | $2,153,000 | ? |
| 1,961,000 | 960,000 | ? |
| 888,000 | 785,000 | ? |
| 1,000,000 | 2,000,000 | ? |

7. Determine corporate liabilities for each of the following:

| Corporate Assets | Corporate Book Value | Liabilities |
|---|---|---|
| $ 800,000 | $ 45,000 | ? |
| 656,000 | 5,300 | ? |
| 796,000 | 596,000 | ? |
| 1,000,000 | 500,000 | ? |

8. Determine the book value in each of the following:

| Corporate Assets | Corporate Liabilities | Outstanding Shares | Book Value per Share |
|---|---|---|---|
| $1,000,000 | $1,000,000 | $ 100,000 | ? |
| 1,500,000 | 3,000,000 | 500,000 | ? |
| 2,000,000 | 1,000,000 | 500,000 | ? |
| 5,000,000 | 1,000,000 | 1,000,000 | ? |

9. For each of the following, determine the minimum number of shares required in a cumulative voting system to vote in preferred candidates:

| Shares Outstanding | No. of Directors Desired by Minority | No. of Directors to be Elected | Required Voting Shares |
|---|---|---|---|
| 1,000,000 | 1 | 10 | ? |
| 1,000,000 | 2 | 5 | ? |
| 1,000,000 | 3 | 10 | ? |
| 1,000,000 | 5 | 10 | ? |

10. Determine the amount of prinicipal you will have after a three-year period for each of the following. Assume semi-annual compounding.

| Original Principal | Annual Interest | After Three Years |
|---|---|---|
| $1,000 | 10% | ? |
| 1,000 | 5% | ? |

11. Determine the total return on the original investment for each of the following.

| Original Investment | Total Annual Dividends | Quarterly Dividends Received | Capital Gains or Losses | Total Return |
|---|---|---|---|---|
| $10,000 | $500 | 7 | $ +300 | ? |
| 10,000 | 600 | 6 | −250 | ? |
| 10,000 | 300 | 8 | +500 | ? |
| 10,000 | 500 | 5 | +1,000 | ? |

12. Determine the value of capital stock and the amount of surplus after the stock dividends indicated below.

| BEFORE DIVIDEND: | | | AFTER DIVIDEND: | |
|---|---|---|---|---|
| Capital Stock | Surplus | Stock Dividend | Capital Stock | Surplus |
| $500,000 | $500,000 | 50% | ? | ? |
| 500,000 | 500,000 | 25% | ? | ? |
| 500,000 | 500,000 | 10% | ? | ? |
| 600,000 | 400,000 | 20% | ? | ? |

13. Determine the book value after the indicated stock dividends:

| Book Value Before Split | Capital Stock | Retained Earnings | Shares Before Split | Stock Dividend | Book Value After Split |
|---|---|---|---|---|---|
| $10 | $500,000 | $500,000 | 100,000 | 50% | ? |
| 10 | 500,000 | 500,000 | 100,000 | 20% | ? |
| 5 | 750,000 | 250,000 | 200,000 | 10% | ? |
| 20 | 750,000 | 250,000 | 50,000 | 10% | ? |

14. Determine the number of shares you will own and their total value after each of the following splits.

| Shares Owned Before Split | Total Value | Stock Split | New Shares Owned | Total $$ Value of New Shares Owned |
|---|---|---|---|---|
| 1,000 | $ 1,000 | 2 for 1 | 2,000 | ? |
| 2,000 | 24,000 | 4 for 1 | 8,000 | ? |
| 1,000 | 8,000 | 1 for 2 | 500 | ? |
| 2,000 | 24,000 | 4 for 1 | 500 | ? |

15. Determine the capital gains or losses on the following:

| Shares Bought | Total Cost for Shares | Buy Commissions | Shares Sold | Amount Received | Sell Commissions | Profit or Loss |
|---|---|---|---|---|---|---|
| 100 | $ 2,000 | $ 60 | 100 | $ 3,000 | $ 90 | ? |
| 100 | 3,000 | 90 | 50 | 2,000 | 60 | ? |
| 200 | 10,000 | 140 | 200 | 10,000 | 140 | ? |
| 500 | 15,000 | 175 | 200 | 10,000 | 220 | ? |

16. Determine the current ratio given the following:

| Current Assets | Current Liabilities | Current Ratio |
|---|---|---|
| $1,000,000 | $ 500,000 | ? |
| 500,000 | 1,000,000 | ? |
| 750,000 | 250,000 | ? |
| 300,000 | 200,000 | ? |

17. Determine the quick ratio given the following:

| Current Assets | Inventory | Current Liabilities | Quick Ratio |
|---|---|---|---|
| $1,200,000 | $200,000 | $ 500,000 | ? |
| 550,000 | 50,000 | 1,000,000 | ? |
| 998,000 | 248,000 | 250,000 | ? |
| 200,000 | 100,000 | 100,000 | ? |

18. Determine the debt-to-equity ratio given the following:

| Owner's Liabilities | Total Assets | Equity Ratio |
|---|---|---|
| $2,000,000 | $1,000,000 | ? |
| 5,000,000 | 3,000,000 | ? |
| 1,000,000 | 2,000,000 | ? |
| 1,000,000 | 1,000,000 | ? |

19. Determine the percent of return on stockholder's equity:

| Net Income | Shareholder's Equity | Return on Stockholder's Equity |
|---|---|---|
| 100,000 | $1,000,000 | ? |
| 300,000 | 1,000,000 | ? |
| 1,000 | 100,000 | ? |
| − 10,000 | 100,000 | ? |

20. Determine the amount of cash (or equivalent) that you must deposit in your account in order to purchase stock under the following initial margin requirements:

| Cost of Stock | Margin Requirement | Deposit Required |
|---|---|---|
| $10,000 | 50% | ? |
| 5,000 | 55% | ? |
| 7,500 | 60% | ? |
| 7,500 | 65% | ? |

21. Determine if the following calls are in-the-money or out-of-the-money:

| Stock | Current Quote | Exercise Price | In or Out |
|---|---|---|---|
| Apache | $13⅝ | $12 | ? |
| Apache | 13⅝ | 10½ | ? |
| Bristol Meyers | 43⅝ | 39 | ? |
| Bristol Meyers | 43⅝ | 45 | ? |

22. Determine if the following puts are in- or out-of-the-money:

| Stock | Current Quote | Exercise Price | In or Out |
|---|---|---|---|
| Apache | 13⅝ | 12 | ? |
| Apache | 13⅝ | 10½ | ? |
| Bristol Meyers | 43⅝ | 39 | ? |
| Bristol Meyers | 43⅝ | 45 | ? |

23. You own 100 shares of XYZ stock currently at $25 per share. You write an at-the-money call. The premium you receive is $2.50 per share. The stock increases to $29 per share. Is it to the advantage or disadvantage of the buyer to exercise his option? _____

24. You own 100 shares of XYZ stock currently at $37 per 1/2 share. You write a call with an exercise price of $42 per share. The premium is $7 per share. The stock advances to $43. Is it to the advantage or disadvantage of the buyer to exercise his option? _____

25. You own 100 shares of XYZ stock currently at $25 per share. You write a put with an exercise price of $30. The premium is $5 per share. The stock increases to $29 per share. Is it to the advantage or disadvantage of the buyer to exercise his option? _____

26. You own 100 shares of XYZ stock currently at $37 per 1/2 share. You write a put with an exercise price of $32 per share. The premium is $6 per share. The stock drops to $30 per share. Is it to the advantage or disadvantage of the buyer to exercise his option? _____

27. Determine the value of each individual right in the following offerings:

| Market Price of Old Shares | Guaranteed Subscription Price | No. of Rights Required for Each New Share | Value of Each Right |
|---|---|---|---|
| $10 | $ 7 | 2 | ? |
| 16 | 12 | 7 | ? |
| 20 | 18 | 19 | ? |
| 20 | 16 | 19 | ? |

28. Determine the value of the following stock rights; assume the new stock has been issued.

| Market Price of Old Shares | Guaranteed Subscription Price | No. of Rights Required for Each New Share | Value of Each Right |
|---|---|---|---|
| $10 | $ 7 | $ 2 | ? |
| 10 | 12 | 7 | ? |
| 20 | 18 | 20 | ? |
| 20 | 16 | 10 | ? |

29. Determine the value of the following warrants:

| Stock Price | Exercise Price | Shares per Warrant | Warrant Values |
|---|---|---|---|
| $28 | $25 | 2 | ? |
| 30 | 25 | 2 | ? |
| 32 | 25 | 2 | ? |
| 34 | 25 | 2 | ? |

30. You purchase 100 shares of RCA at $30 per share, 200 shares of AM International at $5 per share, and 300 shares of Warner Communications at $20 per share. Six months later, you sell the shares of RCA for $27⅜, one-half the shares in AM for $4, and one-third the shares in Warner for $3,000. What is your total profit or loss before all commissions? _____

## APPENDIX    A

# Answers to All Review Questions

## Chapter 1
### A

1. The stock market is the market for corporate stocks created by national and local exchanges around the world. <u>True</u>

2. Since the 1700s, small, informal exchanges have existed in the United States. <u>True</u>

3. In the early days, stock exchanges not only dealt in corporate stocks but also in the slave trade. <u>True</u>

4. The first organized exchange in the United States was established in Philadelphia in the year 1790. <u>True</u>

5. The New York Stock Exchange was originally called the New York Curb Exchange. <u>False</u>

6. There is now only one exchange in the United States: The New York Stock Exchange. <u>False</u>

7. Floor brokers conduct transactions for other members of the same exchange in return for a commission. <u>True</u>

8. Registered brokers are members of an exchange who buy and sell securities for their account. <u>True</u>

9. Odd-lot dealers are those exchange members who buy from, or sell to, customers of commission brokers dealing in fewer than 100 shares. True

10. Block positioners usually handle trades of thousands of shares of stock. True

**B.**

11. A stock exchange is a marketplace for securities already in the hands of the public.

12. The largest regional stock exchange in the United States is the Pacific Stock Exchange.

13. The OTC Market is an electronic marketplace for those securities not sold on any of the exchanges.

14. Through the creation of the National Association of Securities Dealers, the OTC Market has developed into a well-organized electronic auction center representing millions of dollars in trades every day.

15. Another name for la bourse de Montreal is the Montreal Stock Exchange.

16. The Paris Stock Exchange is a legal monopoly in France created for the trading of securities.

17. A limit order means the buyer has specified the highest price he or she is willing to pay.

18. Is it true that there are more than one hundred stock exchanges worldwide? True

19. Are some stocks listed on more than one stock exchange? Yes

20. Are dual listings allowed on the Paris Bourse? <u>No</u>

## Chapter 2

1. The largest exchange in the United States is the New York Stock Exchange. <u>True</u>

2. Yield is the annual (unless otherwise specified) rate of return. <u>True</u>

3. PE ratio refers to the number of times by which the company's latest twelve-month earnings must be multiplied to obtain the current stock price. <u>True</u>

4. Convert the following fractions to parts of a dollar:

    a. ⅛  <u>12-½ cents</u>
    b. ¼  <u>25 cents</u>
    c. ⅜  <u>37-½ cents</u>
    d. ⅝  <u>62-½ cents</u>
    e. 1-¼ <u>$1.25</u>

5. You buy 200 shares of XYZ Corp. at $20-½. The company pays an annual dividend of $.50 per share. How much in dividends will you receive each year from XYZ? <u>$100.00</u>

## Chapter 3

1. In stock listings, "pf" identifies <u>preferred</u> stocks.

2. What is the yield on a stock selling for $40 and paying a $1.50 per year dividend? <u>3.75%</u>

3. What is the P/E ratio on a stock earning $2 per share and selling for $50? <u>25</u>

4. Do preferred stocks carry first rights over common stock in regard to dividend payments? <u>Yes</u>

5. If you own 100 shares of 10% preferred stock with a par value of $50, what would be your annual dividends? <u>$500</u>

6. Are dividends on preferred stocks guaranteed? <u>No</u>

7. <u>Callable</u> preferred stock is that which is redeemable on or after a specified date and at a specified price.

8. <u>Cumulative</u> preferred stock contains provisions which bind the corporation to pay all money due these preferred holders before dividends may be paid on common stock.

9. <u>Convertible</u> preferred stock may be exchanged for common stock.

10. <u>Prior</u> preferred stockholders receive preferential treatment over other preferred holders, much the same as preferred stockholders have preferential treatment over common stock holders.

11. Unless a preferred stock has a <u>sinking fund</u> provision, no eventual payment to the amount of the par value is required from the issuing corporation.

12. Unless a preferred stock is a <u>participating</u> preferred, the shareholders cannot expect any income beyond the fixed dividend of the security.

13. <u>Common</u> stock is the capital stock of the corporation and gives the owners of the common equity, or ownership, in the corporation.

14. <u>Authorized</u> stock is the amount of stock that a corporation may actually issue.

15. <u>Issued</u> stock is the authorized stock actually sold to the public or which has been purchased back by the corporation.

16. Outstanding stock is that which is actually in the hands of the public.

17. Book value is arrived at by finding the difference between assets and liabilities.

18. Analysts generally expect that a stock should be selling at least at its book value.

19. A proxy statement is a written power-of-attorney that a stockholder turns over to another to vote his corporate stock.

20. If a 6% preferred with a par value of $100 is selling at $80, what is the current yield? 7½

21. If a 6% preferred with a par value of $100 is selling at $150, what is the current yield? 4%

22. If a company needs to raise $1 million but can only expect to get $50 per share when they bring the stock to market, how many shares will they have to issue? 20,000 shares

23. Does a new stock issue dilute or increase the value of your current holdings? Dilute

24. If there are 200,000 shares outstanding and the book value of the corporation is $1 million, what is the book value of each share of stock? $5

25. Will book value and liquidiating value always be the same? Theoretically, they should be; but in actuality they never are.

## Chapter 4
1. If you buy 100 shares of stock for $10.00 per share and sell it six months later for $10-¼ per share, what is your profit before commissions? $25.00

2. If you buy 100 shares of stock for $10 per share and sell it five months later for $10-1/2 per share, how much is your profit (or loss) if your buy-and-sell commissions total $65.00? $15.00 loss

3. About where would your break-even point be if you purchased 200 shares of stock at $9.00 per share and the buy commissions were $53.00? $9⁵/₈ per share (Remember, you must consider sell-side commissions.)

4. Will savings in brokerage commissions really enhance your profits if you trade frequently? Most definitely

5. Must you pay a brokerage commission even if you take a loss on a stock transaction? Most definitely

6. Determine the rate of return for each transaction below, each of which represents a common stock purchase.

| Cost of Shares | Annual Dividends | Rate of Return |
|---|---|---|
| $950.00 | $ 45.00 | .047 |
| $2,500 | $125.00 | .050 |
| $6,000 | $295.00 | .049 |

7. Determine the rate of return for each of the transactions below, each of which represents a preferred stock purchase of 100 shares.

| Cost of Shares | Par Value | Div. Rate | Rate/Return |
|---|---|---|---|
| $9,100 | $100.00 | 4½% | .049 |
| $5,000 | $ 50.00 | 5% | .050 |
| $6,200 | $ 50.00 | 6% | .048 |

8. You buy 100 shares of AT&T at $55.00 per share, and 200 shares of PSE&G at $18.00 per share. Each stock declines by 10%. You decide you need the money elsewhere and sell all your holdings? What is your profit or loss? $910.00 loss

9. You buy 200 shares of AM International at $15-⅛. You sell those shares six months later at $15-¾. Buy commissions are $30.00 and sell commissions $32.50. What is your total profit or loss? <u>$62.50 profit</u>

10. You purchase 100 shares of Litton Industries at $75.00, 200 shares of Mobil Oil at $30-⅝, and 300 shares of IT&T at $30-⅞. What is your total cost before commissions? <u>$22,887.50</u>

11. You sell 100 shares of Litton purchased in Question No. 3 above at $86-¼ per share. What is your profit if buy and sell commissions total $165.00? <u>$960.00 profit</u>

12. You sell 200 shares of Mobil purchased in Question No. 10 above at $31-¼ per share. What is your profit or loss if buy-and-sell commissions total $150.00? <u>$25.00</u>

13. Refer to Table 4.2. What is your total profit before commissions if you sold your holdings after the June '86 purchase? <u>$6,386</u>

14. Refer to Table 4.2. Would you have a profit if you sold all your holdings after the August '86 purchase? Before commissions? After commissions? <u>Loss before commissions; loss after commissions</u>

15. Refer to Table 4.2. Would you have a profit if you sold your holdings after the October '86 purchase? <u>No</u>

16. What is the advantage of dollar-cost averaging? <u>Safety</u>

17. True or false? If you play the game of dollar-cost averaging, you need to pick a stock that will be bullish on the long-term—and you've got to stick to your game plan. <u>True</u>

## Chapter 5

1. Opportunity Cost represents the value of that which must be disregarded because some other good or service is to be produced.

2. You invest $5,000 in 100 shares of American Telephone, paying $3 per share in dividends per year. For the same annual period, you could have put your money in certificates that would have paid you 10% in interest. What was your opportunity cost? $200

3. ROI is the abbreviation for return on investment.

4. Determine the ROI in each of the following:

| Cost of Stock | Buy/Sell Commissions | Capital Gain | ROI |
|---|---|---|---|
| $9,600 | $400 | $1,200 | 12% |
| 920 | 80 | 900 | 90% |
| 14,700 | 300 | 500 | 33⅓% |
| 3,850 | 150 | 100 | 2½% |
| 2,380 | 120 | 750 | 30% |

5. Assuming semi-annual compounding, what would be the amount of your principal after a one-year period for each of the following situations:

| Original Principal | Interest | Balance |
|---|---|---|
| $1,000 | 8% | $1,081.60 |
| 1,000 | 9% | 1,092.03 |
| 1,000 | 10% | 1,102.50 |
| 2,500 | 8% | 2,704.00 |
| 2,500 | 9% | 2,730.06 |
| 2,500 | 10% | 2,756.25 |

6. True or false? It is easy to pinpoint the amount of return and the time of that return for stock investments. False

7. True or false? It is worth any amount of money to purchase a stock that can triple in ten years. False, as you must evaluate the risk

8. True or false? Risk-taking should always be kept to a minimum. True

9. You buy 100 shares of XYZ stock at $1,000. The yield at the time is 8%. You receive seven quarterly dividend payments before you sell the stock for a $200 loss. How much did you gain or lose from holding the stock for that period? $60 loss

10. You buy 100 shares of XYZ stock selling at $25.00. Quarterly dividends are 50 cents per share and you receive eight dividends before you sell the stock for a $220 gain. Commissions on the buy and sell transactions were $60 and $65 respectively. Would you have been smarter to have purchased a certificate paying 9% interest compounded semi-annually? Yes; the certificate would have yielded $481.30 for the period; the stock yielded $400 in dividends, and only $95 in capital gains after commissions.

## Chapter 6
1. A margin account is one which allows the investor to borrow money from his broker to help finance the purchase of securities.

2. Initial margin requirements are set by the Federal Reserve.

3. Assume that the equity margin requirement is 35%. You have just purchased two or more securities having a total value of $10,000. Declines in the price of the securities results in paper losses to you of $3,000. Will you be required by your broker to deposit additional funds in your account? Yes

4. True or false? Short selling is a sure way to profit because stocks always eventually go down. False

5. True or false? A margin account is required before an investor may sell short on a stock. True

## Chapter 7
1. Dividends are payments that a corporation makes to its stock- holders.

2. A stock dividend consists of authorized but unissued shares of stock that are paid to stockholders in lieu of cash.

3. Determine the book value for each share of stock before and after the indicated stock dividends:

| Capital Stock | Retained Earnings | Book Value | Stock Dividend | New Book Value After Stock Dividend |
|---|---|---|---|---|
| $500,000 | $500,000 | $10 | 50% | $6.67 |
| 100,000 | 50,000 | 6 | 20% | 5.00 |
| 100,000 | 100,000 | 10 | 10% | 9.09 |

4. If you are holding 1,000 shares of XYZ before a 3 for 1 split, how many shares will you own after the split? 3000

5. If you have $5,000 worth of stock in XYZ Corporation, how much money will you have in XYZ stock after a 3 for 1 split? The same amount of money

6. If you own 1,000 shares of stock in XYZ before a 1 for 2 reverse split, how much stock will you own after the split? 500 shares

7. If you have $5,000 in XYZ stock, what will be the dollar value of your holdings after a 1 for 2 reverse split? The same amount of money.

8. Regular dividends are the cash payments that are paid on shares of stock at the discretion of the board of directors.

9. Extra dividends are those declared in addition to what may be termed the regular dividends.

10. Extraordinary dividends are those paid as a result of annual profits.

11. Cumulative dividends are those which are in arrears on preferred stocks.

12. Liquidating dividends are actually capital distributions and, as such, are not taxable.

13. Interim dividends are partial payments to stockholders from corporate profits.

14. Scrip dividends come in the form of notes which may be payable at any future time or which may be payable in specific installments at fixed intervals of time.

15. True or false? All stockholders are entitled to receive dividend payments. False

## Chapter 8

1. If you purchased 100 shares of Con Edison stock at $26⅝ per share, and later sold them for $27⅜ per share, what would be your profit before commission? $75

2. If you purchased 500 shares of International Aluminum at $15, and later sold them for $12¾, what would be your total loss? $1,125

3. If you sold short 100 shares of Apache Corporation at $10⅜ per share, and later "purchased" the shares for $8⅞ each, what would be your profit or loss? $150 profit

4. True or false? If you hold a stock long enough, you will always realize a profit. False

5. If a stock selling at $80 has a P/E ratio of $10, what are its earnings per share? $8

6. True or false? The P/E ratio is all you need to know to decide whether or not to purchase a stock. False

7. Current assets dividend by current liabilities = current ratio.

8. Current assets (less inventory) divided by current liabilities = the quick ratio.

9. Owner's liabilities divided by stockholders' equity = the debt-to-equity ratio

10. Total operating expenses divided by net sales = the operating ratio.

11. Net income divided by shareholder's equity = ROI.

12. True or false? The price of your stock will always go in the direction of the market in general. False

13. True or false? The most frequently quoted stock index is the Dow Jones Industrial Average. True

14. True or false? The closing price of a stock, when compared to its opening price for the same day, is a dependable indicator of which way the stock will move at the beginning of the next day's trading. False

15. True or false? Never put all your investment money in one security. True

## Chapter 9
1. A call is an option which gives legal right to the buyer to purchase the underlying security at a fixed price until the expiration date of the call.

2. A <u>put</u> is an option which gives legal right to the buyer to sell the underlying security at a fixed price until expiration date of the contract.

3. A <u>premium</u> is the money paid by the buyer of an option to the seller (writer) of the option.

4. The stock on which an option contract is based is called the <u>underlying security.</u>

5. The <u>expiration date</u> is the last date on which the buyer still has the right to exercise his option.

6. The <u>striking price</u>, also known as the exercise price, is the price at which the option buyer exercises his rights.

7. <u>Buyers</u> of call options hope to resell their contracts at a higher price.

8. Define an in-the-money-call. <u>A call having an exercise price below the current quote for the underlying security</u>

9. Define an in-the-money put. <u>A put having an exercise price above the current quote for the underlying stock</u>

10. Define an out-of-the-money call. <u>A call having an exercise price above the current quote for the underlying stock</u>

11. Define an out-of-the-money put. <u>A put having an exercise price below the current quote of the underlying stock</u>

12. True or false? Stock option trading is a sure way to make money. <u>False</u>

## Chapter 10
1. Determine the value for each of the following warrants.

| Exercise Price | Warrant | Shares Per Warrant Value | Stock Price |
|---|---|---|---|
| $20 | $18 | 5 | 10 |
| 20 | 16 | 5 | 20 |
| 20 | 18 | 4 | 8 |
| 20 | 18 | 3 | 6 |
| 18 | 16 | 5 | 10 |
| 16 | 16 | 5 | 0 |
| 16 | 15 | 4 | 4 |

2. When warrants are exercised will stockholders' equity increase or decrease in value? <u>Decrease</u>

3. Do stock rights have exercise prices above or below the current market value of the underlying stock? <u>Below</u>

4. What is the value of each newly issued right having a subscription price of $5 on a stock with a market value of $10 per share? Each right entitles you to the purchase of 2 shares. <u>$2.50</u>

5. Can stock rights be sold? <u>Yes</u>

## Chapter 11
1. Any stock listed on the New York Stock Exchange is a sure winner. <u>False</u>

2. A 30% increase in trading volume from one day to the next indicates that a stock is a sure winner. <u>False</u>

3. Always buy a stock selling at its yearly low. It is sure to go up. <u>False</u>

4. A stock closing at its high for the day will continue to climb in price on the next day. <u>False</u>

5. Stocks with low P/E ratios are always better buys than stocks with high P/E ratios. <u>False</u>

6. Dividends on preferred stocks are guaranteed. <u>False</u>

7. A stock split doubles the stockholder's money. <u>False</u>

8. Book value and par value are the same thing. <u>False</u>

9. There is little risk with stock options. <u>False</u>

10. Everybody makes money in the stock market. <u>False</u>

## Chapter 12

1. Determine the annual and quarterly dividends that will be paid on each of the following preferred shares:

| Par Value | Dividend Rate | Annual Dividend | Quarterly Dividend |
|---|---|---|---|
| $100 | 11% | $11.00 | $2.75 |
| 100 | 5% | 5.00 | 1.25 |
| 50 | 11% | 5.50 | 1.37½ |
| 50 | 5% | 2.50 | .62½ |

2. Determine the current yield on the following preferred stocks:

| Market Value | Par Value | Dividend Rate | Current Yield |
|---|---|---|---|
| $ 55.00 | $100.00 | 11% | 20% |
| 110.00 | 100.00 | 11% | 10% |
| 25.00 | 50.00 | 11% | 22% |
| 100.00 | 50.00 | 11% | 5½% |

3. Determine the P/E ratio for each of the following:

| Market Value | Per Share Earnings | P/E Ratio |
|---|---|---|
| $24.00 | $2.00 | 12 |
| 32.50 | 6.50 | 5 |
| 48.750 | 7.50 | 6.5 |
| 16.625 | 2.50 | 6.65 |

4. Determine the earnings per share in each of the following:

| Market Value | P/E Ratio | Earnings per Share |
|---|---|---|
| $12.50 | 2 | $ 6.25 |
| 24.00 | 5 | 4.80 |
| 48.75 | 2.5 | 19.50 |
| 50.00 | 5 | 10.00 |

5. Determine the number of shares that must be issued in each of the following:

| Money Required | Market Value of Stock | Shares to be Issued |
|---|---|---|
| $12,000,000 | $60.00 | 200,000 |
| 3,500,000 | 25.00 | 140,000 |
| 1,000,000 | 10.00 | 100,000 |
| 500,000 | 40.00 | 12,500 |

6. Determine the book value for each of the following:

| Corporate Assets | Corporate Liabilities | Book Value |
|---|---|---|
| $2,200,000 | $2,153,000 | $ 47,000 |
| 1,961,000 | 960,000 | 1,001,000 |
| 888,000 | 785,000 | 103,000 |
| 1,000,000 | 2,000,000 | −1,000,000 |

7. Determine corporate liabilities for each of the following:

| Corporate Assets | Corporate Book Value | Liabilities |
|---|---|---|
| $ 800,000 | $ 45,000 | $ 755,000 |
| 656,000 | 5,300 | 650,700 |
| 796,000 | 596,000 | 189,400 |
| 1,000,000 | 500,000 | 500,000 |

8. Determine the book value in each of the following:

| Corporate Assets | Corporate Liabilities | Outstanding Shares | Book Value per Share |
|---|---|---|---|
| $1,000,000 | $1,000,000 | $ 100,000 | $ 0 |
| 1,500,000 | 3,000,000 | 500,000 | −3 |
| 2,000,000 | 1,000,000 | 500,000 | 2 |
| 5,000,000 | 1,000,000 | 1,000,000 | 4 |

9. For each of the following, determine the minimum number of shares required in a cumulative voting system to vote in preferred candidates:

| Shares Outstanding | No. of Directors Desired by Minority | No. of Directors to be Elected | Required Voting Shares |
|---|---|---|---|
| 1,000,000 | 1 | 10 | 100,001 |
| 1,000,000 | 2 | 5 | 400,001 |
| 1,000,000 | 3 | 10 | 300,001 |
| 1,000,000 | 5 | 10 | 500,001 |

10. Determine the amount of prinicipal you will have after a three-year period for each of the following. Assume semi-annual compounding.

| Original Principal | Annual Interest | After Three Years |
|---|---|---|
| $1,000 | 10% | $1,340.10 |
| 1,000 | 5% | 1,131.42 |

11. Determine the total return on the original investment for each of the following.

| Original Investment | Total Annual Dividends | Quarterly Dividends Received | Capital Gains or Losses | Total Return |
|---|---|---|---|---|
| $10,000 | $500 | 7 | $ +300 | 11¾% |
| 10,000 | 600 | 6 | −250 | 6½% |
| 10,000 | 300 | 8 | +500 | 11% |
| 10,000 | 500 | 5 | +1,000 | 16¼% |

12. Determine the value of capital stock and the amount of surplus after the stock dividends indicated below.

| BEFORE DIVIDEND: | | | AFTER DIVIDEND: | |
|---|---|---|---|---|
| Capital Stock | Surplus | Stock Dividend | Capital Stock | Surplus |
| $500,000 | $500,000 | 50% | $750,000 | $250,000 |
| 500,000 | 500,000 | 25% | 625,000 | 375,000 |
| 500,000 | 500,000 | 10% | 550,000 | 450,000 |
| 600,000 | 400,000 | 20% | 720,000 | 280,000 |

13. Determine the book value after the indicated stock dividends:

| Book Value Before Split | Capital Stock | Retained Earnings | Shares Before Split | Stock Dividend | Book Value After Split |
|---|---|---|---|---|---|
| $10 | $500,000 | $500,000 | 100,000 | 50% | $ 6.67 |
| 10 | 500,000 | 500,000 | 100,000 | 20% | 8.33 |
| 5 | 750,000 | 250,000 | 200,000 | 10% | 4.54 |
| 20 | 750,000 | 250,000 | 50,000 | 10% | 18.18 |

14. Determine the number of shares you will own and their total value after each of the following splits.

| Shares Owned Before Split | Total Value | Stock Split | New Shares Owned | Total $$ Value of New Shares Owned |
|---|---|---|---|---|
| 1,000 | $ 1,000 | 2 for 1 | 2,000 | $ 1,000 |
| 2,000 | 24,000 | 4 for 1 | 8,000 | 24,000 |
| 1,000 | 8,000 | 1 for 2 | 500 | 8,000 |
| 2,000 | 24,000 | 4 for 1 | 8,000 | 24,000 |

15. Determine the capital gains or losses on the following:

| Shares Bought | Total Cost for Shares | Buy Com- missions | Shares Sold | Amount Received | Sell Com- missions | Profit or Loss |
|---|---|---|---|---|---|---|
| 100 | $ 2,000 | $ 60 | 100 | $ 3,000 | $ 90 | $ +850 |
| 100 | 3,000 | 90 | 50 | 2,000 | 60 | +350 |
| 200 | 10,000 | 140 | 200 | 10,000 | 140 | −280 |
| 500 | 15,000 | 175 | 200 | 10,000 | 220 | +3,605 |

16. Determine the current ratio given the following:

| Current Assets | Current Liabilities | Current Ratio |
|---|---|---|
| $1,000,000 | $  500,000 | 2 to 1 |
| 500,000 | 1,000,000 | 1 to 2 |
| 750,000 | 250,000 | 3 to 1 |
| 300,000 | 200,000 | 3 to 2 |

17. Determine the quick ratio given the following:

| Current Assets | Inventory | Current Liabilities | Quick Ratio |
|---|---|---|---|
| $1,200,000 | $200,000 | $  500,000 | 2 to 1 |
| 550,000 | 50,000 | 1,000,000 | 1 to 2 |
| 998,000 | 248,000 | 250,000 | 3 to 1 |
| 200,000 | 100,000 | 100,000 | 1 to 1 |

18. Determine the debt-to-equity ratio given the following:

| Owner's Liabilities | Total Assets | Equity Ratio |
|---|---|---|
| $2,000,000 | $1,000,000 | 2 to 1 |
| 5,000,000 | 3,000,000 | 5 to 3 |
| 1,000,000 | 2,000,000 | 1 to 2 |
| 1,000,000 | 1,000,000 | 1 to 1 |

19. Determine the percent of return on stockholder's equity:

| Net Income | Shareholder's Equity | Return on Stockholder's Equity |
|---|---|---|
| 100,000 | $1,000,000 | 10% |
| 300,000 | 1,000,000 | 30% |
| 1,000 | 100,000 | 1% |
| − 10,000 | 100,000 | −10% |

20. Determine the amount of cash (or equivalent) that you must deposit in your account in order to purchase stock under the following initial margin requirements:

| Cost of Stock | Margin Requirement | Deposit Required |
|---|---|---|
| $10,000 | 50% | $5,000 |
| 5,000 | 55% | 2,750 |
| 7,500 | 60% | 4,500 |
| 7,500 | 65% | 4,875 |

21. Determine if the following calls are in-the-money or out-of-the-money:

| Stock | Current Quote | Exercise Price | In or Out |
|---|---|---|---|
| Apache | $13⅝ | $12 | In |
| Apache | 13⅝ | 10½ | In |
| Bristol Meyers | 43⅝ | 39 | In |
| Bristol Meyers | 43⅝ | 45 | Out |

22. Determine if the following puts are in- or out-of-the-money:

| Stock | Current Quote | Exercise Price | In or Out |
|---|---|---|---|
| Apache | 13⅝ | 12 | Out |
| Apache | 13⅝ | 10½ | Out |
| Bristol Meyers | 43⅝ | 39 | Out |
| Bristol Meyers | 43⅝ | 45 | In |

23. You own 100 shares of XYZ stock currently at $25 per share. You write an at-the-money call. The premium you receive is $2.50 per share. The stock increases to $29 per share. Is it to the advantage or disadvantage of the buyer to exercise his option? <u>Advantage</u>

24. You own 100 shares of XYZ stock currently at $37½ per share. You write a call with an exercise price of $42 per share. The premium is $7 per share. The stock advances to $43. Is it to the advantage or disadvantage of the buyer to exercise his option? <u>Disadvantage after commissions are taken into account.</u>

25. You own 100 shares of XYZ stock currently at $25 per share. You write a put with an exercise price of $29. The premium is $5 per share. The stock increases to $29 per share. Is it to the advantage or disadvantage of the buyer to exercise his option? <u>Disadvantage</u>

26. You own 100 shares of XYZ stock currently at $37½ per share. You write a put with an exercise price of $32 per share. The premium is $6 per share. The stock drops to $25 per share. Is it to the advantage or disadvantage of the buyer to exercise his option? <u>Advantage</u>

27. Determine the value of each individual right in the following offerings:

| Market Price of Old Shares | Guaranteed Subscription Price | No. of Rights Required for Each New Share | Value of Each Right |
|---|---|---|---|
| $10 | $ 7 | 2 | $1.00 |
| 16 | 12 | 7 | .50 |
| 20 | 18 | 19 | .10 |
| 20 | 16 | 19 | .20 |

28. Determine the value of the following stock rights; assume the new stock has been issued.

| Market Price of Old Shares | Guaranteed Subscription Price | No. of Rights Required for Each New Share | Value of Each Right |
|---|---|---|---|
| $10 | $ 7 | $ 2 | $1.50 |
| 10 | 12 | 7 | 0 |
| 20 | 18 | 20 | .10 |
| 20 | 16 | 10 | .40 |

29. Determine the value of the following warrants:

| Stock Price | Exercise Price | Shares per Warrant | Warrant Values |
|---|---|---|---|
| $28 | $25 | 2 | $ 6 |
| 30 | 25 | 2 | 10 |
| 32 | 25 | 2 | 14 |
| 34 | 25 | 2 | 18 |

30. You purchase 100 shares of RCA at $30 per share, 200 shares of AM International at $5 per share, and 300 shares of Warner Communications at $20 per share. Six months later, you sell the shares of RCA for $27⅜, one-half the shares in AM for $4, and one-third the shares in Warner for $3,000. What is your total profit or loss before all commissions? $737.50

# Dictionary

***abatement.*** A reduction in the amount that would ordinarily be charged for services; a discount. With the advent of negotiated rates, it is possible for an account to bargain for reduced commissions from the firm with which he or she ordinarily does business. It is highly unlikely, however, that if this account represents only an occasional trade, the broker will be receptive to suggestions of reducing his charges on buy or sell trades. For tips on choosing a broker and on paying commissions, see pages 359–363 in United Business Service's *Successful Investing: A Complete Guide to Your Financial Future* (New York: Simon & Schuster, 1979).

***absorb.*** Meeting the volume of sell orders with buy orders. When there are no buyers for shares being offered, the result is downward pressure on stock prices. If 10,000 shares of International Aluminum are being offered at $15 per share but at that price there are only buyers for 5,000 shares, the other sellers will begin lowering their asking price. Thus, if a broker is able to find buyers for the shares being offered, he will, in effect, keep the market from plunging. For an inside look at floor traders and Exchange operations, see Leonard Sloan, *The Anatomy of the Floor, The Trillion-Dollar Market at the New York Stock Exchange* (Garden City, New York: Doubleday, 1980).

***absorption point.*** The price at which potential buyers lose interest in a particular stock. The result is downward pressure on the price of the stock. If you are interested in selling 1,000 shares of AT&T at $65 per share, but there are no buyers at that price, you will try to hold your offer or else begin lowering the price until you can find a buyer. For recommendations on when to buy and when to sell, see Richard A Crowell, *Stock Market Strategy* (New York: McGraw-Hill, 1977). You might also find of interest Ira Cobleigh, *The Dowbeaters; How to Buy Stocks That Go Up* (New York: Macmillan, 1979).

**account.** A business relationship with a broker as well as the actual record of business transactions with that broker. Once you have signed up to do business with a brokerage house, you become one of its accounts. Your buy, sell, interest, dividend, income, and payment records are recorded in a ledger or computer memory, representing your account, for the purpose of maintaining a list of all transactions you undertake with the firm. For further information on the relationship between broker and customer, see Robert J. Schwartz, *You and Your Stockbroker* (New York: Macmillan, 1967). United Business Services, *Successful Investing: A Complete Guide to Your Financial Future* (New York: Simon & Schuster, 1979); Louis Engel, *How To Buy Stock,* 6th rev. ed. Boston: Little Brown, 1976; Conrad W. Thomas, *How To Sell Short & Perform Other Wondrous Feats* (Homewood, Ill.: Dow Jones-Irwin, 1976).

**account analysis.** The review of debit and credit activity in an account as well as the frequency and quality of the transactions. Most investors would be wise to have periodic meetings with the account representative for their broker to determine if their current strategy is sound for the intermediate and long-term. One cannot simply buy stocks and tuck them away; a portfolio must be continually managed. Many individuals buy and sell stock in *street name,* in which case the brokerage house does not transfer the certificates to you and does all the maintenance (recordkeeping) for your account. If your account shows little activity, the broker may convert the record of holdings into actual shares and deliver them to you in your name—or else charge you a small fee for his maintenance services. For further reading on brokerage accounts and legal liabilities between broker and customer, see Robert J. Schwartz, *You and Your Stockbroker* (New York: Macmillan, 1967). See also, United Business Service, *Successful Investing: A Complete Guide to Your Financial Future* (New York: Simon & Schuster, 1979).

***account balance.*** The difference between the money you owe (debit) the broker and the money the broker may owe (credit) you. You may have purchased 100 shares of Public Service Electric and Gas for $2000 including brokerage commissions. But at the same time, you have recorded to your account, but not yet delivered to you, capital gains or dividends totalling $1,200. In this case, you would have a debit account balance of $800. In the case of margin accounts, there would be interest due the broker on the money he had lent you for purchase of part or all of the stock, and that interest would be an additional debit to your account. See "account analysis" for reference texts.

***account day.*** Third and last settlement day on the London Stock Exchange where settlements are made twice each month.

***account executive.*** The representative at a brokerage house with whom you will ordinarily place your buy and sell orders. The account executives at full-service brokerages will often as- sist you in deciding whether or not to purchase certain securi- ties. A good relationship with the account executive is always important, and frequent communications with him or her can often lead to a number of potentially hot stocks which you may want to research further. Account representatives at the discount brokerage houses, however, function mainly as order takers and do not assist in stock selection or other market decisions. Whether or not you will want to deal with full-service broker- ages or discount houses depends upon your own track record and knowledge of the stock market. You can save a lot of money at the discount brokerages if you trade frequently, but, on the other hand, you might make much more when you have at your disposal the research services of the full-service brokerages. See "account analysis" for references.

**action.** Stock market activity. This activity may be in terms of volume or of price movement—for the market in general or a specific stock. Market watchers are usually favorably impressed when the market moves up on high volume, and in general consider unloading holdings if the market is going south on low volume. Some ideal texts for stock watchers are Richard A. Crowell, *Stock Market Strategy* (New York: McGraw-Hill, 1977); Ira Cobleigh, *The Dowbeaters; How To Buy Stocks That Go Up,* (New York: Macmillan, 1979); Joseph E. Granville, *Granville's New Strategy for Daily Stock Market Timing For Maximum Profit* (Englewood Cliffs, N.J.: Prentice Hall); Justin Mamis, *When To Sell: Inside Strategies for Stock Market Profits* (New York: Farrar, Straus & Giroux, 1977).

**active account.** Account of a stock investor who trades heavily. Some investors specialize in high-yield stocks and are mainly interested in current income and/or long-term capital gains; they will purchase securities and hold them for years before they sell. Such a trading philosophy, when adhered to, results in little trading activity. At the other extreme are traders interested in short-term capital gains; they may buy and sell the same security within months, weeks, days, and sometimes hours to turn a profit or cut a loss. This type of trading results in high account-activity. The more account activity, the more money for the broker, who, one must remember, receives commission on both buy and sell orders. See Donald I. Rogers, *How Not To Buy A Common Stock* (New York: Arlington House, 1972); and Richard A. Crowell, *Stock Market Strategy* (New York: McGraw-Hill, 1977) for introductory and intermediate texts on trading stocks.

**active market.** The stock market during a time of heavy trading volume. This is a relative term and does not signify any specific number of shares traded. It may be that in any given year, 25 or 30 million shares traded represents an active market, and in the new year, 130 or 145 million. For further research on the technical aspects of investing, *see* Ira Cobleigh, *The Dowbeaters; How to Buy Stocks That Go Up* (New York: Macmillan, 1979). Joseph E. Granville, *Granville's New Strategy for Daily Stock Market Timing for Maximum Profit* (Englewood Cliffs, N.J.: Prentice Hall, 1976).

***active partner.*** A partner in a brokerage firm—or any business, for that matter—who is involved in the daily operation of the firm or business.

***active securities.*** Securities which are traded daily and for which quotations are listed. "Active Securities" do not indicate the market trend, only the fact that trading is frequent. An active security can very well be on a downward trend. For further research on the techniques of investing, *see* Richard Blackman, *Follow the Leaders; Successful Trading Techniques with Line Drive Stocks* (New York: Simon & Schuster, 1978); Ira Cobleigh, *The Dowbeaters; How to Buy Stocks That Go Up* (New York: Macmillan, 1979). Joseph E. Granville, *Granville's New Strategy for Daily Stock Market Timing for Maximum Profit* (Englewood Cliffs, N.J.: Prentice Hall, 1976).

***actual price.*** The price at which a transaction takes place. First offerings may be for $10⅛, first bids for $9½. But when there is agreement in the offer and the bid, say $10, and a sale is made, that $10 is the *actual price.*

***admitted to dealings.*** When a particular security has qualified for listing and trading on an exchange. Every exchange has its own set of requirements that corporate stock and other securities must meet before they can be listed.

***advance.*** An increase in stock prices. Stocks never continue in one direction without interruption; in every bull phase there are slides in price, just as in every bear phase there are periods of marked increases in price. See "advance-decline indicator" defined below.

**advance-decline indicator.** A technical index used along with the Dow Jones Industrial Average (DJIA) to determine market trend. If the index and the DJIA move in the same direction, whatever the trend, it should continue. If the index peaks, but the DJIA continues to climb, then the market is expected to be approaching a top. If the index bottoms out, but the DJIA continues to plummet, then the market is expected to be approaching a low. This is all theory of course, and one must remember that he invests not in the DJIA or in the market, but in specific securities which may very well perform completely opposite to expected general trends. See Anthony W. Tabell, "Forecasting Stock Prices: The Technician's Approach," in *The Anatomy of Wall Street* (Philadelphia: Lippincott, 1968). For the kind of information that one must consider to make a success of investing, see the following intermediate-level texts on investment: Joseph E. Granville, *Granville's New Strategy for Daily Stock Market Timing For Maximum Profit.* (Englewood Cliffs, N.J.: Prentice Hall); Justin Mamis, *When To Sell: Inside Strategies for Stock Market Profits* (Farrar, Straus & Giroux, 1977); Harry Brown, *Inflation Proofing Your Investments* (New York: Morrow, 1981); Jerome B. Cohen, Edward D. Zinbaire, Arthur Zeikel, *Guide To Intelligent Investing* (Homewood, Ill.: Dow Jones-Irwin, 1977).

**against the box.** A short sale in which the seller actually owns the stock being sold, but cannot, or will not deliver the stock to the buyer. What he does, therefore, is direct his broker to borrow the stock from another account (which may even be the broker's account), and deliver the borrowed stock to the buyer. This topic is more fully discussed in "selling against the box," as the expression more often goes. For a primer on this and other related subjects, see the following: Conrad W. Thomas, *How To Sell Short & Perform Other Wondrous Feats* (Homewood, Ill.: Dow Jones-Irwin, 1976). For additional information on stock market strategies, see Justin Mamis, *Inside*

*Strategies for Stock Market Profits* (New York: Farrar, Straus & Giroux, 1977); Jerome B. Cohen, Edward D. Zinbaire, Arthur Zeikel, *Guide To Intelligent Investing* (Homewood, Ill.: Dow Jones-Irwin, 1977).

**air pocket.** A situation whereby a stock registers sudden and unusual decline in price. This is usually a flag that news had leaked out, or is about to leak to the public concerning adverse economic conditions for a particular stock. Often, an air pocket feeds a bear phase for a given security. The sudden drop excites others to unload their holdings. And, as short-sellers may be forced to cover their positions in the case of an air pocket, there is additional downward pressure on the price of the shares.

**allotment.** A percentage of a new security issue assigned by the sponsoring investment house to a subscriber. As all new offers are made with an allotment provision, the actual number of shares received can be less than the amount for which originally subscribed.

**allotment notice.** A letter distributed to individuals applying for bonds or shares of stock. The letter indicates the actual amount assigned and what is the payment schedule.

**alpha coefficient.** A correlation between a stock's return and some stationery market average.

**Amman Financial Market.** A small stock exchange located in the country of Jordan. For the address of this and other exchanges located throughout the world, see the supplement to this dictionary.

**American Depository Receipts (ADRs).** Forms for the listing of shares in foreign companies on U.S. stock exchanges in a qualified U.S. bank or trust company. These foreign corporations must have on deposit, in a qualified American bank or trust company, an amount equivalent to the number of shares listed. There are exceptions and these apply when the represented securities are easily transferable in New York, are easily exchanged with other certificates still outstanding in the major foreign market, and can guarantee to American stockholders all rights and privileges that accompany ownership of the stock. Many foreign corporations do not register the owners of stock, so legally the individual or institution in posssession of the stock is the true owner; this is not at all in accordance with U.S. practice. Additionally, foreign stock, when evaluated in terms of U.S. currency, often sells for pennies rather than dollars, and as penny stocks have little marketability in the United States, the American bank holding the ADRs may very well have each ADR represent multiple shares of the foreign stock. Also, currency conversion for dividend payments is much more easily executed. And, finally, many foreign companies fail to register new issues with the Securities and Exchange Commission, leaving American stockholders out of the picture when it comes to stock rights; ADRs solve the problem by allowing banks to sell rights in foreign markets for American shareholders.

The procedure works as follows: As the foreign shares are placed on deposit in the other country, a representative number of ADRs are made available to buyers in New York. When normal trading activity in the stock commences, the ADRs are transferred to the new owner—not the original certificates. This solves the awkward problem of having to ship stock certificates back and forth between the United States and foreign countries.

***American Stock Exchange.*** The second-largest exchange in the United States in terms of both the volume of shares traded and the dollar value of the shares traded. Conducting business since about 1849, the exchange actually operated outdoors until 1921. Its members conducted business right on the sidewalk, and it was referred to for years as "The Curb." In 1908, it became the New York Curb Agency; in 1911 the New York Curb Market Association, in 1921, the year it moved indoors, the New York Curb Market; in 1929, the New York Curb Exchange; and in 1953, the American Stock Exchange. The American Gold Coin Exchange (AGCE), a new AMEX subsidiary, has been trading the Canadian Maple Leaf since January, 1982 and is now trading the Austrian 100 Corona, the South African Krugerrand, the Mexican 50 Peso and the Mexican One Ounce. Four types of membership are available on the exchange. *Regular members* handle equities and options, *options principal members* handle principal transactions in options only; *associate members* have wire access to the floor; and *allied members* are general partners, principal executive officers, and individuals who manage member organizations. The exchange is located at 86 Trinity Place, New York. For a history of the exchange, see Robert Sobel, *The Curbstone Brokers: The Origins of the American Stock Exchange* (New York: Macmillan, 1970).

**American Stock Exchange Index.** A price-trend indicator to guide investors. It actually consists of three separate indicators, the Price Change Index, the Breadth of Market Summary, and the Price/Earnings (P/E) Profile. The Price Change Index represents the price level of both common stocks and warrants; the Market Summary indicates across-the-board price changes; and the P/E Profile gives statistical data on price-to-earnings ratios.

**annual report.** Published statement of the last fiscal year's financial activity of a corporation, partnership, or proprietorship. It is distributed to all stockholders. In every case, the financial data included in these reports has already been distributed in one way or another to the financial community. Your broker, as well as many financial news publishers and research organizations will have already been aware of, and reviewed, the accounting data by the time the stockholder reads it. The report includes a description of the corporation's subsidiaries and divisions and its markets, along with a forecast for the year or years ahead. See Chapter 23 in United Business Services' *Successful Investing: A Complete Guide to Your Financial Future*

(New York: Simon & Schuster, 1979). For a more detailed treatment of financial reports, you may want to refer to Leopold Bernstein, *Financial Statement Analyses, Application and Interpretation* (Homewood, Ill.: Richard D. Irwin, 1978).

**anti-trust.** A political/economical policy instituted to control monopolies. In the history of the United States the following federal statutes have been instituted just for this purpose: the Sherman Anti-Trust Act in 1890, which declared any contract or conspiracy which would result in restraint of trade to be illegal; the Clayton Anti-Trust Act in 1914, which prohibited contract, price cutting, or rebates for the purpose of wiping out smaller competitors; the Federal Trade Commission Act in 1914, which directs business operating policy to preserve competition; the Robinson-Patman Act in 1936, which sought to protect independent merchants from the large chains with which they could not ordinarily compete; the Miller-Tyding Act in 1937, which sought to enforce retail price maintenance agreements; and the Wheeler-Lea Act in 1938, which banned false and misleading advertising. See Mark J. Green, *The Closed Enterprise System,* (New York: Grossman, 1972).

**arbitrage.** Trading of specified items in one market and simultaneously selling them in another. The investor engaging in arbitrage will sell short 100 shares of Stock A in one market, while buying 100 shares of Stock A in another market at a different price; he will realize his profit from the difference in price between buy and sell orders. Many stocks are dually listed. For instance, you may see a stock listed on both the Pacific Stock Exchange and the Boston Stock Exchange where it may be selling at prices that can vary up to a couple of points, thereby creating an ideal situation for some arbitrage. Of course, an arbitrageur (as one who deals in arbitrage is called) need not employ this strategy only in stock trades; he may also deal in rights, warrants, convertible bonds, or even convertible preferred shares. Arbitrage requires a great deal of trading sophistication, as well as excellent timing.

**arbitrage house.** A brokerage firm which specializes in arbitrage transactions.

**asking price.** The lowest price at which an owner of stock is willing to sell his holdings. If you own 100 shares of Chrysler Corporation and are offering to sell them for $6¾, that $6¾ is your *asking price*. Whether or not you will get it is another matter.

**at a discount.** When the asking price of a stock is below par value. If you are offering to sell 100 shares of a stock, which has a par value of $10, for $8, you are said to be selling it at a discount. There are specific marketing problems when a stock falls below its par, as most investors will rarely be willing to risk the resulting liability. Stockholders are liable for the balance to par in cases of insolvency.

**at-or-better.** Instructions to a broker to buy or sell at the current quote or a price more advantageous to the buyer than the current quote. For the basics of investing, see the following: Yale L. Meltzer, *Putting Money To Work: An Investment Primer* (Englewood Cliffs, N.J.: Prentice Hall, 1976). Donald I. Rogers, *How Not To Buy A Common Stock* (New York: Arlington House, 1972); United Business Service, *Successful Investing: A Complete Guide to Your Financial Future* (New York: Simon & Schuster, 1979).

**at par.** When the price for a share of stock is equal to the par value of the stock.

**at market price.** Instructions to a broker to buy or sell shares of stock at the current offering price. If Pacific Telephone is listing at $18, and you put in an order to your broker to buy the shares at market, the shares will be purchased at $18. If the stock suddenly jumps in price just before your "market order" is entered, your order will be placed at the latest offering price. Thus, the placing of "market" orders is a somewhat risky approach to purchasing stocks unless one is sure that the stock will remain near, or advance steadily from its opening price. For advice on when to buy, when to sell, see Richard A. Crowell, *Stock Market Strategy* (New York: McGraw-Hill, 1977).

*at opening price.* Instructions to a broker to buy or sell as soon as possible after trading in a stock begins. For advice on when to buy, when to sell, see Richard A. Crowell, *Stock Market Strategy* (New York: McGraw-Hill, 1977).

*at-the-money.* A term used to describe certain tyes of puts and calls which have their exercise price equal to the market price of the underlying stock. See also "in-the-money," "at-the-money," and "options."

*auction.* A public sale of merchandise to the highest bidder by an individual (auctioneer) licensed to assume such responsibility. Every stock exchange is an auction where the price of the securities to be bought and sold is determined solely by the law of supply and demand. For advice on buying and selling securities, see Donald I. Roberts, *How Not To Buy A Common Stock* (New York: Arlington House, 1972); United Business Service, *Successful Investing: A Complete Guide to Your Financial Future* (New York: Simon & Schuster, 1979); Louis Engel, *How To Buy Stock*, 6th rev. ed. (Boston: Little Brown, 1976).

*auction market.* Any environment wherein supply and demand are the only governing factors for the buying and selling of merchandise. "Auction market" is a popular description for any of the stock exchanges, for that is exactly what they are. Stocks are sold to the highest bidder. When supply outweighs demand, stock prices slide. When demand outweighs supply, prices climb. The man or woman performing the role of auctioneer on the exchanges is the specialist whose job it is to bring together buyer and seller.

*authorized issue.* The amount of capital stock as authorized by its charter that a corporation may offer to the public. Whenever a board of directors of a corporation meets to increase this offering, they must first get approval of the majority of stockholders, and then amend the corporate charter. Do not confuse this term with "issued stock" or "outstanding stock," the first of which is a portion of the authorized stock actually sold to the public or which has been purchased back by the corporation, the second of which is stock actually in the hands of the public.

***autonomous investment.*** One that is made regardless of economic trends. When an investor buys shares in a large corporation just for the satisfaction of owning Blue Chip securities, he has, in fact, made an autonomous investment; he has given no consideration to the state of the economoy or the particular industry in which he has invested. For the basics of investing, see Jerome Turille, *Everything the Beginner Needs to Know to Invest Shrewdly* (New Rochelle, N.J.: Arlington House, 1973). For advanced techniques, you may want to refer to Ira Cobleigh, *The Dowbeaters; How to Buy Stocks That Go Up* (New York: Macmillan, 1979); Joseph E. Granville, *Granville's New Strategy for Daily Stock Market Timing for Maximum Profit* (Englewood Cliffs, N.J.: Prentice Hall, 1976).

***averaging out.*** Reducing the mean cost of stock purchases through an investment plan whereby one invests *the same amount of money* in the same stock at equal intervals. For instance, because you are unsure of short-term market trends, or are reluctant to make a lump sum investment at what may be the end of a bull phase, you invest $500 per month in a listed security. When the price of the security is $10 per share, you will be purchasing 50 share. When it is $20 per share you will be purchasing only 25 shares. Thus at the lower price you buy more; at the higher price you buy less. Over the long term of your investment plan, providing the stock has continued to climb except during short-term bear phases, your average cost will be less than your selling price. Averaging is a safe way to invest, but it is hardly full-proof. An investor must still be sure to select a good stock, and he must be willing to stick to his long-term game plan of *equal dollar amounts at fixed intervals*, and never confuse this method with buying equal shares at fixed intervals. (See Chapter 4 in this text.)

*average price.* The mean cost of your investment in a given security over a period of time; or the mean price at which you sold shares in a given security over a period of time. The average price is determined by dividing the total dollar value of the sales or purchases by the number of shares bought or sold.

*averages, stock.* See "Dow Jones Averages," market averages, "price composites," and "stock price averages." Market watchers rely heavily on "averages" as an indication of where the market is going in the future. But the averages are only general guidelines and must be weighted along with a great many other market and economic factors. For a discussion of what "averages" and other indicators mean to investors, see Justin Mamis, *When To Sell: Inside Strategies For Stock Market Profits* (New York: Farrar, Straus & Giroux, 1977).

*baby bond.* Bonds which are issued at a price of $25 each. They are one of the newer categories of corporate offerings on Wall Street. The idea behind their issuance was to attempt to create new interest in the bond market. The majority of corporate bonds are issued at $1,000 each, a price which is not generally attractive to the small investor. The low price of baby bonds enables the small investor to further diversify his portfolio.

*backdate.* Assigning a date to a document which represents a time prior to the date it was actually drawn or conceived.

*backlog.* In general business terms, an accumulation of orders for which shipments will not be made until some future date. To investors, the backlog of orders for a company is one of the variables to be weighted in estimating its profit potential. The term is also commonly used in the securities industry to mean an excess of paperwork in brokerage houses which often results in transfer and delivery problems. Usually, anytime there is an excess of volume in stock trading, back office work in the brokerages begins to pile up and transfers and deliveries run late.

**back office.** The processing department of a brokerage firm. It is where the purchases and sales of securities are recorded, where securities are received and forwarded. Backlogs can often result in credits or debits to the wrong accounts, so it is wise to always check your monthly statements carefully. For insight on investors' rights in dealing with brokers, see Robert J. Schwartz, *You and Your Broker* (New York: Macmillan, 1967).

**back spread.** In arbitrage transactions, a situation whereby the price of the same security, which is listed in different markets, is less than the usual spread. See also "arbitrage."

**bad delivery.** A delivery made *not* in accordance with the rules of the governing stock exchange. Each stock exchange on which a security might be listed stipulates deadlines, assignment procedures, and other technicalities to assure the proper assignment and safe delivery of stock.

**baht.** Monetary unit of Thailand. For current foreign exchange rates, see a copy of *The Wall Street Journal* or any other financial newspaper. See also "foreign currency units."

**bailout.** A plan or procedure to obtain income under a favorable tax situation. Stockholders will benefit by corporate bailout efforts that result in the distribution of payments to them as capital gains rather than as ordinary income—that is, as long as the distribution does not result in a reduction of the stockholder's interest in the corporation. On the subject of tax strategy and shelters, you may find the following text of special interest: Judith H. McQuown, *Tax Shelters That Work For Everyone* (New York: Harper & Row).

***balanced funds.*** Diversified investment companies which have included in their portfolios, the common, preferred, or other securities of many, many companies. The philosophy behind such an investment spread is that there is safety in diversity. *Theoretically*, when one group of stocks being held falls in price, there will be other holdings which will advance to offset them. The method of assuring maximum return for these balanced funds is to increase defensive holdings when the market is at a high, and to move into more aggressive issues when the market is at a low. See John L. Springer, *The Mutual Fund Trap* (Chicago: Henry Regnery, 1973); and Ronald D. Rugg and Norman B. Hale, *The Dow Jones-Irwin Guide to Mutual Funds* (Homewood, Ill.: Dow Jones-Irwin, 1976).

***balanced growth.*** In macroeconomic terms, related growth in all areas of the national economy. Balanced growth requires detailed planning of the investment spread. For instance, if construction of a manufacturing plant is being considered, there must also be considered the construction, organization, and implementation of supply and transportation systems upon which the manufacturing effort will be dependent.

***balance of payments.*** A record indicating the economic transactions between one nation and all others with which it generally conducts business. These transactions include cash and bullion shipments, interest and dividends, goods and services. From an accounting perspective, each time the United States has money due from some country, say France or England, the United States is debited for the full amount, and France and England are credited according to their share of the debt. When the United States total credits are less than its total debits, then it has a deficit; when credits are more than debits, then it has a surplus. Continuing deficits are an indication of serious economic difficulty. See pages 338–343 in Willis L. Perterson's *Principles of Economics: Macro* (Homewood, Ill.: Richard D. Irwin, 1977).

**bankruptcy.** Insolvency, or a financial or business failure. Bankruptcy may be voluntary or involuntary. Voluntary bankruptcy merely requires insolvency on the part of the applicant whenever liabilites are such that resulting obligations cannot be met. Involuntary bankruptcy requires a petition filed by a creditor when the total number of creditors is less than twelve but by *three* creditors when the total number is twelve, or more and total claims by the three creditors equal at least $500.00. Any individual, business, or corporation with the exception of railroads, banks, municipalities, insurance companies, and building and loan corporations can submit voluntary petitions for bankruptcy. Any individual or corporation may be the object of an involuntary petition except for farmers, wage earners, and those excepted above for voluntary petitions. There are certain chapters in the bankruptcy law with which the investor should be generally familiar, as he or she will often see them referenced in financial papers. They are:

— *Chapter 8,* which is concerned with railroads, their reorganization, and debt repayment schedules;
— *Chapter 9,* which is concerned with bankrupt public authorities;
— *Chapter 10,* which is concerned with reorganization of businesses for the purpose of recovering profitability;
— *Chapter 11,* which is concerned with precedures for a businesses' debt settlements;
— *Chapter 12,* which is concerned with debtors who are not incorporated and whose real estate was offered as collateral for their loans;
— *Chapter 13,* which is concerned with governing the arrangements of debt repayments between a debtor and his creditors;
— *Chapter 14,* which is concerned with maritime claims.

**barometer stock.** A stock whose price movement is indicative of general economic conditions or of general stock market price movement.

**bear.** Someone who anticipates, or may seek to profit from a declining market. That market may be in stocks in general or in one stock specifically. Though the "bear" may be negative about the market, he or she is not necessarily negative about his or her chances of making a profit in it. The bear's technique is to *sell short* (see also "short selling") at what is expected to be the higher trading price, and plan to buy the stock back at a lower price sometime in the near future. The bear's method, then, is to actually sell a stock he does not own, and then purchase it back at a future time. The bear revereses the normal stock transaction. His or her profits, however, are still determined by the difference between buy and sell prices. It is important to note that anyone selling short can do so only if a margin account has been established with a broker. Minimum requirement for a margin account is a $2,000.00 deposit. The short-seller (bear) must also put up half the value of the shares he sells short. Thus, if he sells short $8,000.00 worth of shares, he must increase the balance on deposit in his margin account. See Chapter six in this text, and Conrad W. Thomas, *How to Sell Short & Perform Other Wondrous Feats* (Homewood, Ill.: Dow Jones-Irwin, 1976).

**bearish.** An attitude which indicates prices are on a downward trend. If IBM share prices were declining steadily, one would report this as a bearish trend. See Conrad W. Thomas, *How to Sell Short & Perform Other Wondrous Feats* (Homewood, Ill.: Dow Jones-Irwin, 1976).

**bear market.** A market for short sellers. In this case, the stock market in general, as indicated by the "averages" or other barometers, is in rapid long-term decline. But this does not mean there will not be periods of rising prices or no chance for a bull to make a profit. In every bear market there are bullish phases, just as in every bull market there are bearish phases. See Conrad W. Thomas, *How to Sell Short & Perform Other Wondrous Feats* (Homewood, Ill.: Down Jones-Irwin, 1976).

**bear pool.** A fund organized specifically for the purpose of putting downward pressure on market prices. If any exist today, they exist outside the law.

**bear raid.** A situation marked by widespread and aggressive short-selling in either the market in general or a specified stock. The usual result is emergency selling in margin accounts. For a discussion on short-selling and how to sell short, see Conrad W. Thomas, *How to Sell Short & Perform Other Wondrous Feats* (Homewood, Ill.: Dow Jones-Irwin, 1976).

**beating the gun.** Soliciting orders for stocks not yet officially registered. The Securities and Exchange Commission frowns on this, and will seriously penalize those who engage in this practice.

**below par.** A stock price less than the face value assigned to it when it was issued. Par value is an arbitrary assignment for recordkeeping purposes, though many years ago it was related to a company's balance sheet. There is some danger, however, to purchasing a stock at a price below its par value. This is because, legally, stockholders are liable for the balance to par in cases of insolvency; par value must be fully paid in order for a stock to remain non-assessable (which means that the stockholder has limited liability). When stock is issued with no par value, the subscription price must still be paid in full, even though the declared value is only a small percent of the subscription price.

**best bid.** The highest price a perspective stock purchaser is willing to pay for a share of stock. The best bid is actually what determines the value of stock you may own—not its par value or its dividend.

**bid.** An offer to buy a stock at a certain price. A bid is actually an order, though, in all possibility, it may not actually be executed. In making a bid, specify the type of order, the number of shares, the company name, and the price you are willing to pay. For example, "Mr. Broker, please enter a day order for 100 shares of Ranger Oil at $12¼.

**bid and asked price.** The bid price is that at which an investor is willing to purchase a security; the asked price is that at which another investor is willing to sell the stock. What the price finally goes for may be some compromise between the two. See "bid" for reference texts.

**bidding up.** Increasing the offering price for a security to successively higher price levels. You may be interested in buying 100 share of American Motors for $5 per share, and place an order at that price. When the stock rises to $5½ per share before your order can be executed, you decide to offer $5½ now for the shares. Before this second order can be executed, the stock jumps to $6 per share and you raise your bid accordingly. In so "chasing after" the stock you have been *bidding up* the price of AM.

**bid price.** Th highest price anyone is willing to pay for shares of stock. The bid price is the true value of your stock at any given time.

**Big Board.** Nickname for the New York Stock Exchange, which is the largest exchange in the world. The exchange is located at 11 Wall Street in New York City. For a history of the exchange, see Robert Sobel, *The Big Board, A History of the New York Stock Market* (New York: Free Press, 1965).

**Black Friday.** September 24, 1869, the day of the famous attempt by James Fisk and Jay Gould to corner the gold market. (See headlines on next page.) Days before, they began purchasing all the gold they could in New York City, so that by the 24th they owned enough of the commodity to bid the price up more than 20 points. This sudden and unexpected price movement threw investors into wild confusion and put down-

ward pressure on the stock market. If it weren't for the inter-
vention of the U.S. Treasury, which made available $4 million
of its gold reserves, many more companies and investors would
have been ruined than eventually were. Fisk and Gould report-
edly made a profit in excess of $10 million. See Robert Sobel,
*Panic On Wall Street, A History of America's Financial Disasters*
(New York: Macmillan, 1968).

---

VOL. XIX........NO. 5619.

# THE GOLD EXCITEMENT

**The Panic in the Gold Room Yes-
terday.**

---

**Culmination of the Great Bull Move-
ment.**

---

**The Rise and Fall of Thirty
Per Cent.**

---

DISMAY OF ALL PARTIES.

---

**The Scenes and Incidents In and Around
Wall-street.**

---

**The Action of the Secretary of the
Treasury.**

---

Copyright © 1869 *The New York Times.* Reprinted by permission.

***blind pool.*** A special investment fund which puts contributions
by members under the management of another member who
invests the money as he sees fit, and in utmost secrecy, until
his objectives have been obtained.

***block.*** A large amount of shares. Technically, "block" refers
to 10,000 shares or more, but the word is in such wide usage
that almost any round lot over 100 shares is sometimes referred
to as a block.

## STOCKS COLLAPSE IN 16,410,030-SHARE DAY, BUT RALLY AT CLOSE CHEERS BROKERS; BANKERS OPTIMISTIC, TO CONTINUE AID

**LEADERS SEE FEAR WANING**

Point to 'Lifting Spells' in Trading as Sign of Buying Activity.

GROUP MEETS TWICE IN DAY

But Resources Are Unable to Stem Selling Tide—Lamont Reassures Investors.

HOPE SEEN IN MARGIN CUTS

Banks Reduce Requirements to 25 Per Cent—Sentiment in Wall St. More Cheerful.

---

**240 Issues Lose $15,894,818,894 in Month; Slump in Full Exchange List Vastly Larger**

The drastic effects of Wall Street's October bear market is shown by valuation tables prepared last night by THE NEW YORK TIMES, which place the decline in the market value of 240 representative issues on the New York Stock Exchange at $15,894,818,894 during the period from Oct. 1 to yesterday's closing. Since there are 1,279 issues listed on the New York Stock Exchange, the total depreciation for the month is estimated at between two and three times the loss for the 240 issues covered by THE TIMES table.

Among the losses of the various groups comprising the 240 stocks in THE TIMES valuation table were the following:

| Group. | Number of Stocks. | Decline in Value. |
|---|---|---|
| Railroads | 25 | $1,128,686,488 |
| Public utilities | 29 | 5,135,734,327 |
| Motors | 15 | 1,680,840,902 |
| Oils | 22 | 1,332,617,778 |
| Coppers | 15 | 824,403,820 |
| Chemicals | 9 | 1,621,687,597 |

The official figures of the New York Stock Exchange showed that the total market value of its listed securities on Oct. 1 was $87,073,630,423. The decline in the 240 representative issues therefore cut more than one-sixth from the total value of the listed securities. Most of this loss was inflicted by the wholesale liquidation of the last week.

---

**CLOSING RALLY VIGOROUS**

Leading Issues Regain From 4 to 14 Points in 15 Minutes.

INVESTMENT TRUSTS BUY

Large Blocks Thrown on Market at Opening Start Third Break of Week.

BIG TRADERS HARDEST HIT

Bankers Believe Liquidation Now Has Run Its Course and Advise Purchases.

---

Copyright © 1929 The New York Times. Reprinted by permission.

**Black Tuesday.** October 29, 1929, the day that the Dow Jones Industrial Average fell more than 30 points (almost 12 percent) on trades of about 16.5 million shares. Many economists and historians claim Black Tuesday heralded the Great Depression. For further reading on the subject of crashes and depressions, see Charles Poor Kindleberger, *Manias, Panics and Crashes: A History of Financial Crises* (New York: Basic Books, 1978); and John Kenneth Galbraith, *The Great Crash 1929* (New York: Houghton, Mifflin, 1979).

**blotter.** A temporary register where security transactions and related data are kept until the information can be transferred and formalized in permanent accounting records.

**blue chip.** High-quality common stocks. Blue chip companies have a long-standing record of profitability as well as consistent and increasing dividends. They are all nationally known companies. Blue chip investments are usually made for what is called "total return." Investors purchase these shares **not** because they expect excessive capital gains or especially high dividends, but because stock in blue chips offer them safety, some steady income from dividends, and a good possibility of capital gains over the intermediate and long term. Some blue chip stocks are General Motors, International Business Machines, AT&T, and Alcoa. Even blue chips, however, cannot guarantee an investor success. Their stock cannot be guaranteed to be on a steady advance; sometimes their dividends are lowered or cancelled, and they, too, can find themselves in such difficult times that when an investor finally sells out, his capital losses will have seriously diminished, or completely wiped out, any gain he was realizing from dividends.

**blue sky laws.** Nickname for various state laws which offer the public protection against security fraud rackets. The laws not only regulate operating practices of those in the financial community, but also seek to punish fraudulent security dealers.

**board.** Group of directors in a corporation (see "board of directors"). The term is also a synonym for "exchange."

**board lot (round lot).** 100 shares of stock. When an investor buys in other than board lots, he must pay a premium on each share purchased.

**board of directors.** Corporate officers elected by stockholders to oversee the business of the firm.

**board room.** The room in which trades take place at an exchange. The term also applies to a type of V.I.P. room at a brokerage office which is generally reserved for customers who wish to keep on top of security prices.

**bolivar.** Venezuelan monetary unit. For current foreign exchange rates see *The Wall Street Journal* or any other financial newspaper. See in this dictionary "Foreign Currency Units."

***boom.*** A time of extreme economic optimism characterized on a macroeconomic scale by rapidly increasing supply and demand, full employment, high income, and extensive investment. Stock market activity during this time reflects widespread interest in speculative issues. Neophyte investors are generally careless during boom periods, for they create such a bullish atmosphere that investments are made more on faith and hope than on sound financial analysis. See "The Problem of Growth" in Robert L. Heilbroner's *Understanding Macroeconomics* (Englewood Cliffs, N.J.: Prentice-Hall, 1968).

***borrowed stock.*** Stock borrowed by brokers in order to execute short sales for their clients. See "short selling."

***Boston Stock Exchange.*** A large regional exchange located in Boston, Massachusetts which has been in operation since 1834. Trading volume here is roughly 100 million shares per year. Since 1965, the exchange has had a full-time president and staff to manage operations. Among the more well-known securities that are listed on the exchange are the Cape Cod Bank, AM International, and Texas Air preferred. You will find a partial listing of this exchange's securities in any of the financial newspapers or in the financial section of the major dailies. Please refer to the supplement to this dictionary for the address of this exchange, as well as a listing of all exchanges worldwide.

***bottomed out.*** The situation in which a security has reached its low point and is now in what is expected to be a narrow trading range preceding a strong advance.

***Bourse.*** Stock exchanges on the European continent. Note that the word is capitalized. See also "Paris Bourse."

***box count.*** An audit of securities held in street name by a broker. When a brokerage house closes its doors for the day, it secures all its certificates in metal containers, each one simply referred to as the "box;" here the certificates remain for safekeeping until accessed to make deliveries and transfers. Periodically, the contents of these boxes are checked against accounting records, and this check is called the box count. For an introduction to the legal liabilities which exist between broker and customer, see Robert J. Schwartz, *You and Your Stockbroker* (New York: Macmillan, 1967).

**break.** A sudden drop in market quotations. It usually occurs after a period of light trading in which stock prices move in a narrow range. It may or may not indicate price trend—depending upon other market indicators. This is to say that a break in itself should not be interpreted as a sign for reversing strategy. If you are interested in researching the technical aspects of investing in stocks, you may enjoy Joseph E. Granville, *Granville's New Strategy for Daily Stock Market Timing for Maximum Profit* (Englewood Cliffs, N.J.: Prentice Hall, 1976); Conrad W. Thomas, *How to Sell Short & Perform Other Wondrous Feats* (Homewood, Ill.: Dow Jones-Irwin, 1976).

**breakeven point.** To the stock investor, this is the point at which a stock trade neither makes nor loses money. Traders rarely, if ever, break even on any stock trade because of the fees associated with evey stock transaction, particularly the brokerage commissions. For instance, you may buy 100 shares of XYZ stock for $16, then sell the stock a year later for $16. It may appear that you have neither won nor lost money, until you count the brokerage fees for the buy transaction and the brokerage fees for the sell transaction, which would probably total around $70. In other words, you broke even on the stock trade itself, but lost $70 in commissions. You have a capital loss, and tax write-off, of $70.

**breakout.** The advance of a stock to a new trading range.

**broad market.** A situation in which there is indication of massive interest in all listed stocks, and many shares are changing ownership. A broad market usually indicates wide participation by the independent investor. It is indicative of a bullish mood in the investment community. If you are interested in how to read the market and have some experience in investing, any of the following books may be of interest to you: Ira Cobleigh, *The Dowbeaters; How to Buy Stocks That Go Up* (New York: Macmillan, 1979). Joseph E. Granville, *Granville's New Strategy for Daily Stock Market Timing for Maximum Profit* (Englewood Cliffs, N.J.: Prentice Hall, 1976); Conrad W. Thomas, *How to Sell Short & Perform Other Wondrous Feats* (Homewood, Ill.: Dow Jones-Irwin, 1976).

**broker.** The go-between in a contract negotiation. Investors sometimes confuse stockbrokers with dealers. There is, however, an important distinction. The broker works for his customer's account, and he can sue his customer should he incur any losses as the result of an oral order. The dealer works for his own account, and does not have the same legal recourse as the broker. See Robert J. Schwartz, *You and Your Stockbroker* (New York: Macmillan, 1967).

**broker's free credit balance.** Unmanaged money in brokerage accounts.

**broker loans.** Money borrowed by a broker to finance margin accounts as well as the normal brokerage activity which includes underwriting and investment.

**bucketing.** Illegal procedure of accepting money with which to purchase stock, but using it for other means. If the stock for which the money was originally planned goes in the opposite direction than the "buyer" expected, then those engaged in the scam benefit; when the stock is sold, they get to keep the "loss." If the stock moves as expected, then the scam becomes a losing game.

**bucking.** Going against the market trend. When the market is advancing, you are selling short; when the market is declining, you are buying long. Market indicators may or may not play a part in determining your strategy.

***bulge in prices.*** Signifies a strong advance in prices. A bulge in prices must not be considered by itself as a trend; other market indicators must be evaluated, also. There is actually no single indicator upon which an investor can depend. If you are interested in learning some of the basics about buying stocks, you will enjoy Louis Engle's *How to Buy Stocks,* 6th rev. ed. (Boston: Little, Brown, 1976); Kiril Sokoloff, *The Thinking Investor's Guide to the Stock Market* (New York: McGraw-Hill, 1978).

***bull.*** Anyone who buys long or has a generally optimistic attitude toward the economy or the stock market. The bull is not likely to chance any short selling, although he or she may try to take advantage of technical corrections in price. This is to say that the bull may well be positive about general market activity, but rather bearish about a particular stock or stock groups at certain intervals.

***bull campaign.*** A continuing, though uncoordinated, effort by independent investors or investment groups that has as its objective upward pressure on stock prices.

***buy and put away.*** Purchasing a stock and filing the certificate away for a lengthy period. You may buy a stock with the *intention* of holding it for sometime, but you must never forget about it; *changing economic forecasts* or particular industry activity may make unloading it at any given time a wise move.

***buyer's market.*** When little demand causes a decline in price and there is little pressure on buyers who can now wait for what they may feel is the best deal possible. See Louis Engel, *How to Buy Stocks,* 6th rev. ed. (Boston: Little, Brown, 1976); Kiril Sokoloff, *The Thinking Investor's Guide to the Stock Market*

(New York: McGraw-Hill, 1978).

***buying power.*** The amount of money in an account which is available for the purchase of securities.

***buying signals.*** Market activity which normally indicates that it is time to take positions in stock. Every investor has his own list of what he feels are "buying signals"; these may range from an investigation of fundamental financial data to simply patterns on a stock chart, or they may consist of an extensive list of trading patters, national economic policy, and expectations of the investment community. See Stanley S. Hueng, *Investor's Intelligence: A New Technical Approach to Stock Market Timing* (Larchmont, New York: Investor's Intelligence, 1973); and Richard A. Crowell, *Stock Market Strategy* (New York: McGraw-Hill, 1977).

***buying on a scale.*** The purchase of a set number of shares of stock at certain intervals during a period of their general decline in price. Investors who buy on scale are trying to average down the cost of their investment in securities that they feel are ready for an upswing, but which they are not sure have yet bottomed out.

***call.*** An option contract to purchase stock at a specified price during a set period of time. Calls are generally used as a means for entering into market transactions at a cost much lower than would ordinarily be required if one were to purchase shares of stock in sufficient number to make the investment worthwhile. Calls are also purchased as insurance to cover short positions. When the price of a call goes up, the money paid (or what is called the premium) for the call also goes up. Buyers of call options, therefore, hope to resell their contracts at a higher price. They will buy a call if they anticipate strong performance by the stock of the underlying security. See Chapter Eight in Jerome B. Cohen, Edward D. Zinburg, and Arthur Zeikel's *Guide to Intelligent Investing* (Homewood, Ill.: Dow Jones-Irwin); Gary

L. Gastineau, *The Stock Option Manual,* 2nd ed. (New York: McGraw-Hill, 1979).

**callable.** A type of preferred stock or bond which the issuer has the right to retire before the scheduled maturity date. This is often done when the issuer expects that "redeeming" the stock early is to his advantage, for the price in weeks, months, or years to come may quite conceivably be higher. There is usually a premium paid to holders for the right to call in a preferred before its maturity date.

**call loan.** A loan which has no specified date of maturity, though it must be paid on twenty-four-hours notice. Call loans facilitate security transactions. For the most part, repayment is generally at the convenience of the borrower. In the case of the brokerage community, government securities are often used as collateral, and the broker is liable for repayment on as little as two-hours notice.

**call money.** Money borrowed by brokers that they must pay back to the lenders on demand. Call money is also referred to as demand money.

**call-money market.** A market formed by financial institutions specifically for the purpose of providing demand loans for brokers and other businesses.

**call price.** The actual redemption price for securities that are callable.

**capital.** (1) In a strictly economic sense, all goods which are employed for the purpose of producing other goods; this includes plants and machinery. (2) In a strictly accounting sense, assets less liabilities. (3) In a strictly business sense, the total assets of a firm, including intangible assets like trademarks and patterns.

**capital gains.** The profit made from the sale of stock. If you purchase 100 shares of MGM for $500 and one year later sell them for $700, you will have made a capital gain of $200. A capital gain is either long-term or short-term. The specific period which qualifies a capital gain as either short-term or long-term is indicated by current tax law. Long-term capital gains receive special tax treatment; they are taxed at one-half the taxpayer's regular rate, but at no more than 25 per cent. Short-term capital gains are taxed at the taxpayer's regular rate. The current tax law in the U.S., however, does not distinguish short and long term capital gain; all gains are treated as income.

**capital gains tax.** A tax upon any profits received from the sale of capital items such as stocks and bonds or options.

**capital-output ratio (capital coefficient).** A ratio between the book value (net of depreciation) of plant and equipment and the gross value of output, used by economists to determine capital utilization and capital interests in specific industries.

**capital stock.** Shares which prove legal ownership in a corporation. The term capital stock includes both common stock and preferred stock. Preferred stockholders have preference over common stockholders in the distribution of dividends or, in the case of liquidation, of any assets. However, the claims of common and preferred stockholders always are second to those of creditors, including bond holders.

**capital stock subscribed.** An accounting term for capital stock not issued to the subscriber because all subscription fees have not yet been recovered.

**capital structure.** The way in which a corporation divides its capital into stocks, bonds, and surplus.

***classified stock.*** Issued stock which contains special provisions for either limiting or enhancing the privileges of the stockholder. Classified stock may be either common or preferred. The usual designations are Class A, Class B common; Class A, Class B preferred, etc. But other designations are also used: prior preferred, convertible preferred, etc.

***closing out.*** The final selling of securities in a margin account to meet the customer's obligations. Besides the 50% initial margin imposed on margin accounts by the Federal Reserve, brokers and/or stock exchanges require that margin accounts maintain a certain amount of equity. In this way, the broker is assured of repayment of his loan on any extensive slide in the price of the stock or stocks in the account. Generally, the maintenance requirement for margin accounts is 50% on one-position accounts and 35% on two or more position accounts, but this can change from broker to broker, and from exchange to exchange. When an investor's equity drops below those guidelines, the broker will send a "call" for the additional funds required to boost the cash position in the account. If the "call" is not responded to, the broker has the right to sell off as much stock as may be required to cover the margin requirement.

***closing price.*** The last price at which stock was sold on a trading day.

***common stock.*** Capital stock giving legal proof of ownership of corporate assets. Stockholders of common shares are generally privileged with voting rights. When dividends are declared on common shares, the dividends are only distributed after the corporation has met its obligations to holders of its bonds, debentures and preferred stocks. If you are interested in buying common stocks for the first time, you will want to read Louis Engel, *How to Buy Stocks,* 6th rev. ed. (Boston: Little, Brown, 1976); C. Colburn Hardy, *Dun & Bradstreet's Guide to Your Investments* (New York: Lippincott, 1981).

*contingent order.* An order which instructs a broker to buy or sell a security only on the condition that another order is executed first. For instance, you may wish to buy 100 shares of Public Service Electric and Gas at $19 per share, but haven't the cash on hand. Therefore, you instruct your broker to enter such an order, but only on condition that he is able to sell 50 shares of Dow Jones at $39 per share.

*continuous market.* A market for securities which ensures that there is always stock available during regular exchange hours.

*contraction.* A general decline in market prices.

*controlled account.* An account which is handled by someone other than the person in whose name it was opened. You may very well open an account and give your broker insructions to buy and sell for it as he sees fit. (However, few brokers, nor most individuals for that matter, are eager for such awesome responsibility.)

*controlling interest.* Ownership of more than 50% of a corporation's stock.

*conversion.* The exchange of one type of security for another, as in the exchange of preferred stock for common stock.

*conversion price.* The exchange rate when a corporation's bonds are converted to stock.

*convertible debenture.* A corporate certificate that signifies debt, and which can be converted into common or preferred stock at the option of the owner of the certificate. In cases of default, debenture holders have the same rights as general creditors. For further research, see James Karanfilian, "Investing in Bonds," in *The Anatomy of Wall Street* (New York: Lippincott, 1968).

**convertible hedge.** Selling short on a corporation's common stock while taking a long position in that corporation's convertible bonds.

**convertible preferred stock.** A class of preferred stock which may be exchanged for common stock. Provisions are usually made so that there is a minimum length of time the preferred must be held before it can be coverted. Convertible stocks appeal to investors because they "promise" some chance of stability, and yet give the investor the opportunity to cash in on a rapidly rising common stock should the situation present itself.

**crossed transaction.** When a broker handles both the sell and buy side of a transaction; he buys the stock from one customer for another customer.

**cruzeiro.** Monetary unit in Brazil. For current foreign exchange rates see *The Wall Street Journal* or any other financial newspaper. Also see "foreign monetary units" in this dictionary for a list of the monetary units used by the major countries throughout the world.

**cum-dividend.** Signifies stock purchased, including the right to the coming dividend. (See also exdividend).

**cumulative dividend.** Dividends which are due stockholders because they were not paid when previously scheduled. The cumulative feature is usually attached to holders of certain preferred stocks. There is a caveat here, however, and you must note that dividends are never guaranteed. That is, a corporation has no legal obligation to pay dividends, and may cancel or postpone them at any time. Therefore, the cumulative feature on preferred is dependant upon the next dividend declared by the corporation. The corporation must pay the cumulative preferred stockholders before they pay dividends to other stock holders.

**curb broker.** Name of historical significance for a broker on the American Stock Exchange which, at one time, was referred to as the "Curb"—for that is exactly where its membership auctioned securities. See Robert Sobel, *A History of the Amreican Stock Exchange, 1921-1971* (New York: Weybright & Rally, 1972); and Robert Sobel, *The Curbstone Brokers, The Origins of the American Stock Exchange* (New York: Macmillan, 1970).

**Curb Exchange.** The name of the American Stock Exchange from 1929 until 1953. The name was a throwback to its humble beginnings on the sidewalks of New York. See "curb broker" for reference texts.

**currency.** Money, though most often only paper money. In the United States, currency consists of Federal Reserve notes as well as treasury notes and coins. Most of the U.S. money supply (about 75%) is actually made up of demand deposits and checking accounts. For further reading: John Kenneth Galbraith, *Money, Whence It Came, Where It Went* (New York: Bantam, 1975).

**current price.** The price at which the shares of a corporation's stock last changed hands.

**current ratio.** Ratio of current assets to current liabilities. Thus, if a company's assets are $500,000 and the current liabilities are $300,000, the current ratio is 5 to 3. For a review of those ratios which an investor may use to get a 3-dimensional view of a corporation's financial picture, see Chapter 8 in this text.

**cyclical stocks.** Stocks which *supposedly* follow regular and, therefore, predictable cycles.

*day order.* An order which is automatically cancelled if it is not executed on the same day it is entered. When entering a day order, specify that fact and then the number of shares, name of the corporation, and the price of the bid. For example, "Mr. Broker, I would like to enter a day order for 100 shares of IT&T at $29 ⅛." For advice on when to buy, when to sell, see Richard A. Crowell, *Stock Market Strategy* (New York: McGraw-Hill, 1977).

*day trader.* A speculator who tries to buy and sell on the same day. Usually he maintains a margin account, and if he is successful in his attempts to turn the shares over on the same day, he can realize a profit without having to put up any money.

*dead assets.* Holdings of a short-or long-term nature which are unproductive.

*dead market.* A market showing little trading activity and hardly any price movement.

*dealer.* A securities professional who buys and sells securities for his own account rather than for someone else's. Investors often confuse dealers with brokers. The primary distinction is that dealers trade for their own accounts, while brokers trade for others.

*debenture.* A certificate which serves as evidence of a debt.

*deferred stock.* A stock on which the dividend payment is conditional; certain financial prerequisites or time requirements must first be met.

*direct financing.* When a corportion offers securities directly to investors without seeking the special services of underwriters.

**directors.** Persons elected by the stockholders to oversee the general policy of the corporation.

**discount house.** Any banking concern dealing in the purchasing and discounting of trade and bankers acceptances and various forms of commercial paper.

**discounting the market.** Market trades in anticipation of future development. People buy or sell stocks not for what they are worth today, but for what they hope, or are afraid, they will be worth at some future date. For instance, if you buy a stock because you feel that in six months certain economic or marketing developments will put upside pressure on the price of the stock, you are said to be discounting the market.

**disclosure.** The publication by a corporation of any news which may positively or negatively effect the value of its stock. The exchanges are rather explicit in their demand for such disclosure and will severely penalize a company which does not adhere to its policies.

**discount.** When the selling price of a security is less than its par value.

**discounting the news.** The tendency of the market to anticipate the news in the price of its listings. Thus, on Monday the price of the shares of AT&T may move to a new level in anticipation of financial disclosure on the coming Friday. When Friday comes and the news headlines new profits by AT&T, the shares may very well remain unchanged in price from the preceding day, as the news was discounted days before.

**distress selling.** Selling securities only because the owner cannot otherwise meet margin requirements.

**distribution.** Stock or cash dividend to investors; also, the widespread selling of securities by the more experienced investors who recognize the end of a bull phase and want to cash in on their profits.

**diversify.** Investing one's money in a number of different securities instead of in a single investment vehicle. For example, instead of investing $10,000 in MCA Corportion, the money is divided for investment in IT&T, Litton Industries, and General Motors as well as MCA.

**dividends.** The share of corporation's net earnings paid to stockholders, although cases do occur when a company pays a dividend from past earnings. See Chapter Seven in this text.

**dividend yield.** Rate of return from ownership in corporate stocks. It is determined by dividing the dividend by the purchase price of the stock. (Sometimes broker commissions are added to the calculation.)

**dollar.** Monetary unit not only in the United States but also in Australia, Canada, Hong Kong, New Zealand, Singapore, and Taiwan. For current foreign exchange rates see a copy of *The Wall Street Journal* or any other financial newspaper.

**dollar cost averaging.** A system of buying shares of stock at regular intervals with close to the same fixed dollar amount used for each purchase. In dollar cost averaging, stocks are purchased by the dollar rather than by the share. In this way, more stock can be purchased when prices are low and fewer shares will be purchased when prices are high. See Chapter Four.

**double bottom.** A price plateau which a stock has twice tested on declines, but from which it has successfully bounced back. Investors often read this as a *possible* indication that a downward trend has been temporarily halted, and there may even follow an upside movement.

**double taxation.** The taxing of corporate profits as income to the corporation, and the taxing of them again when they are paid as dividends to the shareholders.

**double top.** A price plateau which a stock has twice tested during advances but failed to break through. Investors often interpret this as a *possible* indication that any bullish phase has been temporarily concluded, and there may now be some downside risk.

**Dow Jones Averages.** The averages of certain industrial, utility, and transportation stocks which *The Wall Street Journal* and many other news and financial publications use as a means of measuring the overall performance of the stock market. The stocks which make up the averages appear in *The Wall Street Journal* every Monday. You will find of interest Chapters Five and Six in Justin Mannis' *When To Sell: Inside Strategies For Stock-Market Profits* (New York: Farrar, Straus and Giroux, 1972).

**down tick.** A trade that takes place below the last transaction price.

**Dow Theory.** A method of analyzing stock market activity orginated by the late Charles H. Dow, the man who founded *The Wall Street Journal.* The method uses the Dow Jones Industrial and Transportation Averages to forecast trends. Dow's ideas were later perfected by his successor William P. Handon. Basically, the Dow Theory looks for coincidence in the Industrial and Transportation Averages. When the Industrials and Transportation climb on heavy volume, *theoretically* they point to a coming bull market. When they fall on heavy volume, *theoretically* they point to a coming bear market. But they must move in the same direction together to indicate coming bear or bullish phases.

**dual listing.** When a stock is represented on more than one exchange.

**dump.** To unload stock as quickly as possible—and usually at the current market price.

**each way.** An expression to indicate that situation when a broker receives a commission for both the buy and sell sides of transaction.

**earned income.** See "earned revenue."

**earned revenue.** Income received as a result of sales or services. The term is a synonym for "earned income."

**earned surplus.** The undistributed profits of a corporation. These are the profits retained after distributions to shareholders.

**earning power.** A reference to a corporation's ability to operate profitably.

**earnings.** Income over a given fiscal period, also expressed as "net income." For an investor's perspective on the meaning of per-share earnings, see Chapter Twelve in Benjamin Graham's *The Intelligent Investor* (New York: Harper & Row, 1973).

**earnings multiple.** See "P/E ratio."

**earnings per share.** The total earnings of a corporation divided by the number of shares. The earnings per share may be stated in terms of common stock. To obtain the earnings per common share, the net income of the corporation is divided by the number of common shares. For the earnings per preferred share, the number of preferred shares becomes the divisor. becomes the divisor.

**enforced liquidation.** Selling under pressure. This is to say that the investor must convert his assets into cash for one reason or another, and cannot hold his securities long enough to waid for rising prices; he must sell them for what he can presently get in the marketplace. Margin account holders often find themselves in this predicament. The equity in their accounts falls below the equity requirement set by the broker or stock exchange, at a time when the investor is short of the cash needed to maintain his account. The result is that he must sell his stock, and use part or all of the proceeds to cover his debt.

**equity.** The amount by which a company's assets exceeds its liabilities. In the type of corporation that you and I might invest, equity is represented by the capital stock and the retained earnings.

**equity capital.** The total amount invested in an enterprise by the owner or owners. A corporation secures equity capital every time it brings its stock to market. The stockholders, of course, are guaranteed nothing more than to share in the profits of the corporation and to participate in any dividends which may be declared, although it must be noted that those dividends are never guaranteed.

**escudo.** Portugese monetary unit. For current foreign exchange rates see *The Wall Street Journal* or any other financial newspaper. See also "foreign currency units" in this dictionary.

**estimated market price.** The most recently quoted price of which someone is aware, though an immediate investigation may turn up new price information. Estimated market prices are given in those cases where replies to queries (say, in the OTC market) may be a long time in coming and the querying investor or broker is not really interested in making a purchase, but only getting an idea of current status. Usually, if an investor is asking about an over-the-counter stock that is not frequently traded, he is given an estimated market price. Generally, prices of stock listed on any of the major exchanges or available through NASDAQ are exact.

**exchange acquisition.** The combining of sell orders from a number of brokers on an exchange floor when there is suddenly an unusually large buy offer which cannot be facilitated without seriously disrupting normal trading activities.

***exchange distribution.*** The opposite of an exchange acquisition. The combining of buy orders from a number of brokers on the exchange floor when there are unusual sell offers which cannot be facilitated without seriously disrupting normal trading activities.

***exchange floor.*** Where brokers and dealers conduct their trading. See Leonard Sloane, *The Anatomy of the Floor: The Trillion-Dollar Market of the New York Stock Exchange* (New York: Doubleday, 1980).

***exchange of securities.*** The offering of securities in one corporation for those of another during mergers and acquisitions.

***exchange rate.*** The number of units of a given currency required to purchase one unit of another country's currency. Money is rarely exchanged on a one-for-one basis. If you were to refer to *The Wall Street Journal* or one of the other financial papers, you would see the foreign exchange rates for American dollars.

***exchange seat.*** Not actually a "seat," but rather membership on an exchange. Membership seats are sold on the open market. There are always a limited number of seats available, so new applicants, in almost every circumstance, must purchase seats from other members. The price of these seats can vary stubtantially from exchange to exchange, and from year to year. Prices of seats on the New York Stock Exchange have been as high as hundreds of thousands of dollars, and, in recent decades, as low as tens of thousands. Membership requires licensing by the National Association of Securities Dealers. For a history of securities trading in America, see Robert Sobel, *The*

*Big Board: A History of the New York Stock Market* (New York: Free Press, 1965).

**ex-dividend.** The stock being purchased is done so without any right to the coming dividend, although the buyer has the right to subsequent dividends. The market price of a stock when it becomes ex-dividend is automatically adjusted down to compensate for the loss to the buyer. Dividends remain of primary importance to investors, thus their willingness to bid up the price of a stock before the ex-dividend date, and their general disinterest during the ex-dividend period.

**execute.** Completing a buy or sell order. Your order to a broker is not necessarily guaranteed to be executed. He must meet your price requirements, and the stock must be in trading. For further reading on the legal obligations existing between customer and broker, see Robert J. Schwartz, *You and Your Stockbroker* (New York: Macmillan, 1967).

**exercise.** The subscription to special offerings of bonds or stocks which a corporation may offer to current shareholders as incentive to invest additional funds in the company.

**exhaust price.** The debit to a margin account which will necessitate either the emergency selling of holdings to cover margin requirements, or the depositing of additional funds into the account.

**expiration date.** The date on which special subscription rights or other offers associated with stock ownership become null and void. For instance, stock options and warrants have expiration dates after which they become worthless; owners of the options or warrants must exercises their rights or privileges prior to the expiration date.

**firm bid.** An offer for a security at a stated price which the offerer has no intention of negotiating or changing.

*firm-commitment offering.* Taking the entire risk associated with underwriting a stock offering to the public.

*firm-price.* An offer to sell a security at a stated price which the seller has no intention of negotiating or changing.

*first lien.* The first legal claim against the assets of a corporation.

*first preferred stock.* A class of preferred which offers its holders first claim to dividend distributions.

*fiscal dividend.* A term applying to the funds made available to the president and to the Congress for the purpose of expanding federal programs currently in operation, to create new federal programs, to reduce and federal taxes that may be in existence, or for the purpose of managing the economy.

*fiscal policy.* Plans for spending and producing revenue for a given accounting period, usually a year.

*floor broker.* An exchange member who buys and sells securities for other brokers. His is commissioned only to handle listed securities of that exchange. See Part Four in Leonard Sloane, *The Anatomy of the Floor: The Trillion-Dollar Market of the New York Stock Exchange* (New York: Doubleday, 1980).

*floor partner.* The representative of a brokerage firm who handles trades for his firm right on the exchange floor.

*floor quote.* A security price received directly from the floor of an exchange.

*floor report.* A confirmation of a transaction received directly from the exchange floor.

*flotation.* The offering of new corporate securities to the marketplace.

*flurry.* Short-term and unexpected activity in a stock or in the market in general. The word may relate to turnover or price movement. Many independent investors react quickly to flurries, usually to their own disadvantage. The flurry should be taken as a flag that a security should be researched, not as a signal to buy or sell. See Benjamin Graham's *The Intelligent Investor* (New York: Harper & Row, 1973).

*foreign currency units.* The names of the major currency units used throughout the world are given in the table on the next page. For up-to-date foreign exchange rates, see a copy of *The Wall Street Journal* or the financial section of major U.S. dailies. Do not assume that the Australian dollar is equal to the Canadian dollar or any foreign currency having the same name, or the Norwegian krone is equal to the Danish krone, etc. Record of past exchange rates can easily be found in the Statistical Abstract of the United States, available at any library (see Table on next page).

*formula investing.* A plan for the buying or selling of securities which calls for automatic placement of orders when certain price levels are reached or when certain indicators point to new market phases. For instance, some institutional investors will automatically sell a percentage of their holdings whenever the Dow Industrial Averages reach a certain level.

*franc.* Monetary unit used in Belgium, France, and Switzerland. For current foreign exchange rates see a copy of *The Wall Street Journal* or the financial section of one of the major daily newspapers. For a list of currency units by country, see in this dictionary "foreign currency units."

*full lot.* 100 shares of stock or multiples thereof. Same as "even lot" or "round lot."

*fully-paid stock.* Any stock on which no further payments are due.

| Country | Currency unit | Country | Currency Unit |
|---------|---------------|---------|---------------|
| Algeria | Dinar | Kenya | Shilling |
| Argentina | Peso | Korea(Rep) | Won |
| Australia | Dollar | Kuwait | Dinar |
| Austria | Shilling | Liberia | Dollar |
| Belgium | Franc | Libya | Dinar |
| Bolivia | Peso | Malaysia | Ringgitt |
| Brazil | Cruzeiro | Mexico | Peso |
| Canada | Dollar | Netherlands | Guilder |
| Chile | Peso | New Zealand | NZ Dollar |
| Columbia | Peso | Nicaragua | Cordoba |
| Costa Rica | Colon | Norway | Krone |
| Denmark | Krone | Pakistan | Ruppee |
| Egypt | Pound | Peru | Sol |
| Finland | Markka | Philippines | Peso |
| France | Franc | Portugal | Escuado |
| Germany | | Saudi Arabia | Riyal |
| (Fed. Rep.) | D. Mark | Singapore | Dollar |
| Ghiana | New Cedi | South Africa | Rand |
| Greece | Drachma | Spain | Peseta |
| Honduras | Lempira | Sri-Lanka | Rupee |
| India | Rupee | Sweden | Krona |
| Indonesia | Rupiah | Switzerland | Franc |
| Iran | Rial | Tanzania | Shilling |
| Iraq | Dinar | Thailand | Baht |
| Poland | Pound | Turkey | Lira |
| Israel | Shekel | United Kingdom | Pound |
| Italy | Lira | Urguay | New Peso |
| Ivory Coast | CFA Franc | Venezuela | Bolivar |
| Jamaica | Dollar | Zaire | Zaire |
| Japan | Yen | Zambia | Kwacha |

*fundamentalist.* A securities analyst who is primarily concerned with general economic factors in determining whether or not the stock of particular corporations is worth considering. Rather than just looking at stock market activity (the averages, indicators, etc.), he looks specifically at the national economic picture, the industrial markets, the current business cycle, the supply of and the cost of money. See Chapter Ten in the following text: Jerome B. Cohen, Edward D. Zinbarg, Arthur Zeikel, *Guide to Intelligent Investing* (Homewood, Ill.: Dow Jones-Irwin, 1977)

*going short.* To sell a security in the hope of making a profit from its decline in price. There is a great risk in selling short, for, from a theoretical standpoint, there is no limit to how high a stock can go. That is, a stock can only go as low as zero, so if you buy it at $50 per share, you known the most you can lose is $50 per share. But if you sell the same stock short at $50, well, it can go to $200 or more, wherein the loss is at least $150 per share. For further detail, see "bear" and "selling" short."

*gross spread.* The difference between the price paid for securities being underwritten and the price at which they will be made available to the public.

*guaranteed stock.* A stock for which another company has guaranteed to pay dividends, should the issuing company fail to meet its commitments to its stockholders.

*guilder.* Monetary unit in the Netherlands. For current foreign exchange rates see a copy of *The Wall Street Journal* or any other financial newspaper. For a list of currency units for major countries throughout the world see in this dictionary "foreign currency units."

*heavy market.* A market in decline because there are not enough buyers around. Stock prices are based solely on the law of supply and demand. If there is an abundance of stock and few buyers, the price of the stock will decline until the price is low enough to create demand.

**hedging.** An investment technique which usually results in dual orders, one to offset the other in case of unexpected moves in the market price. Buying long and also purchasing a put on the same stock would be an example of hedging.

**holder of record.** The owner of a particular security as of a certain date. The record date here is rather important, for when dividends or other special offerings are offered to shareholders, it is always to the holders of those shares as of a specific date.

**holding company.** The corporation which owns the majority of the stock in all subsidiary corporations. Corporations usually need specific authorization to have holdings in other corporations. They need not only legal permission, but also to have such authority expressly provided for in their corporate charters. The great financial advantage to a holding company is that it offers control of numerous businesses with minimal investment. The great legal advantage is the liability of the holding corporation is limited to the degree of investment in each subsidiary.

**hypothecation.** The offering of securities or other assets as collateral, yet retaining legal title to them.

**immediate order.** A floor order calling for immediate execution at some state price. The order contains an automatic cancellation "agreement" if even part of if cannot be executed according to the instructions. In this way, the buyer or seller is assured that the order is placed in regard to the exact quantity of stock desired for purchase or sale.

**inactive market.** The stock market when volume is relatively low. It does not mean that there is no activity at all. In today's market, 15 million shares traded would represent an inactive market.

**inactive securities.** Securities in which there is relatively low trading or no trading at all.

**in-and-out.** Generally, stock bought and sold on the same day or over a period of days or weeks. The in-and-out trader is the speculator. For a perspective on trading versus investing, see Chapter One in Benjamin Graham's *The Intelligent Investor* (New York: Harper & Row, 1973).

**income.** Specifically, any gain from investments in labor or capital. Income is generally specified as being "before" or "after" taxes. Wages, of course, are one example of income; interest on savings, or corporate dividends on stock owned, are other examples. Profits, however, are considered gains from investments, and there is an important distinction for tax purposes. Your dividends from stock will be treated as income by Internal Revenue, but your profits from stock transactions will be considered capital gains. Capital gains receive tax treatment.

**indicated yield.** The rate of return that will probably be realized from ownership in a particular stock. It is important to remember, however, that dividends are never guaranteed; that is why the term "indicated yield" is so appropriate. Corporations are not required to pay dividends unless they actually declare them. If you purchase a stock currently paying a dividend of $2.00 per year, you, by no means, have any guarantee that this dividend will be continued. Corporations not only do not have any legal obligation to pay dividends on common stock, but do not have any legal obligation to pay them on preferred stock.

**industrial stocks.** Common and preferred stock in corporations engaged in manufacturing and merchandising, as opposed to corporations in banking and finance or to utilities. Some of the major categories of industrial stocks include: automobile, brewing, broadcasting, business machines, metals, textiles, trucking. See Chapter Eight in this text for a listing.

*insider report.* Monthly report required by the Securities and Exchange Commission from officers, directors, and the larger stockholders of a corporation; it indicates their trading activity in their corporation's stock, as well as their current holdings. The report is only necessary if a trade has taken place.

*insiders.* Directors, officers, and the larger shareholders of a corporation. Like anyone else in a corporation, these people may not trade securities in their corporation as a result of special information they may receive as a result of their top-level information; they must wait until there has been public disclosure of any news which may effect stock prices. Stock watchers like to keep tabs on insider trading, for many believe such trades are an indication of the level of confidence top management has in the future performance of the stock.

*interim dividend.* A dividend distributed to shareholders before the regular dividend is distributed. For a discussion of the types of dividends, see Chapter Seven in this text.

*intermediate trend.* The tendency of the market in general, or of a stock in particular, to experience bull, bear, or levelling phases from which it may reverse, climb, or decline over the long term. See "The Investor and Market Fluctuations" in Benjamin Graham's *The Intelligent Investor* (New York: Harper & Row, 1973).

*in-the-money.* Term used to describe certain types of puts and calls. When the exercise of a *call* is less than the current quote for an underlying stock, the call is said to be in-the-money. When the exercise price of a *put* is higher than the current quote for the underlying stock, the put is said to be in-the-money. Thus the meaning of the term changes depending upon whether one is referring to a put or a call option.

*irregular market.* A market showing no indication of consistency. Some stock groups may move impressively high, others low. One general market indicator may contradict another. For instance, the Dow Jones Industrials may advance impressively, but there may be more stocks declining than advancing. You will find of interest, "The Investor and Market Fluctuations" in Benjamin Graham's *The Intelligent Investor* (New York: Harper & Row, 1973).

*issue.* Securities available for purchase.

*issued price.* The price at which a new issue of securities is offered to the public by an underwriter. See "underwriter" for a description of the terms under which stock is generally underwritten.

*issued stock.* A percentage of, or all of, the authorized stock actually sold to the public or which has been bought back by the corporation. See also "authorized stock."

*krona.* Monetary unit of Sweden. For current foreign exchange rates see a copy of *The Wall Street Journal* or any other financial newspaper. For a list of currency units by country, see in this dictionary, "foreign currency units."

*krone.* Monetary unit of Norway and Denmark. For current foreign exchange rates see a copy of *The Wall Street Journal* or any other financial newspaper. For a list of currency units by country, see in this dictionary "foreign currency units."

*leverage.* Making a little money do the work of more money. Margin purchases are an example of leverage. With $2,000 of his own money, an investor may purchase up to $4,000 of securities, the other $2,000 coming automatically from his broker—providing he has a margin account with enough buying power. If the stocks he has purchased double in the price, then he stands to make $6,000 ($8,000 less the $2,000 owed to the broker). Of course, if the stock went down 50% instead of up, he would lose everything! Leverage is a good means of increasing profits, and a good way to accelerate losses.

**limit order.** An order to a broker to buy or sell at a certain price and in certain quantity. An order to sell 100 shares of AT&T at $60½ is an example of a limit order. You will find of special interest, Louis Engel, *How To Buy Stock*, 6th ed. (Boston: Little, Brown, 1976).

**liquidating dividend.** Payments made to creditors and shareholder when a company is selling off certain assets and going out of business.

**liquidation.** Selling off the assets of a company in order to pay off all debt obligations. Also, selling all securities in an account and withdrawing the proceeds.

**liquidity.** A strong cash position to cover losses and to continue to operate normally. Liquidity also refers to a market situation wherein high volume does not result in much of a price change.

**liquidity dividends.** Non-taxable capital distributions representing payments to stockholders from their original investment. Each payment of a liquidity dividend results in a reduction of the value of each share held.

**liquidity preference.** When there is a trend toward the maintenance of cash positions (or checking accounts) rather than investment in securities. This results from a need or preference to have cash on hand for everyday activities because of fear of unexpected financial needs, or because of fear of rising interest rates which tend to reduce the value of securities.

**liquidity ratio.** The relationship of cash and ready assets to total current liabilities. If cash and ready assets total $500,000 and current liabilities total $250,000, the liquidity ratio is 2.0.

*lira.* Monetary unit used in Italy. For current foreign exchange rates see a copy of *The Wall Street Journal* or any other financial newspaper.

*listed securities.* Securities which are listed on an exchange. Each exchange has its own requirements which a corporation's stock must meet before it may be listed, yet the listing itself is no guarantee of investment worth. Some of the smaller exchanges have less rigid listing requirements than the New York Stock Exchange, yet there may very well be stocks on these smaller exchanges that are better investments than the ones on mainstream exchanges, given the current market trend and overall economic forecasts.

*listing requirements.* The rules and regulations an exchange sets forth for any corporation wishing to have its stock listed. These rules and regulations are by no means standard, and they vary considerably from exchange to exchange. They always specify the tangible assets, amount and value of publicly-held shares, net income, and capital requirements for all corporations seeking to be listed. Listing requirements can be acquired by simply writing to the exchange in which you are interested. For the addresses of exchanges located throughout the world, see the supplement to this dictionary.

*locked-in.* When an investor must hold on to a security because he will otherwise have to face extensive capital losses, or because there is little tax advantage in any capital gains during the current tax year.

*London Stock Exchange.* One of the oldest and most important stock exchanges in the world. It was first organized in 1773, but like the New York and American Stock Exchanges, it existed long before that on London streets. U.S. financial newspapers only list a portion of the stocks on the exchange. There are actually more than ten thousand stocks in its listing. It is a tightly structured organization, and is free of any government control. Its members are prohibited from advertising their services. Among the better known stocks listed on the exchange are: British GE, Reed International, and United Biscuit. You will find a partial listing of this exchange's securities of the major dailies. Please refer to the supplement to this dictionary for the address of this exchange, as well as listing of all exchanges worldwide.

*long.* Actually having ownership of a security. For instance, if you purchase 100 shares of RCA, you are "long on RCA." This means you have purchased the security with the intention of selling it later at a higher price. See "short sale."

*long pull.* The long-term objectives of someone purchasing a security. He is not looking for short-term capital gains, and probably will ignore intermediate trends. He is the investor rather than the speculator. For a comparison of investment and speculative approaches to the market, see Chapter One in Benjamin Graham's *The Intelligent Investor* (New York: Harper & Row, 1973).

*manipulating the market.* Using improper and often illegal methods to stimulate interest or disinterest in stocks, or possibly, even the market in general. Manipulation usually occurs through releasing information about a company's finances or market perspectives which may be interpreted in more than one way, and will probably be interpreted in the way the manipulator hopes.

*margin account.* A special account set up for a customer that allows him the privilege of purchasing securities with the additional funds provided by the broker. See Chapter Six in this text.

*margin call.* The payment request from a broker to his customer specifying the amount of funds which must be deposited in his margin account to offset losses incurred by an advancing or declining (if he has been a short-seller) market. The customer is required to send the money to his broker on notification, or else sell off securities from his account to cover the obligation. If the customer fails to act in a short time, the broker has the authority to sell off securities in the account to cover the margin requirement.

**margin requirements.** The amount of deposit required to purchase securities on margin. Margin requirements are set by the Federal Reserve Board. Stock exchanges often have their own additional requirements for margin accounts. The actual amount of money that may be borrowed from brokers on margin purchases varies according to Federal Reserve policies. In times past, margin requirements have varied considerably. (See Chapter 6 in this text.)

**mark.** Monetary unit of West Germany. For current foreign exchange rate see a copy *The Wall Street Journal* or any other financial newspaper.

**market.** Any place where buyers and sellers congregate for the purpose of conducting their transactions. The word does not necessarily indicate a physical place; it can also represent a means of business or a business environment in general.

**marketability.** The chances of successfully marketing securities; security; the chances of finding a buyer at some specific price.

**market averages.** Averages of stocks selected randomly, by industry, by market, or by exchange which are used along with other trend indictors to predict the direction of stock prices in general. Often, too much emphasis is placed upon the meaning hidden behind the averages. It is important for every investor to realize that the averages are only one of many guidelines to use in predicting the short-term or intermediate term of the market. For an introduction to "averages" and other indicators, see Justin Mannis, *When To Sell: Inside Strategies For Stock Market Profits* (New York: Farrar, Straus & Giroux, 1977).

***market cycle.*** The trend of the market to have first periods of advance which are followed by periods of leveling-off, and then declines before another major advance takes place. During any one of its major cycles, the market will normally experience bullish and bearish phases. The market rarely bee lines consistently in only one direction. See "Business Cycle analysis" in the following text: Jerome B. Cohen, Edward D. Zinbarb, Arthur Zeike, *Guide To Intelligent Investing* (Homewood, Ill: Dow Jones-Irwin, 1977)

***market letters.*** These are periodic reports that are published by brokerage firms and financial advisors for customers or subscribers. Generally, these letters are only available for a fee. Some of them are highly expensive. Usually the letters circulated by brokers are either free or low in subcription price. Those letters published by independents may run into hundreds of dollars per year. The letters generally evaluate the current economic situation, and try to predict both the overall stockmarket trend and the price movement of certain selected issues.

***market liquidation.*** When demand for stock is so low that sellers must continually lower their offering price to make a trade. The law of supply and demand governs stock prices, and as long as there is no one interested in buying a stock, its price will come down until a buyer can be attracted.

***market liquidity.*** A market which is able to float through trading sessions without sinking from the weight of reduced demand or rising from a wave of increased demand. There is generally high volume and relatively stable prices during periods of market liquidity. One must not confuse this expression with that of market liquidation.

***market is off.*** Prices have been on a decline: the number of shares being offered outweighs the current demand at present offering prices.

**market is on.** Prices have been advancing; the demand for securities exceeds the supply of shares willing to be offered at current bid prices.

**market order.** An order to purchase or to sell stock at whatever the current quote happens to be. The danger in market orders is that a stock may be selling at $10 at the time the market order is given to the broker, but at $11 by the time the order can be executed. A one dollar change in price, of course, does not sound like much to worry about, but when you are dealing in hundreds of dollars, the loss mounts up. For advice on when to buy and when to sell, see Richard A. Crowell, *Stock Market Strategy* (New York: McGraw-Hill, 1977).

**market price.** The price at which a security can be traded at any given moment. The market price of a stock is what the stock is actually worth. Many confuse par value or book value with market value, but these three terms have completely different meanings.

**market ratio.** The ratio of a company's sales to the sales of all companies in any particular industry in which it is marketing its goods. The ratio is important to analysts because it shows the strength of a particular corporation in relation to its competition. Whether or not the particular market it is in has any economic stability or growth potential is another important consideration in determining whether or not the stock is a worthwhile buy.

**market securities.** Securities which are offered to the public either through any of the formal exchanges or through the over-the-counter market. The exchanges and OTC markets are secondary markets for securities already sold to, and in the hands of, the public.

**market sentiment.** The optimism, pessismism, or indifference of the trading public. Many theories prevail about the effect of market sentiment on the long-term trend of stock prices. One holds that when optimism is at its highest, the business cycle is about to go into its recessionary phase and stock prices will herald the event by retreating toward new lows; and when pessisism is at its greatest, the business cycle is ready to rebound toward new highs.

***market value.*** The value of stocks and other securities based on what someone is willing to pay for them.

***markka.*** Monetary unit of Finland. For current foreign exchange rates see a copy of *The Wall Street Journal* or any other financial newspaper.

***Midwest Stock Exchange.*** One of the larger regional stock exchanges in the United States. It came about as the result of a merger in 1949 of exchanges then in existence in Cleveland, Minneapolis, St. Louis, and Chicago. See the supplement to this dictionary for the names and addresses of all major and most secondary stock exchanges worldwide.

***Montreal Stock Exchange.*** Canadian Exchange founded in 1874. Like its American counterparts, it had humble beginnings: a coffee house. In 1974, the exchange merged with the Canadian Stock Exchange—just one year after it had established a market surveillance department. Some of the securities listed on the exchange are the Bank of Montreal, National Bank of Canada, and the Royal Bank. Trading on the exchange is in Canadian dollars. (For current foreign exchange rates see a copy of *The Wall Street Journal* or any other financial newspaper.) The Montreal Exchange is not the only exchange in Canada; there are also exchanges in Canada, Toronto, Vancouver, and Winnipeg. You will find addresses of all exchanges worldwide listed in the supplement to this dictionary.

***narrow market.*** The stock market when volume is lower than usual and there is little price fluctuation. Even hard-and-fast speculators who will play certain stocks for movements of a quarter of a point or less cannot find suitable opportunities.

*National Association of Securities Dealers (NASD).* All brokers and dealers who specialize in trades of those securities in the over-the-counter market. It is a very well organized association of individuals and firms making their business in securities, and it has its own computer-based quotation system (NASDAQ). Not all over-the-counter stocks are included in NASDAQ, and the association is currently requiring those companies that wish their stocks listed on NASDAQ to meet certain financial and marketing requirements. The association is located at 1735 K Street, N.W., Washington, D.C. 2006.

*natural monopoly.* Control of a given market as a natural result of the size and efficiency of a particular company. Natural monopolies are perfectly legal in the United States as, by definition, they exist only in highly limited markets which can sustain only one producer anyway. Public utilities are a form of natural monopoly. You may find of special interest the following text on anti-trust and monopolies: Mark J. Green, *The Closed Enterprise System* (New York: Grossman, 1972).

*new high.* Top price reached by a particular security during some period of time, usually twelve months—however, the expression is relative and can relate to a single day's trading, a month's, or whatever period of time has been established as the measure. For instance, AT&T can be said to have reached a new high for the day or for the year—or for its entire history. Many analysts use the "new high" listings as "flags" for stocks which might be on their way to even further price advancement. But the new high that is reached by any given security should never by the only criteria for determining whether or not it is worthwhile buy. For what the investor should consider in tackling the market, see Benjamin Graham's *The Intelligent Investor* (New York: Harper & Row, 1973).

***new issue.*** Any security which is made available to the public for the very first time. Corporations usually bring out new issues to acquire the money for new capital investment or for expansion. New issues are not brought to the public through the stock exchanges, for the stock exchanges are secondary markets for shares already in the hands of the public.

***New York Stock Exchange.*** The world's largest stock exchange and the one with perhaps the most rigid requirements for corporations applying to have their securities listed. Known as the Big Board, it was founded in 1792 as a loosely knit association of brokers and financiers who traded in salves as well as securities. See the supplement to this dictionary for names and addresses of stock exchanges worldwide. For further research see Robert Sobel, *The Big Board, A History of the New York Stock Market* (New York: Free Press, 1965).

***New York Stock Exchange Index (Composite).*** One of the more popular indexes followed by investors. It records the changes in prices for all common stocks listed on the exchange. Financial sections of daily newspapers as well as the major financial publications usually publish the results. *Barron's*, a weekly financial which can be found on many newsstands, is a fine source for such statistics.

***no-limit order.*** An order to trade a security at the current market price. There is always the danger that from the time the order is given to the broker to the time it is finally executed, there will be a severe jump in the price of a security. Long-term investors will generally place no-limit orders, as they will generally hold their stock for a year or more and are not generally concerned with daily price fluctuation. The speculator, however, rarely places a market order, as he often "plays the point," which is to say he will often sell a stock after it has registered a one-point gain (or even less).

***no-load fund.*** A mutual fund, the shares of which can be purchased without having to pay a commission. The commission is referred to as the *load*. No-load refunds make their offerings directly to the public. *See* Donald D. Rugg, Norman B. Hale, *The Dow Jones Guide to Mutual Funds* (Homewood, Ill.: Dow Jones-Irwin, 1976).

**nominal price.** A price so low that is is hardly worth taking into account in deciding whether or not to enter into a transaction. Thus, unfortunately, the reason why many investors tend not to think twice about purchasing penny stocks. "At that price, it is worth the gamble,' is an expression heard many times. But if someone wants to turn a profit in the stock market, every dollar counts. Every investment decision should be taken seriously, whether it is in a 25 cent OTC stock or a $100 Big Board security.

**non-assessible stock.** A stock which cannot be assessed for any amount should the issuing corporation be declared insolvent. For the most part, all stocks are non-assessible. *See also* "par value."

**non-callable securities.** Securities which are not subject to a call-back by the issuing company.

**non-clearing house stock.** Stocks which have not been cleared by an exchange's clearing house because they are relatively unknown and inactive and hardly worth making a market in.

**non-cumulative dividends.** These are dividends on non-cumulatie preferred stock which need not be accumlated for payment by the corporation should they be omitted at any time. Thus, if the dividend payment on a non-cumulative preferred should be ommitted for any reason, the holders of that preferred have no legal claim against the corporation.

**non-stock moneyed corporation.** A corporation which is sub-

ject to banking or insurance law. It is, therfore, any corporation wich is not either a stock or a public corporation. Credit
unions and savings banks are examples of non-stock corporations.

***non-voting stock.*** Stock which does not allow shareholders
voting privileges. Most common stocks offer the owners the right
to vote for corporate directors, but preferred stocks never do
except under unusual circumstances.

***no-par stock.*** Stock issued without a specific dollar value. Par
value has little significance in the case of common stock; it is
simply an arbitrary amount for bookkeeping purposes. Old
timers will remember when the par value of a stock had something to do with the balance sheet of a corporation, but this is no
longer so. See also "par value."

***obsolete securities.*** In reference to corporate stock, this expression means those securities which no longer have any value
because the corporation no longer exists or exists in name only.
This term, however, is probably more frequently used to describe bonds which have matured or other securities, such as
warrants, which have also passed their expiration date and are
of no use to the holder.

***odd-lot.*** Any number of shares which total less than one hundred. The word is an antonym for round-lot which represents
shares in multiples of a hundred. There is a premium attached
to the cost of each share purchased in odd-lots. See "odd-lot
differential."

***odd-lot broker.*** A broker who specializes in arranging trades
of shares available in lost of less than one hundred. He services only other brokers, and has no dealings at all with the public.

***odd-lot differential.*** This is a price added to each share traded
in odd-lots; it compensates the odd-lot broker executing the

transaction. While the actual amount added to each share will differ with exchanges, it is generally 12½ cents per share.

*odd-lot theory.* One of those unusual concepts which tend to expect the market to move in a direction opposite to general expectation. Behind the theory is the idea that the small investor is generally ill-informed and will probably buy toward the end of a bull phase and sell toward the end of a bear phase. Thus, the theorists tally odd-lot trades to try and get a feel of the general trend of the public at large.

*offer.* The price at which someone is willing to sell a security. Thus, if you have 100 shares of American Motors and you give an order to your broker to sell them at $5½, you are *offering* your shares for that amount. That does not mean you will be able to unload them, for the closest bid may be $5¼.

*offered ahead.* Sell orders which have been submitted before yours and which will naturally have preference. Thus, if you offer to sell 500 shares of General Motors at $48 per share, there may be some 30,000 shares being offered at that same price that were entered before yours. General Motors may very well trade at $48 per share during the day, but there may not be enough buyers at that price to reach your 500.

*offer wanted.* An expression which indicates that there is a seller of stock seeking out bids.

*offset.* Buying or selling securities, long or short, to balance positions previously taken. There are, actually, a number of different transactions which investors enter into for the purpose of covering their positions, for heding, or for limiting risk. If you are interested in further research on investment tactics, see Richard A. Crowell, *Stock Market Strategy* (New York: McGraw-Hill, 1977).

*off-the-board.* Securities transactions which are conducted anywhere except one of the organized exchanges.

*on a scale.* Buying and selling securities at different price levels. These buy and sell orders are triggered automatically.

*on margin.* The expression refers to purchase of stock which has been made on margin. An investor may go long or short on margin purchases, as long as he has the minimum balance on account and can put up 50% of the purchase price for additional securities. Margin accounts are not for the beginner. While an individual can win big with the leverage afforded by margin, he can also lose big. See "Margin Yourself Into Debt" in Donald I. Rogers' *How Not to Buy A Common Stock* (New York: Arlington House, 1972).

*open-end investment company.* A mutual fund which investors can buy in and out of with no problem at all. See Donald D. Rugg, Norman B. Hale, *The Dow Jones—Irwin Guide to Mutual Funds* (Homewood, Ill. 1976), and John L. Springer, *The Mutual Fund Trap* (Chicago: Henry Regnery, 1973).

*opening price.* The price of the first transaction for the day in any given security, or, the opening offer of a new issue. For further reading, see "How The Opening Is Arranged" in Justin Mannis' *When To Sell: Inside Strategies For Stock Market Profits,* (New York: Farrar, Straus & Giroux, 1977).

*open order.* An order given to a broker which directs him to keep the order entered until it can be executed or until it is canceled or changed. It is no different from a good-till-canceled order and is given in the following matter: "Mr. Broker, please enter an open sell (or buy) order for 200 shares of Warner Communications at $60." For information on how to buy stocks, see Louis Engel, *How to Buy Stocks,* 6th rev. ed., Little,

Brown, Boston, 1976; Kiril Sokoloff, *The Thinking Investor's Guide to the Stock Market* (New York: McGraw-Hill, 1978).

**opportunity cost.** Generally, what it costs an individual to keep his money. In other words, if it is possible to earn $1,000 from a securities investment, but an individual prefers to leave his money in a savings account where he may only earn $200, his opportunity cost is $800. When the opportunity cost of money is high, individuals will generally convert that money into more valuable assets rather than hold onto it.

**option.** There are basically two types of stock options, one is termed a *put* and the other a *call.* The call option gives legal right to the buyer to purchase the underlying security at a fixed price until the expiration date of the call; anyone may be either a buyer of seller (writer) of a call. The put option gives legal right to the buyer to sell the underylying securiety at a fixed price until the expiration date of the put; anyone may either buy or sell a put. Buying options has become quite popular with large and small investors alike. They can get a relatively high return from a relatively small amount of money; they can diversify their portfolios because the low price of the options allows their money to be distributed over many contracts or some combination of stock, bond, warrant, rights, and options purchases; they can be assured that their losses will be no more than what they had to put up for the option plus any broker commission. Sellers of options are usually after the premiums (selling price) the puts or calls will bring to them, but their motives may go beyond simply the receipt of the premium, and may be writing the puts or calls as part of any number of investment strategies. See also "put" and "call." For further research, see Jerome Turille, *Everything The Beginner Needs To Know To Invest Shrewdly* (New Rochelle, NY: Arlington House 1973); and Gary L. Gastineau, *The Stock Option Manual,* 2nd ed. (New York: Mc-Graw-Hill, 1979).

**optional dividend.** A dividend which is offered to a shareholder in cash or in some form other than cash, the actual form of the payment being left up to the shareholder.

**option writer.** An investor dealing in options whose objectives include quick income in the form of the premiums for which the option may be bought. For further detail, see Chapter 9 in this text and the recommended reading list under "option" in this appendix.

**out-of-the-money.** Term used to describe certain types of puts and calls. When the exercise price of a call is higher than the current quote of the underlying stock, the *call* is said to be out-of-the-money. When the exercise price of a put is lower than the current quote of the underlying stock, the *put* is said to be out-of-the-money. See also "at-the-money" and "in-the-money."

**outside market.** Any market which has been created for the purpose of trading unlisted securities.

**outsiders.** Individuals who trade without the the financial community. The term has come to mean just about any independent investor who does not depend on market trades for his or her primary income.

**outside securities.** Any securities which have no listing on any of the recognized exchanges. The fact that they are not listed, however, is not an indication that they represent pure gambles by the trading public. Many unlisted securities are worthwhile investments.

**overbought.** When a stock has met with such interest that speculators have forced the price of its shares to unusually high levels and there is strong probability that prices will drop back considerably. See William L. Jiler, *How Charts Can Help You In The Stock Market,* (New York: Trendline, 1962).

*overcapitalization.* When capital investments of a corporation far outweigh the potential return from these investments. *Note:* this term is also used to convey a very different meaning: that a corporation's capital is not equal in value to the property which secures it.

*Over-the-Counter (OTC).* A market created for the trading of all securities, both those listed on the major exchanges as well as those which are unlisted. The quality of the stocks traded on the OTC differs markedly. Some are penny stocks, some new issues. But there are also high-quality stocks which the investors would be wise to investigate. Just about all U.S. government securities and almost all municipal and corporate bonds are traded here. The main problem in dealing with OTC issues in the past was that the investors and researcher could not expect a minimum standard for the issues being offered. However, through the creation of an organization titled the National Association of Securities Dealers (NASD), the OTC Market has developed into a well-organized electronic auction center. The secret to NASD's success has been the automatic quotation system call NASDAQ (National Association of Securities Dealers Automatic Quotation System). OTC stocks are now divided into two main categories: those that subscribe to NASDAQ and those that do not. Subscribers must meet certain financial and market requirements to remain a part of the automatic quotation system. See Leo M. Loll and Julian Buckley, *The Over-the-Counter Securities Market,* 4th ed. (Englewood Cliffs, N.J.: Prentice Hall, 1981)

*overtrade.* To buy and sell with speculative fever; the result is a constant turnover of one's portfolio and usually more profit to the broker than the investor. See Jerome B. Cohen, Edward D. Zinborg, Arthur Zeubel, *Guide To Intelligent Investing* (Homewood, Ill. Dow Jones-Irwin, 1977).

*owner of record.* The shareholder who has legal ownership of a given security as of a certain date and is entitled to whatever dividends or other distributions are owed stockholders up until that time.

**Pacific Stock Exchange.** A large regional exchange in the United States. It came about as the result of a merger of the Los Angeles and San Francisco stock exchanges. The San Francisco Stock Exchange had its beginnings back in 1882; and the Los Angeles Stock Exchange, originally the Los Angeles Oil Exchange, dates back to 1899. The Pacific Stock Exchange still maintains separate trading floors in the cities of Los Angeles and San Francisco; however, the floors are teleconnected to each other for the swift relay of information. You will find a partial listing of this exchange's securities in any of the financial newspapers or in the financial section of the major dailies. Please refer to the supplement to this dictionary for the address of this exchange as well as a listing of all exchanges worldwide.

**paid-in capital.** Capital which comes to a corporation as a result of stockholder contributions and which is accounted for as other than capital stock.

**panic.** Unusually high volume selling. The panic may be resulted to a specific issue or to the market in general. There are many technical theories about the cause of panics, but they all generally point to overspeculation in the market during times of tight money and rising prices. See Charles D. Ellis, *The Second Crash: How The Stock Market Went the 1929 Route in 1970* (New York: Simon & Schuster, 1973); and John Kenneth Galbraith, *The Great Crash 1929* (New York: Houghton Mifflin, 1970).

**paper.** Commerical paper: notes, drafts, and any other type of negotiable paper used for commercial transactions.

**paper profits.** Profits which have not been actually realized. In terms of tax strategy, investors will often tend to take their losses for the resulting reduction in taxes, but keep their profits "on paper" for as long as it may be practical; however, if a stock has peaked, and the investor can realize the fact, it is always best to realize the actual profit regardless of tax consequences; investor preoccupation with tax saving schemes can result in greater losses than if he or she traded without tax implication. For example, you may have purchased 100 shares of McGraw-Hill at $32 per share, and now it is $42 per share. You have a $10 per share profit to date—but it is only on paper. You cannot actually realize the gain until you sell the shares in your posession. If you decide not to realize that profit by cashing in the stock because you are afraid of the tax consequences, you may be in the awfully embarrassing position of watching your profits, and possibly principal, disappear if the stock suddenly goes south. Be careful about tax selling, and always consult your accountant and broker before making any major decisions.

**par.** In a strictly technical sense, 100 per cent quality. It is the value represented by the number printed on the face of a certificate. In terms of stock certificates, it is important for the investor to note that the only true value of a security is what someone is willing to pay for it, which is to say that its only true value is its market price.

**par amount (value).** The face value of a share of stock. Par value has a completely different application for preferred shares than for common shares. Common shares may very well be issued without any par value, as par has little significance to common; in this case the shares are assigned a capital value simply for accounting purposes. (Those of us who have been around for sometime may remember when the par value of common had something to do with a company's balance sheet; but no longer is this true.) The par on preferred is used as a basis for determining the dividend payment. See also "preferred stock."

**peseta.** Monetary unit used in Spain. For current foreign exchange rates see a copy of *The Wall Street Journal* or any other financial newspaper.

*peso.* Monetary unit of Argentina, Colombia, Mexico, the Philippines and Uruguay. For current foreign exchanges rates see a copy of *The Wall Street Journal* or any other financial newspaper.

*playing the market.* Generally, investing for short-term capital gains. When someone is playing the market, he or she is generally trading quite heavily, often selling out or covering short positions after price movements of only a point. Playing the market is no easy game, and the percent of one's savings invested in market trading should be minimal; many financial counselors recommend no more than 10% of one's savings be tied up in the stock market. Before one even invests a penny, he or she should become aware of stock investing basics; economics (particularly in the area of the money supply and interest rates and their effect on the stock market), and, of course, the fundamental arithmetic involved in the buying and selling of securities.

*point.* Each one-dollar movement in the price of a shares. Thus, if someone reports that RCA has just advanced two points, he or she is indicating that the price per share has increased $2.

*portfolio.* Holdings of stocks or other securities. It is always recommended that one keep their portfolio of stocks as diverse as possible. For many small investors, this is not always possible, for they have not the funds to take worthwhile positions in more than one or two securities at a time. Thus, the particular popularity of stock options as well as warrants and rights.

*position.* One's present holdings in certain securities. For example, if you own stock in AT&T and Warner Communications, one would say that you have a position in both AT&T and Warner Communications.

*pound.* Monetary unit used in Britain and Lebanon. For current foreign exchange rates see a copy of *The Wall Street Journal* or any other financial newspaper.

**precedence.** When one buy or sell order has priority over another.

**preferred stock.** Capital stock in a corporation which gives the holder the right to his share of the dividends before they are distributed to any common shareholder. In the cases of reorganization or bankruptcy, preferred stockholders also have precedence over common stockholders during the distribution of remaining assets. Preferred stocks generally trade in a rather narrow range, usually pay higher dividends. Preferred stock may be *cumulative, non-cumulative,* or *participating.* Cumulative preferred requires that all delinquent dividends must be paid in full before any distributions are made to common shareholders. Non-cumulative does not guarantee payment of delinquent dividends. Participating means the shareholder is not only entitled to regular dividends, but also special payments should the corporation realize excess profits of some predetermined amount. Preferred shares generally do not offer the holder voting privileges. See also "dividends."

**premium.** Generally, the difference between the original price at which a security is offered and the increased price which you may actually pay for it. Thus, if a security is offered at $100 and you purchase it at $110, you have paid a premium of $10. The term applies more to the bond market than to the stockmarket, for bonds are always either selling at a discount from their face value or at a premium from their face value.

**premium stock.** This expression has come to mean a stock of superior quality, one that offers its oner relatively steady and safe income, and relatively good chances of capital gains over the long term. Premium stocks will always fluctuate in price much like any other stock, but his changes will usually not be as extreme as those of what be called "more speculative issues."

Investors generally look to premium stocks for "total yield"—
that is, both a fair dividend and the possibility of good capital
gains when the stock is finally sold.

**Price-Earnings (P/E) Ratio.** The market value of a company's stock divided by the per-share earnings of the company.
Thus, if a company's stock is selling at $20 and its earnings per
share is $5, then the P/E ratio is 4. Stock listings do not give
the earnings per share but they do give the P/E ratio and the
current market quote. Simply by dividing the price by the P/E
ratio one determines, then, the current earnings per share for
the listed stock. The average P/E ratio will be different for stocks
in various industries, so there is no standard price-to-earnings
ratio at which at stock should sell. The P/E ratio, however, is
one of the criteria used in selecting stocks, but by no means the
only one. See United Business Service, *Successful Investing, A
Complete Guide to Your Financial Future* (New York: Simon &
Schuster, 1979).

**put.** A contract which gives its owner the right to sell stock at
a specific price over a period of time. It is a type of option contract, and the opposite of a call. It is important to note that what
the buyer and seller of the contract are dealing in are contracts
rather than the actual stock itself. If, after the time period has
elapsed, the holder of the contract fails to exercise his option
to sell the stock, then he simply loses the amount he paid for
the contract. That is to say, that if he purchased the right to sell
XYZ Corporation at $70 because he thought it would fall in
price, and he paid $800 for that contract, if, by the expiration
date, XYZ is still at $70 and there is no profit in exercising the
option, then all he loses is $800. If XYZ dropped to $50 within the time period, he stands to make a great deal by exercising his option. Investors tend to favor put and call options as
a means for "insuring" their positions and for diversifying their
porfolios. Options are tricky business, however, and you should
consult your broker or an investment specialist before attempting
to buy either puts or calls on your own. There are strict margin

requirements in some cases. See Chapter Fourteen in United Business Service's *Successful Investing, A Complete Guide to Your Financial Future* (New York: Simon & Schuster, 1979).

**quarter stocks.** Stocks which have a par value of $25.

**quick assets.** Current assets excluding inventories. Assets termed "quick" are those which can be converted into cash in less than a year.

**quick ratio.** The ratio of a company's current liquid assets to its current liabilities. Thus, if the current liquid assets equal $200,000 and the current liabilities are $100,000, then the quick ratio is 2 to 1.

**quotation.** The listed price of a security. It represents the highest offer and/or the lowest bid.

**quotation board.** The scoreboard of stock transactions that used to be found spread across one of the walls in a brokerage office before the age of electronics.

**rand.** Monetary unit of South Africa. For current foreign exchange rates see a copy of *The Wall Street Journal* or any other financial newspaper.

**refunding.** The retiring of earlier securities with the proceeds of a newer issue. The earlier issue need not be fully refunded, and the refunding can be effected anytime before the maturity date on the older securities.

**regional exchange.** Security exchanges located in cities other than New York. These exchanges generally do not have the same stringent requirements as the larger exchanges: however, many of the securities they list are for corporations worth researching. Profits can be made anywhere in the stock market, on the large exchanges, on the regional exchanges, in the over-the-counter. Money also can be lost anywhere. Where a stock is listed is no indication of its value as an investment. Stocks on the regionals are often potential moneymakers. Many of the stocks they list also have listings on the New York, American, or other stock exchanges. See the supplement to this dictionary for a list of all regional and foreign exchanges.

**registered representative.** An individual who has met the requirements to deal in securities for either the firm with which he is employed or for his own clients. You may know him as the account executive or the customer's broker in the firm through which you buy and sell securities. You may find of special interest the comments in Chapters Eight and Nine of Donald I. Rogers, *How Not To Buy Common Stocks* (New York: Arlington House, 1972) in which he discusses the role of the broker and how to get the most out of him.

**registered trader.** Any member of the New York Stock Exchange who has earned the right to trade for his individual account right on the exchange floor. For an inside look at the people and activities on an exchange floor, see Leonard Sloane *The Anatomy of the Floor: The Trillion-Dollar Market at the New York Stock Exchange* (Garden City, N.Y.: Doubleday, 1980).

**registration statement.** A document detailing the investment characteristics of a new issue to be offered to the public. The securities which the statement defines and explains generally are not made available until thirty days after the filing date—the time it usually takes for the statement to become effective. For further information on new issues see the chapter on "New Security Issues" in John Prime's *Investment Analysis* (Prentice Hall, N.J.: Englewood Cliffs, 1967).

**regular dividend.** The amount of money that a corporation usually distributes to its shareholders. Sometimes, in addition to this regular payout, when business so warrants, there are extra dividend payments to either common or preferred shareholders.

*regular way sale.* Generally, when someone takes a long position in a security.

*Regulation Q.* A banking regulation which establishes the maximum rates that are available on time deposits from the U.S. commercial banking system. Regulation Q is one of the Federal Reserve system's tools for controlling the flow of money without affecting the money supply.

*Regulation T.* A Federal Reserve regulation that controls the amount of credit made available to investors by brokers and dealers. Investors who trade securities on margin are greatly influenced by Reg. T requirements, for they depend heavily on broker credit to get the leverage they need to make their investments worthwhile. See also "margin." For information on margin accounts, see the following: United Business Service *Successful Investing: A Complete Guide to Your Financial Future* (New York: Simon & Schuster, 1979); Conrad W. Thomas, *How To Sell Short & Perform Other Wondrous Feats* (Homewood, Ill,: Dow Jones-Irwin, 1876).

*reorganization.* Mainly, the recapitalization of a corporation which is in serious financial difficulty. The objectives are to see that all debt obligations can be met and that the enterprise itself can continue to operate successfully.

*return on investment.* A synonym for yield, it is the income received from an investment. Interest from bank accounts or bonds represents a return on investment just as dividends do. The return on investment is almost always given in percent. Thus, if you paid $1,000 for shares of stock in a corporation, and the total dividends you receive from then comes to $100 per year, then your return on your investment is 10% ($100 divided by $1,000). See "tell-tale ratios" in Chapter 8 of this text.

**reverse split.** When a corporation reduces the number of shares outstanding. It does this by distributing to its stockholders a lesser amount of shares in return for what they now hold. Thus, the corporation may return to you one share of its corporate stock for every two that you have, making obsolete the former shares. You still have the same percent of ownership in the corporation, although the price of the stock has now doubled. For example, suppose that you have 100 shares in a corporation worth $2 per share. The total value of your holdings is $200. After the one-for-two split you now have 50 shares, but each is worth $4 and the total value of your holdings is still $200. Corporations generally ask permission from their stockholders for reverse splits when the market price of the shares is at an usually low level. For a primer on this and other related subjects, see Chapter Seven in this text.

**ringgit.** Monetary unit of Malaysia. For current foreign exchange rates see a copy of *The Wall Street Journal* or any other financial newspaper.

**riyal.** Monetary unit of Saudi Arabia. For current foreign exchange rates see a copy of *The Wall Street Journal* or any other financial newspaper.

**round lot.** One hundred shares of stock, or multiples thereof, although technically a round lot is any normal unit of trading adopted by a securities exchange. In the United States, the round lot is 100 shares, except for certain inactive issues (in which case the round lot, or normal trading lot, is 10 shares). See also "odd-lot" and "odd-lot differential." See United Business Service, *Successful Investing, A Complete Guide To Your Financial Future* (New York: Simon & Schuster, 1979).

**round-lot orders.** Orders for shares of stock in multiples of 100. See "round lot."

**run off.** Late ticker tape printouts as a result of extraordinarily heavy trading.

**rupee.** Monetary unit of India. For current foreign exchange rates see a copy of *The Wall Street Journal* or any other financial newspaper.

**rupiah.** Monetary unit used in Indonesia. For current foreign exchange rates see a copy of *The Wall Street Journal* or any other financial newspaper.

**saddled.** Being caught with a stock that is now selling at a price less than for what it sold. The investor has little choice but to hold onto the stock and thus tie up his money, or else sell it and take the loss. For advice on when to buy and sell, see the following texts: Richard A. Crowell, *Stock Market Strategy,* (New York: McGraw-Hill, 1977); Ira Cobleigh, *The Dowbeaters; How To Buy Stocks That Go Up* (New York: Macmillan, 1979); Justin Mamis, *When To Sell: Inside Strategies for Stock Market Profits* (New York: Farrar, Straus & Giroux, 1977).

**saturation point.** When buyers have lost interest in a stock after an extended buying spree, and the price of the shares begins to decline. The decline may be moderate and short-lived, or it may possibly be extensive and long-term, depending upon other market conditions. For intermediate-level texts on this and related subjects, see Kiril Sokoloff, *The Thinking Investor's Guide To The Stock Market* (New York: McGraw-Hill, 1978); Harry Brown, *Inflation Proofing Your Investments* (New York: Morrow, 1981); Jerome B. Cohen, Edward D. Zinbaire, Arthur Zeikel, *Guide To Intelligent Investing* (Homewood, Ill.: Dow Jones-Irwin, 1977).

**schilling.** Monetary unit of Austria. For current foreign exchange rates see a copy of *The Wall Street Journal* or any other financial newspaper.

**scrip.** Any certificate or form which can be used as money, though only in certain environments. In the case of stock, scrip represents the right to receive money or shares of stock in some amount determined by the face value of the scrip.

**scrip dividend.** A dividend which is distributed in the form of a promissary note to pay the holder, at some time in the future, cash, stock, or some other negotiable instrument.

**seasoned stocks.** Securities issued by corporations which have a long history of stability. These corporations usually have a record of continued and increasing dividends and price appreciation. They are favored by investors because of their relatively low risk.

**seat.** A membership in any exchange. The word is a throwback to a time when members actually were given seats on an exchange. Today there are no longer any seats, but the term has been carried over to mean simply membership. The price of membership on exchanges varies, determined simply by the law of supply and demand. A seat must be purchased from another member. Prices of seats have ranged from a mere $500 to several hundreds of thousands of dollars. See Robert Sobel *The Big Board, A History of the New York Stock Market* (New York: Free Press, 1965). For additional reading you might want to see Leonard Sloane, *The Anatomy of the Floor: The Trillion Dollar Market of the New York Stock Exchange* (New York: Doubleday, 1980); Anthony W. Tabell, *The Anatomy of Wall Street* (Philadelphia: Lippincott, 1968).

**secondary market.** The market for securities which comes into being after the shares are first issued to the public. This is the market in which you and I presently trade securities; that is, the market created by the stock exchanges. For a listing of stock markets around the world, see the supplement to this directory. For information on how to trade stocks and options, see Yale L. Meltzer, *Putting Money To Work: An Investment Primer* (Englewood Cliffs, N.J.: Prentice Hall, 1976); Donald I. Rogers, *How Not To Buy A Common Stock* (New York: Arlington House, 1972); United Business Service, *Successful Investing: A Complete Guide to Your Financial Future* (New York: Simon & Schuster, 1979); Louis Engel, *How To Buy Stock*, 6th rev. ed. (Boston: Little Brown, 1976); Conrad W. Thomas, *How To Sell Short & Perform Other Wondrous Feats* (Homewood, Ill.: Dow Jones-Irwin, 1976).

**secondary movement.** Bull phases during a bear market, or bear phases during a bull market. The stock market never moves in one direction only. It moves in pulse-like patterns, up and down, up and down—with each jump or decline going a little bit further than the last. In every bull market there exists opportunities for short sellers, and in every bear market opportunities for those who buy long.

**secondary stocks.** These are corporate stocks which are usually volatile because investors are unsure of their long-term possibilities and tend to pull out of them when they weaken under certain market conditions. They may offer the possibility for high income and extensive capital gains, but they also offer extensive risk. For intermediate-level texts on this and related subjects, Ira Cobleigh, *The Dowbeaters; How To Buy Stocks That Go Up* (New York: Macmillan, 1979); Joseph E. Granville, *Granville's New Strategy for Daily Stock Market Timeing For Maximum Profit* (Englewood Cliffs, N.J.: Prentice Hall, 1976).

**second preferred stock.** A class of preferred stock which takes second place to other preferred issues when it comes to the distribution of dividends during regular business or the dividing of assets during liquidation.

**security.** Any legal certificate or document that gives evidence of ownership of property. To the investor, a security is any stock, bond, option, or other note of indebtedness in which he may trade.

***Securities and Exchange Commission (SEC).*** An independent U.S. government agency which has as its sole purpose the protection of the public from investment fraud. The commission consists of a five-member board, each member appointed by the president for a five-year term. The commission not only seeks to prohibit all types of security fraud, but also any manipulative practices, intentional or unintentional, which leave the unsuspecting public at a disadvantage in dealing with brokers and dealers on the registered exchanges or in the over-the-counter market.

***selling against the box.*** A technique used by investors to protect their paper profits. It involves selling short on a security to the extent of your present ownership in the stock. For example, suppose you have 100 shares of stock which you are afraid will soon decline in price. To insure your position, you sell short 100 shares of the stock, but engage your broker to buy 100 shares to make the delivery. You still have the 100 shares you own. If the stock does indeed decline, the loss is offset by the profit accumulating from your short sale. If the stock should advance, the profit accumulating will compensate for the loss from the short sale. You have the option of closing out your short sale whenever you feel it necessary by simply buying back the 100 shares sold short and having your broker return them to the lender. Why all this complicated trading just to stay even before commissions? Well, investors sell against the box to postpone any tax liabilities that would otherwise result.

***selling climax.*** A mass selling of positions, it usually heralds the end of a bear market and the beginning of a bull market.

***shareholder.*** Synonym for stockholder. The shareholder, unlike the bond owner, actually owns a piece of the corporation and shares in its profits. If an investor is a common shareholder, then he probably also has the right to vote, although all classes of common do not carry voting privileges.

**shareholder's equity.** This is an accounting expression and it means exactly the same as net worth or owner's equity. It is revealed in every balance sheet and is simply the difference between all assets and liabilities. For a very effective introduction to the balance sheet and other accounting terminology, see Allen Sweeney, *Accounting Fundamentals For Nonfinancial Executives* (New York: AMACOM, 1972).

**shares.** The amount of stock which is owned. Stock is distributed in unit amounts. Each unit is called a share. The amount of shares that anyone may own is represented by certificates which may be printed with almost any face value. This face value is not the par value of the stock. One shareholder may own 100 shares of stock represented by two $50 certificates; another may own 100 shares of stock represented by one $100 certificate.

**shekel.** Monetary unit used in Israel. For current foreign exchange rates see a copy of *The Wall Street Journal* or any other financial newspaper.

**short.** To sell a stock, which you do not own, with the intention of buying it back at a lower price. For instance, you may feel that IBM is about to decline in price, so you give the following order to your broker: "Mr. Broker, please sell short 100 shares of IBM at $70 per share for my account." The broker, in turns, borrows the 100 shares from some other account, so he can execute the transaction. If IBM declines to $60 per share, then you can give the following order to your broker: "Mr. Broker, I would like to cover my short position on 100 shares of IBM. Please put in my bid at $60 per share." If the transaction is executed you will have made a $10 per share profit. However, if the stock had increased in price, then you would have lost money. See also "bear" and "short sale" for further clarification and for reference texts.

**short account.** An account which specializes in short sales. See "bear," "short," "short against the box," and "short sale."

**short coverage.** Terminating a short position in a security by entering a buy order for the same amount of shares of the stock sold short. See "bear," "short," "short against the box," and "short sale." For the details of short-selling, see Conrad W. Thomas, *How to Sell Short & Perform Other Wondrous Feats*, (Homewood, Ill.: Dow Jones-Irwin, 1976).

**short interest.** The total amount of short sales which are outstanding. The short interest may be in a given security, an entire account, or on an exchange. Stock exchanges usually publish short interest statistics on a weekly basis.

**short sale.** The selling of a stock or stocks that are not actually owned by the seller. The short sale is made in anticipation of declining prices. The short seller is looking to either insure the paper profits he has as a result of a long position, or else he is looking for capital gains as a result of a declining market in the subject shares. See also "bear," "short," and "short against the box." For further reading, see Justin Mannis, *When to Sell: Inside Strategies For Stock Market Profits* (New York: Farrar, Straus & Giroux, 1977); Conrad W. Thomas, *How to Sell Short & Perform Other Wondrous Feats* (Homewood, Ill.: Dow Jones-Irwin, 1976).

**short seller.** One who sells stock that he does not own in the hopes of buying it back at a lower price. He reverses the normal trading situation. His profit or loss, however, is still determined by the difference between buy and sell prices. See "short." For a discussion of how short sales can be used in tax planning, see Jack Crestol and Herman M. Schneider, *Tax Planning For Investors: A Guide to Securities Investment and*

*Tax Shelters* (Princeton: Dow Jones Books, 1979); Conrad W. Thomas, *How to Sell Short & Perform Other Wondrous Feats* (Homewood, Ill.: Dow Jones-Irwin, 1976)

**short side.** The side of market activity which is favored by the bears, those who see profit from a declining market in a given security or securities. See "short" and "short sale."

**short stock.** Stock that has been sold by someone who does not own it and has not yet covered his position by buying an equal number of shares. See "short" and "short sale."

**short term.** From strictly a tax standpoint, any security which has not been held long enough to take advantage of long-term capital gains rates. The actual period which a security must be held to qualify for long-term capital gains status depends upon current legislation. See "capital gains," "selling against the box," and "short." For tax strategies, see Jack Crestol and Herman M. Schneider, *Tax Planning For Investors: A guide To Securities Investment and Tax Shelters* (Princeton: Dow Jones Books, 1979).

**short term notes.** Any obligations which must be met in a year or less.

**special offering.** The selling of an unusually large block of shares that, if handled in the normal way, would put unfair pressure on the price of the subject security. These special offerings must be approved by the exchange on which they will be traded. On some occasions, there is such interest in an offering of this sort that the stock becomes oversubscribed. In these instances, shares are allotted according to bid sizes.

**specie.** The gold or silver on which currency value is based and—theoretically—for which the currency should be able to be redeemed.

**speculate.** To buy and sell securities frequently in the hopes of securing capital gains. The speculator is generally not interested in long-term investments or dividend income. He is generally a margin account and will sometimes turn over stock so quickly that he need not put up any money. Those who prefer to speculate in the market are often willing to take risks that the income-oriented investor would wince at. Speculating is risky business. See Chapter One in Benjamin Graham's, *The Intelligent Investor* (New York: Harper & Row, 1973).

**speculator.** The investor who is willing to take great risks to turn over a quick profit. He will usually play the market both ways, which is to say that he will go long or short depending upon where he believes the profit will come from. The speculator is good business for the broker who is receiving a commission on each buy and sell transction. Speculation often make hundreds of each buy and sell transaction. Speculator often make hundreds of trades in the course of a year. Should you be interested in speculating, first read Donald I. Rogers, *How Not To Buy Common Stocks* (New York: Arlington House, 1972); Jerome B. Cohen, Edward D. Zinburg, Arthur Zeubel, *Guide To Intelligent Investing* (Homewood, Ill.: Dow Jones-Irwin, 1977); and Benjamin Graham, *The Intelligent Investor* (New York: Harper & Row, 1973).

**stock market.** The market created for the purchase and sale of corporate securities by any of the stock exchanges in the world today. The prices of stocks are controlled solely by the law of supply and demand, and often stock prices will go in the opposite direction that current corporate earnings are going. Stocks are assigned a par value for bookkeeping purposes and have a book value based on corporate earnings, but the only real value of a stock is what someone else is willing to pay for it. The underlying factors that create demand for stocks in general or one stock in specific are many, and every investor must be alert to these variables that control market activity. For texts on the market and related subjects, see the following: Leonard

Sloane, *The Anatomy of the Floor: The Trillion Dollar Market of the New York Stock Exchange* (New York: Doubleday, 1980); Anthony W. Tabell, *The Anatomy of Wall Street* (Philadelphia: Lippincott, 1968).

**stock option.** A contract which gives to the purchaser the right to buy or sell corporate stock at a certain price but within a specified period of time. Investors dealing in options are simply dealing in "right," not actually in the corporate stock itself. Buying and selling options has become a popular means of speculating for both large and small investors alike. This is because options ofer a relatively high return from what is, when compared to an investment in stock, a relatively small amount of money, offer the small investor the opportunity to diversify his portfolio with little money, offer the investor insurance that his or her losses will be no more than what was required to buy the option. See also "puts," "calls," "spreads," and "straddles." For a good reference text on stock option, see Gary L. Gastineau, *The Stock Option Manual,* 2nd ed. (New York: McGraw-Hill, 1979). You will find of additional interest the following books which deal with options and related topics: *Successful Investing: A Complete Guide To Your Financial Future,;* (New York: Simon & Schuster, 1979); and Jack Crestol and Herman M. Schneider, *Tax Planning For Investors: A Guide To Securities Investment and Tax Shelter* (Princeton: Dow Jones Books, 1979).

**stock purchase warrants.** Options that entitle an owner to purchase shares in an underlying stock for a certain period of time. Stock purchase warrants are often considered equity privileges as they are usually made available only to holders of certain corporate securities; but they may also be issued to the public. Some warrants are issued without an expiration date. If you are the holder of a warrant, you must realize that you own the warrant—or the right to purchase the stock—not the stock itself. And, you must purchase the stock the warrant entitles you to before the warrant reaches beyond its expiration date. When dividends are declared on the stock, you receive nothing because you are owner of the warrant not owner of the stock. The basic value of a warrant is closely related to the current value of the stock for which it has been issued. To determine the value of a warrant, substract the exercise price of the warrant from the current market price of the common stock for which it has been issued; when you derive the answer, multiply it by the number of shares the warrant entitles you to purchase; the answer is the (theoretical) value of the warrant.

**stock ratings.** The assignment of alpha codes to grade the quality of common and preferred stocks. For instance, A + indicates highest rating, A the next highest, A- above average and so on. The alpha characters used to grade preferred stocks differ from those used for common. For instance, in the Standard & Poor's rating guide for preferreds:

$$
\begin{aligned}
AAA &= \text{Prime} \\
AA &= \text{High Grade} \\
A &= \text{Sound} \\
BBB &= \text{Medium Grade} \\
BB &= \text{Lower Grade} \\
B &= \text{Speculative} \\
C &= \text{Submarginal}
\end{aligned}
$$

It is important for the investor to realize that these ratings are only meant as a flag, and before any decision is made to buy or sell either a common or preferred stock, a thorough analysis is necessary.

**stock rights.** Corporate offers to stockholders which allow them to purchase additional stock in some ratio to the shares they presently own. For instance, a corporation may give the stockholder the privilege of purchasing at a discount from market one share of a new issue for each ten that they own. Corporations offer special rights such as these to raise additional funds from stockholders, as well as create further interest in their securities.

**stock split.** Dividing the corporation's capital stock into a greater number of shares, each of these shares, however, having their par value reduced accordingly. This is to say that if a corporation has 10 million shares of stock with a par value of $20 before a split, after the split it will have outstanding 20 million shares of stock at $10 par. Corporations usually split stock when they are anticipating near-term issuance of new stock and want the price at a favorable level. The stockowner winds up with twice as many shares, but the same proportionate share of ownership in the corporation as well as the same total dollar value of holdings. However, stock investors usually like the idea of a split because it gives them leverage. Before a split, a stockholder may have 100 shares at $20 each. Each $1 increase in market price is $100 in paper profits for him. After the split he has 200 shares at $10 each. Each $1 increase in the share of the stock now, however, is $200 in paper profits for him. Of course, if the price of the stock heads south instead of north, he is in for twice the losses he would ordinarily incur. See "Stock Dividends" in Chapter Seven of this text.

**stock transfer.** Transfer of stock ownership from one individual to another. Until that transfer takes place, the first individual remains entitled to all the privleges guaranteed by the stock. With every purchase of stock, the old certificates must be cancelled and new ones issued. Corporations or banks usually employ someone who acts as the transfer agent for these title changes; and it is the responsibility of this transfer agent to see that all stock transfers are carried out swiftly and correctly.

**stop limit order.** A type of market order which instructs the broker to sell a certain security but at no less than some specified amount. See also "stop loss order."

**stop loss order.** An order to a broker which establishes the minimum price at which his customer is willing to trade. For instance, if AM International is selling at $10 per share and a shareholder fears there may be downslide pressure on the issue, he may want to unload the stock as soon as it depreciates to $8 per share, fearing that if it goes that low it will likely go even lower. So, he gives the following instructions to his broker: "Sell 100 shares of AM Interntional at $8 stop limit." The broker will do all in his power to execute the order at $8 or as close to, or below—that price as possible. For a primer on this and other related subjects, see the following: Yale L. Meltzer, *Putting Money To Work: An Investment Primer* (Englewood Cliffs, N.J.: Prentice Hall, 1976); Donald I. Rogers, *How Not To Buy A Common Stock* (New York: Arlington House, 1972; United Business Service, *Successful Investing: A Complete Guide To Your Financial Future* (New York: Simon & Schuster, 1979); Louis Engel, *How To Buy Stock* (Boston: Little Brown, 1976); Conrad W. Thomas, *How To Sell Short & Perform Other Wondrous Feats* (Homewood, Ill: Dow Jones-Irwin, 1976).

**stop order.** Same as a stop-loss order.

**stop price.** The price at which a broker is instructed to execute a stop order.

**straddle.** An option contract that gives to the holder the right to buy or sell stock at a certain price during a specified time. It is, in effect, a combination of put and call option contracts. But if the one side of the contract is executed, the other still remains available. Thus, both the buy and the sell sides of the contract may quite possibly be completed. For intermediate-level texts on this and related subjects, see Gary L. Gastineau, *The Stock Option Manual*, 2nd. ed. (New York: McGraw-Hill, 1979).

**street.** Generally, the New York financial markets. The term, however, is often used to refer to Wall Street.

**street broker.** Any broker who is not a member of one of the stock exchanges and specializes, therefore, in buying unlisted securities for his customers.

**street name.** Term used to describe a method of stock purchase in which the buyer, who may be a margin account or else someone just uninterested in receiving the actual certificates because of the frequency of his trades, does not require, or has not the right to expect, the broker to transfer his securities to him. The certificates due him are actually transferred in blank, and are negotiable when delivered; there is no need for any additional endorsement or to transfer the stock on the corporate book—no matter how many time the certificates may actually be bought and sold.

**striking price.** A term used in options trading which refers specifically to put and call contract prices. Specifically, the term relates to the price at which an option owner may exercise his right. The striking price is also called the exercise price.

**strip.** Stock option contracts which are made up of two puts and one call. See "straddle."

**subscription price.** The original offering price for new corporate issues. New corporate issues are not made available through the stock exchanges but through investment bankers. The stock exchanges function only as secondary markets for securities already in the hands of the public.

**subscription right.** Opportunities given to shareholders to purchase additional stock at a price lower than that which is quoted on the open market. The privilege may also relate to convertible debentures. Stockholders need not exercise these rights, they may also sell them in secondary markets. If, however, a stockholder does not exercise his subscription rights or is not able to sell them, then he loses the privilege to exercise the rights as well as any money he would have made by selling them.

**subsidiary.** Any corporation which is managed and controlled by another corporation. Subsidiaries have their own corporate charter and independent management structure. The larger corporations obtain or create subsidies through the purchase of controlling shares or by founding new corporations and remaining as majority stockholders.

**sucre.** Monetary unit used in Ecuador. For current foreign exchange rates see a copy of *The Wall Street Journal* or any other financial newspaper.

**taking a position.** Buying long or short in a security. Investors who buy long are hoping to realize capital gains from accelerating prices. Investors who buy short are playing the market to go down and are expecting to profit from declining prices. Those who buy long are taking a bullish position; those who buy short are taking bearish position. See "bull," "bear," "long position," and "short sale." For further information on investing techniques, see Richard A. Crowell, *Stock Market Strategy* (New York: McGraw-Hill, 1977). For the fundamentals of investing, see Yale L. Meltzer, *Putting Money To Work: An Investment Primer* (Englewood Cliffs, N.J.: Prentice Hall, 1976); Donald I. Rogers, *How Not To Buy A Common Stock* (New York: Arlington House, 1972); United Business Service, Successful Investing: A Complete Guide to Your Financial Future (New York: Simon & Schuster, 1979); Louis Engel, *How To Buy Stock*, 6th rev. ed. (Boston: Little Brow, 1976); Conrad W. Thomas, *How To Sell Short & Perform Other Wondrous Feats* (Homewood, Ill.: Dow Jones-Irwin, 1976).

**tax-exempt dividend.** A percent of some dividends paid by public utilities are which distributed without any tax liabilities. It all depends upon the basis on which the dividends are paid.

**tax selling.** The unloading of securities to offset gains or losses for tax purposes. Tax selling becomes extremely heavy during the last two months of the year. During this time investors will usually unload their securities hurriedly—and, therefore, at market—the stock exchanges often become a buyer's market, and prices decline accordingly. See Jack Crestol and Herman M. Schneider, *Tax Planning For Investors: A Guide to Securities Investment and Tax Shelters* (Princeton: Dow Jones Books, 1979).

**technical divergence.** When market averages or other indicators are not in coincidence, and it is impossible to detect any trend in price movement.

**technical factors.** These are trading trends or characteristics which are often indicative of price movement in securities dealings. Some of the data contributing to what are called technical factors are odd-lot purchases, rotating group leadership, the ratio of new highs to new lows, margin purchases, etc.

**technical position.** Market performance as a result of contributing technical factors.

**tender.** A formal offering to buy securities, usually within a specified time frame.

**tender price.** The price to be paid for a security involved in a tender offer.

**ten share units.** Stocks which trade in round lots of 10 shares.

**ticker.** An electromechancial printer which prints out price and trade details shortly after transactions are completed on the exchange floor.

**ticker symbol.** The abbreviation by which a stock is recognized. In many cases the abbreviation is not taken from the actual name of the stock because some other security is already identified by those call letters.

**top-heavy.** A market which is overbought; its prices are about to topple.

***Toronto Stock Exchange.*** One of Canada's major exchanges. You will find a partial listing of this exchange's securities in any of the financial newspapers or in the financial section of the major dailies. Please refer to the supplement to this dictionary for the address of this exchange as well as a listing of all exchanges worldwide.

***trade.*** To buy and sell shares of stock. This may be done on a long term basis. Generally, the short term investor is referred to as a trader, for his main interest is in short-term capital gains and he will trade his securities frequently going in and out of a stock sometimes daily. The long-term investor is generally interested in *total yield*, which is a combination of dividend income and capital appreciation over a year or more. For a discussion of the pros and cons of speculating, see Chapter One in Benjamin Graham's *The Intelligent Investor* (New York: Harper & Row, 1973). For study on stock trading, see also Richard Blackman, *Follow the Leaders; Successful Trading Techniques with Line Drive Stocks* (New York: Simon & Schuster, 1978); David Darst, *The Handbook of the Bond and Money Markets* (New York: McGraw-Hill, 1981); C. Colburn Hardy, *Dun & Bradstreet's Guide to Your Investments* (New York: Lippincott, 1981).

***trader.*** See "trade."

***trader's market.*** A market which fluctuates enough to allow the trader to go in and out almost as he pleases and turn a profit—sometimes selling short, sometimes buying long. For discussion of the investor in a fluctuating market, see Chapter Eight in Benjamin Graham's "*The Intelligent Investor*" (New York: Harper & Row, 1973).

***transfer agent.*** The member of a corporation whose responsibility it is to manage the issuing, transferring, and cancellation of stock certificates.

**transfer of stock.** The successful delivery of a certificate to the purchaser of the stock it represents—or, in the case of stocks being held in street name, to the broker.

**transportation (Dow Jones).** Refers to the twenty stocks which make up the Dow Jones Transportation Averages. The stocks which are used to obtain this average will change on occasion, but for a current listing, see Chapter Eight in this text.

**turnover.** The number of transactions completed. The word is a synonym for volume. High turnover and increasing share value is usually indicative of an upward trend in stocks prices. Low turnover on a downward trend in stock prices is generally thought to be indicative of a failing market.

**two-dollar ($2) broker.** A broker's broker who executes the trades other exchange members are too preoccupied to handle. The name $2 broker has historical significance, as there was a time when the commission for their efforts amounted to $2 per share. For a primer on this and other related subjects; see Leonard Sloane, *The Anatomy of the Floor: The Trillion Dollar Market of the New York Stock Exchange* (New York: Doubleday, 1980).

**underwrite.** To guarantee the sale of new corporate issues. Underwriters generally work for the profits to be made from the difference between the price they pay for the security and the price they can get from the public. Many new corporate issues are too extensive for one underwriter to handle, so two or more often team up to share the risk. Coming sales of new issues are reported in the financial news. New corporate issues are not introduced through the stock exchanges, as the exchanges function as secondary markets for stocks already in the hands of the public.

**underwriter.** The investment banks who sponsor the underwriting of new corporate issues.

**unloading.** Selling out positions taken in a security or securities or selling all holdings in an account.

**unrealized profits.** Paper profits; profits which can be realized if a short position is covered or a long position is sold.

**unregistered stock.** A security which is not registered with the Securities and Exchange Commission. Its market is, therefore, highly limited, and investors who take positions in it may not be able to unload their holdings in the future. Still, this type of stock is often attractive to investors because it comes to market at a discount. Unregistered stock is not illegal as long as it is issued with prior agreement from the SEC that the latter will not take action against the issuer.

**upgrading.** Building a stronger portfolio by unloading riskier securities with those of greater investment quality. For research on stock selection and trading, see United Business Service, *Successful Investing: A Complete Guide to Your Financial Future* (New York: Simon & Schuster, 1979); Louis Engel, *How To Buy Stock,* 6th rev. ed. (Boston: Little Brown, 1976); Conrad W. Thomas, *How To Sell Short & Perform Other Wondrous Feats* (Homewood, Ill.: Dow Jones-Irwin, 1976); Ira Cobleigh, *The Dowbeaters; How to Buy Stocks That Go Up* (New York: Macmillan, 1979).

**uptick.** An increase in price.

**utilities.** Generally refers to the fifteen utility stocks which make up part of the Dow Jones sixty-five stock averages. The stocks which make up the utility list will change from time to time but a current listing is available in Chapter Eight.

**velocity of money.** The number of times each dollar is spent during any one-year period. The velocity of money is used to identify saving and spending trends. When there is an increasing trend in the velocity, people are spending rather than holding onto their money. On the other hand, if there is a decreasing trend in the velocity statistics, the money supply is going to dry up. As the money supply is an important indicator in business forecasting, the velocity of money figures help in economic planning.

***voting rights.*** The right of a stockholder to vote at a stockholders' meeting. Generally, only common shareholders have voting privileges. See also "common stock" and "preferred stock."

***voting trust.*** A trust which, in taking custody of a corporation's stock, receives the authority to vote its shares. These voting trusts are normally organized when a company is undergoing restructuring or preparing to merge with another. Special arrangements are made to provide stockholders with temporary certificates until the trust is terminated. The temporary certificates may be traded as ordinary stock would be.

***warrant.*** A certificate which may be used to buy securities at at discount. The offering is generally for a limited period of time, but not always. Investors may trade the warrants as they do stock. Prices of warrants are listed along with stocks in the financial papers.

***won.*** Monetary unit of South Korea. For current foreign exchange rates see a copy of *The Wall Street Journal* or any other financial newspaper.

***Wilshire 5000 Equity Index.*** Market index based on the value of all New York and American Exchange stocks and the more active OTC stocks.

***yen.*** Monetary unit of Japan. For current foreign exchange rates see a copy of *The Wall Street Journal* or any other financial daily.

**yield.** Return on investment. For instance, if you buy a share of stock for $100 and it is paying a $10 dividend per year, your return on investment—or your yield—is 10%.

**yuan.** Monetary unit of China. For current foreign exchange rates see a copy of *The Wall Street Journal* or any other financial newspaper.

# SUPPLEMENT TO DICTIONARY
## Principal Stock Exchanges Worldwide

## ARGENTINA

Buenos Aires: Mercado de Valores de Buenos Aires, S.A., Sarmiento 299, P.B. 1353, Buenos Aires 1353

Cordoba: Bolsa de Comecio De Cordoba, Rosario de Santa Fe 231, Cordoba 5000

Mendoza: Bolsa De Comercio De Mendoza, Mercada De Valores De Mendoza, S.A., Sarmiento 199 esq. Espana, Mendoza 550

## AUSTRALIA

Adelaide: Stock Exchange of Adelaide, LTD., 55 Exchange Place, Adelaide, S.A.

Brisbane: Brisbane Stock Exchange, LTD., MM1, Bldg. 344, Queen Street, Brisbane, 4000

Hobart: Hobart Stock Exchange, 86 Collins Street, Hobart, Tasmania

Melbourne: Stock Exchange of Melbourne, 351 Collins Street, Melbourne, Vic.

Perth: Stock Exchange of Perth, LTD., Exchange House, 68 St., George's Terrace, Perth, W.A.

Sydney: Australian Associated Stock Exchanges, King George Tower, 388 George Street, Sydney, N.S.W.

Sydney: Sydney Stock Exchange, 20 Bond Street P.O.B. 224, Australia Square, Sydney, N.S.W. 2000

## AUSTRIA

Wipplingerstrasse: Wierner Borsekamma, 1011 Wien, Wipplingerstrasse 34

## BARBADOS

Bridgetown: Barbados Stock Exchange, Bridgetown

## BELGIUM

Antwerpen: Fondsen-En Wisselbeurs Van Antwerpen, Korte Klarenstraat, 1, 2000 Antwerpen

Brussels: Commission de la Bourse de Bruxelles, Palais de la Bourse, Place de la Bourse, Brussels

Gent: Fondsen-En Wisselbeurs Van Gent, Kouter, 29, 9000 Gent

Liege: Bourse De Fonds Publics De Liege, Bd. D'Avroy, 3/022, 4000 Liege

## BRAZIL
Porto Algre: Bolsa De Valores Do Extremo Sul, Rua dos Andradas, 1234, 9 Andar, cx. Postal 1641.

Rio de Janeio: Bolsa de Valores do Rio de Janeiro, Praca XV de Novembro 20, Rio de Janeiro, RJ

Sao Paulo: Bolsa de Valores de Sao Paulo, Rua LIbero Bandaro 471, 3, Sao Paulo, SP

## CANADA
Calgary: Alberta Stock Exchange, 300 5th Avenue, S.W., 3rd Floor, Calgary, Alberta, T2P3C4

Montreal: Montreal Stock Exchange, P.O.B. 61, 800 Place Victoria, Montreal

Tornoto: 234 Bay Street, Toronto, Ontario M5J 1R1

Vancouver: Vancouver Stock Exchange, 536 Howe Street, Vancouver, B.C., Canada V6C2E1

Winnipeg: 303-167 Lombard Ave., Winnipeg, Manitoba, Canada

## CHILE
Santiago: Bolsa de Comercio, La Bolsa 64, Casilla 123-D, Santiago

Valparaiso: Bolsa de Volores, Prat 798, Casilla 218-V, Valparaiso

## COLOMBIA
Bogota: Bolsa de Bogota, Carrera 8A, No. 13-82, Piso 8, Bogota

Medellin: Bolsa De Medellin, S.A., Carrera 50 50-48 Piso 2, Medellin

## COSTA RICA
San Jose: Bolsa Nacional de Valores, S.A., AVDA. 1 Calle Central, Edif Cartagena, 7° PISO, Apdo. 1736, San Jose

## DENMARK
Copenhagen: Copenhagen Stock Exchange, Nikolaj Plads 6, 1067 Copenhagen K

## ECUADOR
Bolsa De Valores e Quito C.A., Av. Rio Amazonas 540 y Jeronimo Carrion, Piso 8, Apartado Postal 3772, Quito

## EGYPT
Cairo: Cairo Stock Exchange, 4-A Cherifein Street, Cairo

## EL SALVADOR
San Salvador: Bolsa de El Salvador, 7a Avda. Norte 30, San Salvador

## ENGLAND
See "United Kingdom"

## FINLAND
Helsinki: Helsinki Stock Exchange, Fabianinkatu 14, 00100 Helsinki 10

## FRANCE
Bordeaux: Bourse De Bordeaus, Palais de la Bourse,2 place Gabriel 33075 Bordeaux Cedex

Lille: Bourse De Lille, Palais de la Bourse, Place du Theatre, 59040 Lille Cedex

Lyon: Bourse De Lyon, Palais Du Commerce, Place de la Bourse, 69289 Lyon Cedex

Marseille: Palais de la Bourse, BP 300, 13215 Marseille

Nancy: Bourse De Nancy, 25 bis, rue Stanislas, BP 815, 54011 Nancy Cedex

Nantes: Bourse De Nantes, Palais de la Bourse, Place du Commerce, 44000 Nantes

Paris: La Bourse de Paris, Palais de la Bourse, 75080 Paris Cedex 02

## GERMANY (Federal Republic)
Berlin: Borse, 1000 Berlin 12, Hardenbergstrasse 16-18 Berlin

Bremen: Bremen Wertpapierborse, 2800 Bremen 1, Langenstrasse 12, Postfach 10 07 26

Dusseldorf: Rheinisch-Westfalische Borse zu Dusseldorf, Ernst-Schneider-Platz 1

Frankfurt: Frankfurt Wertpapierborse, Borsenplatz 6, Franfurt-am-Main

Hamburg: Hanseatische Wertpapierborse Hamburg, 2000 Hamburg 11, Borse

Hanover: Niedersachsische Borse zu Hanover, 3 Hanover, Rathenaustr. 2

Munich: Bayerische Borse, 8 Munich 2, Lenbachplatz 2A/I

Stuttgart: Baden-Wurttenbergische Wertpapierborse zu Stuttgart, 7 Stuttgart 1, Hospitalstrasse 12.

## GREAT BRITAIN
See "United Kingdom."

## GREECE
Athens: Athens Stock Exchange, 10 Sophocleus Street, Athens 121

## HONG KONG
Far East Exchange Ltd., 8th Floor, New World Tower, 16-18, Queen's Rd. Central

Hong Kong Stock Exchange, Ltd, 21st Floor, Hutchinson House

Kam Ngan Exchange, 7th Floor, Connaught Centre, Connaught Rd. Central

Kowloon Stock Exchange, Kowloon

(On October 6, 1986, these exchanges merged and now operate as the Stock Exchange of Hong Kong).

## INDIA
Ahmedabad: Ahmedabab Share & Stock Broker's Association, Manekchowk, Ahmedabab 1

Bangalore: Bangalore Stock Exchange, Indian Bank Bldg., Kempegowda Rd., Bangalore 560009

Bombay: Bombay Stock Exchange, Dalal Street, Bombay 400001

Calcutta: Calcutta Stock Exchange Association LTD., 7 Lyons Range, Calcutta 700001

New Delhi: Delhi Stock Exchange Association LTD. 3 and 4/4B Asaf Ali Rd., New Delhi 110002

Madras: Madras Stock Exchange LTD, Exchange Bldg. 11 Second Line Beach, Madras 600001

## INDONESIA
Jakarta: Badan Pelaksana Pasar Modal (BAPEPAM), Jalan Medan Merdeka Selatan 13, Jakarta

## IRAN
Teheran: Teheran Stock Exchange, Taghinia Bldg., Saadi Ave., Teheran

## IRELAND
Dublin: Irish Unit, London Stock Exchange, 24-28 Anglesea St., Dublin 2

## ISRAEL
Tel-Aviv: Tel Aviv Stock Exchange, 113 Allenby Rd., Tel-Aviv, 65127

## ITALY
Bologna: Borsa Valori Di Bologna, Piazza della Constituzone, 8, Palazzo degli Affari, 40100—Bologna

Firenze: Borsa Valori Di Firenza, Piazza Mentana, 2, 50122—Firenze

Genoa: Borsa Valori Di Genoa, Via G. Boccardo 1, 15121 Genoa

Milan: Borsa Valori Di Milano, Piazza Affari 6, 20123—Milan

Naples: Borsa Valori Di Napoli, Piazza Bovio, Palazzo Borsa, 80133—Naples

Palermo: Borsa Valori Di Palermo, Via E. Amari, 11, 90139—Palermo

Rome: Borsa Valori, Via dei Burro 147, 00186, Rome

Trieste: Borsa Valori Di Trieste, Via Cassa di Risparmio, 2, 34100—Trieste

Turin: Borsa Valori, Via San Francesco da Paoloa, 28, Turin

## JAMAICA
Jamaica Stock Exchange. LTD., P.O.B. 621, Bank of Jamaica Tower, Nethersole Place, Kingston

## JAPAN
Fukuoka: Fukuoka Stock Exchange. 2-14-12 Tenjin. Chuo-ku. Fukuoka

Hiroshima: Hiroshima Stock Exchange. 14-18. Kanajama-Cho. Hiroshima

Kyoto: Kyoto Stock Exchange. 66 Tateuri Nishimachi, Tohdohin Higashihairu, Shijohdohri. Shimokyoku. Kyoto

Nagoya: Nagoya Stock Exchange. 3-17 Sakae-Sanchome, Naka-ku. Nagoya

Niigata: Niigata Securities Exchange. 1245 Hachibancho. Kamiohkawamaedohir. Niigata

Osaka: Osaka Securities Exchange. 2-chome. Kitahama. Higashiku. Osaka

Sapporo: Sapporo Stock Exchange. 5-14-1 Nishi. Minami Ichizo. Naka-ku. Sapporo

Tokyo. Tokyo Stock Exchange. 6 1-chome, Nihonbaski-Kabutocho. Chuo-ku. Tokyo

## JORDAN
Amman: Amman Financial Market, P.O.B. 8802, Amman

## KENYA
Nairobi: Nairobi Stock Exchange, Stanbank House, Moi Ave., P.O.B. 43633, Nairobi

## KOREA
Seoul: Korea Stock Exchange, 1-116 Yoido-Dong, Youngedeungpo-Ku, Seoul

## KUWAIT
Kuwait City: Kuwait Stock Exchange, Kuwait City

## LUXEMBOURG
Bourse de Luxembourg S.A., B.P.65, 2011, Luxembourg

## MALAYSIA
Kuala Lumpur Stock Exchange, 4th Floor Block C, Damansara Heights, Kuala Lumpur 23-04

## MEXICO
Bolsa Mexicana de Valores, S.A. de C.V., Uruguay 68, Mexico 1, D.F.

## MOROCCO
Casablanca: Bourse Des Valeurs de Casablanca, Chamber of Commerce Building, 98 blvd Mohammed V., Casablanca

## NETHERLANDS
Amsterdam: European Options Exchange, P.OB. 19164 1000 GD, Amsterdam

Amsterdam: Vereniging voor de Effectenhandel, Beursplein 5, P.O. Box 19163, 1000 GD Amsterdam

## NEW ZEALAND
Auckland, Auckland Stock Exchange, CML Centre, Queen Street, Auckland 1

Christchurch: Christchurch Invercargill Stock Exchange Ltd., 128 Oxford Terrace, Christchurch

Dunedin: Dunedin Stock Exchange, Queens Building, 109 Princess Street, Dunedin C.1

Wellington, Wellington Stock Exchange, Government Life Insurance Building, Brandon Street, Wellington C.1

## NICARAGUA
Managua: Actividades Busatiles De Fomento S.A., Apartado P.O. 4126, Managua, D.N.

## NIGERIA
Lagos: Nigerian Stock Exchange, P.O.B. 2457, 63/71 Broad Street, Lagos

## NORWAY
Aalesund: Aalesunds Bors, Roysegaten 15, Aalesund

Bergen: Bergens Bors, Olav Kyrresgate 11, 5000 Bergen

Drammen: Drammens Bors, Drammen

Frederikstad: Fredrikstad Bors, Nygaardsgaten 5, Fredrikstad

Haugesund: Haugesund Bors, Haugesund

Kristiansand: Christianssand Bors, Kristiansand

Kristiansund: Kristiansund (N.) Bors, Kristiansund

Stavanger: Stavanger Bors, Stavanger

Trondheim: Trondheim Bors, Dronningensgt

Oslo: Oslo Bors, Tallbugt 2, Oslo

## PAKISTAN
Karachi: Karachi Stock Exchange Ltd., Stock Exchange Rd., Karachi 2

Lahore: Lahore Stock Exchange Ltd, 17 Bank Square, Lahore

## PANAMA
Panama City Stock Exchange, Panama 5

## PERU
Lima: Bolsa de Valores de Lima, Jiron Miro Quesada 265, Lima 1

## PHILIPINES
Manila: Makati Stock Exchange, Mokati Stock Exch. Building, Ayala Ave., Makati, Metro Manila

Manila: Manila Stocke Exchange Bldg., Muelle de la Industria and Prenso Sts., Binondo, Manila

Manila: Metropolitan Stock Exchange, 2nd Floor, Padilla Arcade, Greenhills Commerical Center, San Juan, Metro Manila

## PORTUGAL
Lisbon: Bolsa de Valores de Lisboa, Praca do Comercio, 1100 Lisbon

## SINGPORE
Stock Exchange of Singapore, 1402 Hong Leong Bldg., Raffles Quay, Singapore 0104

## SOUTH AFRICA
Johannesburg: Johannesburg Stock Exchange, P.O.B. 1174, Johannesburg

## SPAIN
Barcelona: Bolsa Oficial de Commercio de Barcelona, Paseo Isabel II, Barcelona

Bilbao: Bolsa de Bilbao, Calle J.M. Olabarri 1, Bilbao

Madrid: Bolsa de Madrid, Palacio de la Bolsa, Plaza de la Lealtad 1, Madrid

Valencia: Sindico General de la Bolsa, Pascal Cenes, Valencia

## SRI LANKA
Colombo: Colombo Brokers' Association, P.O.B. 101, 201 De Sakram Place, Colombo 10

## SWEDEN
Stockholm: Stockholm Stock Exchange. Kallargrand 2. Box 1256. 111 82 Stockholm

## SWITZERLAND
Basel: Basel Stock Exchange, 3 Freie Str., Postfach 244. 4001. Basel

Berne: Bourse de Berne, Berne

Geneva: Bourse de Geneva: 8-10 rue Petitot, 1211 Geneva

Lousanne: Bourse de Lousanne: c/o Societe de Banque Suisse. 1002. Lousanne

Neuchatel: Bourse De Neuchatel, Coq d'Inde 24, 2000 Neuchatel

Zurich: Bourse de Zurich, Bleicherweg 5. 8021 Zurich

Zurich: Bourse Suisse de Commerce. 8023 Zurich

## TAIWAN
Taipei: Taiwan Stock Exchange. 9th Floor, City Bldg., 85 Yen-ping South Rd., Taipei

## THAILAND
Bangkok: Securities Exchange of Thailand, 965 Rama 1 Rd., Bangkok

## TUNISIA
Tunis: Bourse Des Baleurs Mobilieres De Tunis, 19 Bis, Rue Kamel Ataturk, Tunis

## TURKEY
Istanbul: Borsa Komiserligi Menkul Kizmetler ve Kambiyo Borsasi, 4 Vakif Han, Bahcekopi, Istanbul

## UNITED KINGDOM (Great Britain)
Belfast: London Stock Exchange, Belfast Unit, 10 High Street, Belfast, Northern Ireland

Birmingham: London Stock Exchange, Midlands and Western Unit, Margaret Street, Birmingham B3 3J1

Dublin: London Stock Exchange, Irish Unit, 28 Anglesea St., Dublin 2

Edinburgh: London Stock Exchange, Scottish Unit, 12 Dublin Street, Edinburgh EH1 3PP

Glasgow: London Stock Exchange, Scottish Unit, Box 141, Glasgow, Scotland

Liverpool: London Stock Exchange, Northern Unit, Silkhouse Court, Tithebarn St., Liverpool L2 2Lt

London: London Stock Exchange, Old Broad Street, London, EC 2N 1 HP

London: London Stock Exchange, Provincial Unit, Room 402, 4th Floor, London EC2N 1HP

Manchester: London Stock Exchange. Northern Unit, 2/6 Norfolk Street, Manchester M2 1 DS

## UNITED STATES
Boston: Boston Stock Exchange, 53 State Street, Boston, Massachusetts 02109

Chicago: Midwest Stock Exchange, 120 South LaSalle Street, Room 1243, Chicago, Illinois 60603

Chicago: Chicago Board Options Exchange, 141 West Jackson Boulevard, Chicago, Illinois 60604

Cincinnati: Cincinnati Stock Exchange, 205 Dixie Terminal Building, Cincinnati, Ohio 45202

Los Angeles: Pacific Stock Exchange, 618 South Spring Street, Los Angeles, California 90014

New York: American Stock Exchange, 86 Trinity Place, New York, New York 10006

New York: New York Stock Exchange, 11 Wall Street, New York, New York 10005

Philadelphia: Philadelphia Stock Exchange, 17th Street & Stock Exchange Place, Philadelphia, Pennsylvania 19103

Salt Lake City: Intermountain Stock Exchange, 39 Exchange Place, Salt Lake City, Utah 84111

San Francisco: Pacific Stock Exchange, 301 Pine Street, San Francisco, California 94104

Washington: Spokane Stock Exchange, 225 Peyton Building, Spokane, Washington 99201

Washington, D.C.: National Association of Securities Dealers, 1735 K Street, N.W., Washington, D.C. 20006

## URUGUAY
Montevideo: Bolsa de Valores de Montevideo, Edificio de la Bolsa de Comercio, Misiones 1400, Montevideo

## VENEZUELA
Caracas: Bolsa de Valores de Caracas, CA., Torre Financiera del Banco, Central de Venezuela 19, Santa Capilla, Avda, Urdaneta, Caracas 1010

Caracas: Bolsa de Comercio del Estado Miranda, Edif, Easo, Loc.H. Avda, Miranda, Caracas

Valencia: Bolsa de Comercio de Valencia, Valencia

## ZIMBABWE
Harare: Zimbabwe Stock Exchange, Pearl Assurance House, Samora Machel Ave., P.O.B. UA 234 Harare